A HISTORY OF NORTHERN IRELAND

Patrick Buckland

A HISTORY OF
NORTHERN IRELAND

HM

HOLMES & MEIER PUBLISHERS, INC.
NEW YORK

First published in the
United States of America 1981 by
HOLMES & MEIER PUBLISHERS, INC.
30 Irving Place, New York, N.Y. 10003

Library of Congress Cataloging in Publication Data

Buckland, Patrick.
    A history of Northern Ireland.

    Bibliography: p. 195
    Includes index.
    1. Northern Ireland – History.   I. Title.
DA990.U46B79   1981   941.6082   81-909
                                         AACR2

ISBN 0–8419–0700–5

Printed in Great Britain

CONTENTS

To Yve
and
To My Mother and Father

PREFACE

This book is an attempt to present a non-specialist political history of Northern Ireland from its foundation in the early 1920s to its disintegration into violence in the early 1970s. It seeks to combine an outline of major events with a discussion of important questions. Why was Ireland partitioned? Why and in what circumstances were a separate and subordinate government and parliament established in the six north-eastern counties? What problems did Northern Ireland encounter? What was the calibre of its politicians? How did it develop a reputation as a Protestant state for a Protestant people? Why did Stormont fall and political initiatives fail against a background of political murder?

If there is a theme drawing the book together, it is the ungovernability of Northern Ireland. It provides a probe with which to examine the complex cross-currents which led one Ulsterman to remark 'Anyone who isn't confused here doesn't really understand what is going on.'[1] Pessimistic though it is, the theme also represents reality. In view of its unwanted and traumatic birth, its divisions, its decaying economy, its dearth of political talent and its irridentist Southern neighbour, Northern Ireland would never have been an easy or even a satisfying place to govern. It was always likely to develop into a one-party state rendered potentially unstable by economic difficulties and a minority problem. The likelihood was turned into virtual certainty by the ill-thought-out system of parliamentary devolution established in 1920-21, which accentuated rather than alleviated the problems facing a deeply divided and under-developed society. Ungovernable or not, the continued existence of the Ulster question is eloquent testimony to the inability of parties and politicians in Britain and both parts of Ireland to realise the inappropriateness of conventional notions of parliamentary government to Northern Ireland. In fact, a secondary theme of this book is the failure of statemanship.

ACKNOWLEDGMENTS

I am once more most grateful to those people who have always encouraged my interest in Irish history, particularly Professor J. C. Beckett, Dr D. G. Boyce, Mr K. Darwin, Professor D. W. J. Johnson, Professor D. B. Quinn and Mr B. Trainor, Director of the Public Record Office of Northern Ireland, and all his staff. Without their assistance and friendship the research underpinning the first four chapters of this book would have been a far less enjoyable undertaking. I would very much have liked to have based the second half on the same sort of research into cabinet and departmental papers, but this was impossible owing to the thirty-year rule and other restrictions on access to public records in Britain and Northern Ireland. Thus in the last four chapters I have had to draw largely on published material, including diaries, memoirs, newspapers and official reports, but my biggest debt is to those authors who have researched into and thought about the years 1945 to 1974 much more thoroughly than I. The references clearly indicate the extent of my debt to Mr D. Boulton, Dr F. Burton, Mr J. Darby, Mr M. Farrell, Dr K. Heskin, Dr I. MacAllister and Drs P. Bew, P. Gibbon and H. Patterson. I wish also to thank Miss Yvonne Jones for unstinting help in all stages of writing and proof-reading.

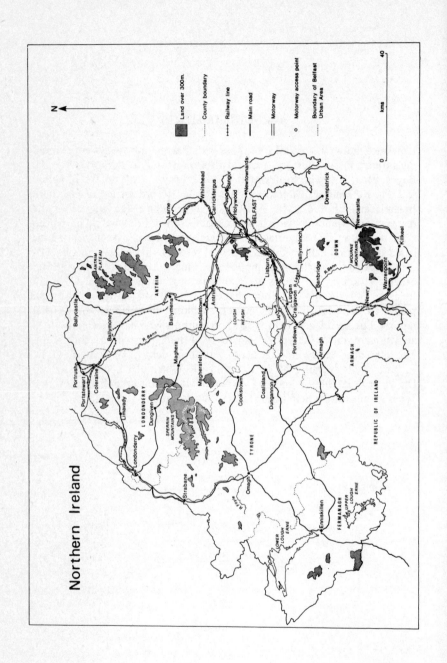

Northern Ireland

ABBREVIATIONS

APL	Anti-Partition League
BDA	Bogside Defence Association
CDU	Campaign for Democracy in Ulster
CSJ	Campaign for Social Justice in Northern Ireland
DUP	Democratic Unionist Party
GAA	Gaelic Athletic Association
ICTU	Irish Congress of Trade Unions
IPP	Irish Parliamentary Party
IRA	Irish Republican Army
ITUC	Irish Trade Union Congress
LAW	Loyalist Association of Workers
MP	Member of Parliament
NICRA	Northern Ireland Civil Rights Association
NILP	Northern Ireland Labour Party
OIRA	Official Irish Republican Army
PD	People's Democracy
PIRA	Provisional Irish Republican Army
PR	Proportional Representation
RIC	Royal Irish Constabulary
ROIA	Restoration of Order in Ireland Act, 1919
RUC	Royal Ulster Constabulary
SDA	Shankill Defence Association
SDLP	Social Democratic and Labour Party
UAC	Ulster Army Council
UCDC	Ulster Constitution Defence Committee
UDA	Ulster Defence Association
UDR	Ulster Defence Regiment
UPA	Ulster Protestant Association
UPV	Ulster Protestant Volunteers
USC	Ulster Special Constabulary
UUC	Ulster Unionist Council
UULA	Ulster Unionist Labour Association
UUUC	United Ulster Unionist Council
UVF	Ulster Volunteer Force
UWC	Ulster Workers' Council
VUPP	Vanguard Unionist Progressive Party

Chapter 1

UNIONISM VERSUS NATIONALISM

Nobody really wanted to partition Ireland in 1920-21. Still less had any-body expected the creation of the separate government and parliament of Northern Ireland. However much they may have disagreed over whether it should be ruled from London or Dublin, Irishmen instinctively thought of Ireland as a single geographical and political unit. A minority wanted it to remain an integral part of the United Kingdom governed directly from Westminster, as had been the case since the Act of Union in 1800. The majority of Irishmen, on the other hand, sought an end to British rule and its replacement by a more or less independent government and parliament in Dublin ruling over the whole island. Nor, contrary to many popular notions, was there any burning or sinister desire in Britain to divide Ireland and shower it with parliaments. Rather partition and the establishment of two Irish parliaments represented a compromise. The former was the most realistic, the latter the most convenient, way of resolving a serious conflict of interests that threatened the peace and stability of the United Kingdom in the early twentieth century. They were the devices adopted by the British government to extricate itself from Ireland and yet redeem contra-dictory commitments to the two powerful but opposed political move-ments that divided Irishmen in the late nineteenth and early twentieth centuries — Irish nationalism and Ulster Unionism.

I

The deeper roots of this conflict lay in the seventeenth century. Until then Ulster had been the most Gaelic as well as the most northerly of Ireland's four provinces, not because it was completely immune from outside influences and English and Scottish colonisation, but because English authority had made least progress there. After its conquest in 1603, however, Ulster developed differently from the other provinces and was later regarded as the most British part of Ireland. Despite the impression created by later propaganda, it never became a wholly Protes-tant province: indeed, Catholics always constituted the largest single *denomination*. Nevertheless, Ulster became the home of a distinctive community which was separated from the rest of Ireland by history, religion and economic development. Most Irishmen were Catholics, agri-culturalists and sometimes conscious of their Gaelic heritage, but in the North there were many Protestants of English and Scottish descent, engaged in trade and industry as well as farming.

1

The latter had first arrived in Ulster in any strength at the beginning of the seventeenth century as part of private and official plans to colonise the area with settlers from Britain. Two Scottish adventurers successfully carved out for themselves what became a prosperous domain in Co. Down, thus providing a bridgehead through which a steady stream of Lowland Scots flowed into Ulster for the rest of the century. The official plantation, James I's plan, covering Counties Armagh, Cavan, Coleraine (later Londonderry), Donegal, Fermanagh and Tyrone, was more ambitious, part of the Crown's policy to subdue the recently conquered province and suppress its Gaelic, Catholic and pastoral culture by establishing towns and giving over most of the fertile and accessible parts of their hinterlands to agricultural development by further groups of Protestant colonists. The introduction of Protestants from England and Scotland had been tried elsewhere but never on such a scale. From the early seventeenth to the early twentieth centuries Protestants comprised the social, economic and political elite of Ireland, but only in Ulster did they constitute an almost self-contained community, a numerical majority at most levels of society instead of an aristocratic and professional minority. In the North they were weavers, farmers, farmhands and merchants instead of being confined to the ranks of clergy, professional men and landowners.

Had the official plantation achieved its original objective, or had the process of assimilation been complete, the history of Ulster and Ireland would have been very different. The aim was to sweep away the existing occupiers and replace them with settlers from England and Scotland, but it soon proved impossible to displace the natives altogether or attract sufficient immigrants to Ulster. On the other hand, there was insufficient assimilation to prevent the development in Ulster of two separate but interlocked communities, one Catholic, the other Protestant. The former was strongest in the south and west, the latter, re-inforced by immigration, predominated in the east, particularly in Counties Antrim and Down. The 'very essence' of the Ulster question was not that the two communities could not live together but that they *do* live together, and have done for centuries. They share the same homeland, and, like it or not, the two diametrically opposed political wills must coexist on the same narrow ground.'[1]

The census returns for 1911 illustrate something of the demography and topography of the Ulster question. Taken as a whole, its religious composition set Ulster apart from the other provinces:

	Population	Catholics	Non-Catholics
Ireland	4,390,219	3,242,670 (73.9%)	1,147,549 (26.1%)
Ulster	1,581,696	690,816 (43.7%)	890,880 (56.3%)
Rest of Ireland	2,808,523	2,551,854 (90.9%)	256,669 (9.1%)

Within Ulster, however, there were marked variations in the distribution of Catholics and Protestants, as is partly revealed by the county figures:

2

	Population	Catholics	Non-Catholics
Antrim	193,864	39,751 (20.5%)	154,113 (79.5%)
Armagh	120,291	54,526 (45.3%)	65,765 (54.7%)
Cavan	91,173	74,271 (81.5%)	16,902 (18.5%)
Donegal	168,537	133,021 (78.9%)	35,516 (21.1%)
Down	204,303	64,485 (31.6%)	139,818 (68.4%)
Fermanagh	61,836	34,740 (56.2%)	27,096 (43.8%)
Londonderry	99,845	41,478 (41.5%)	58,367 (58.5%)
Monaghan	71,455	53,363 (74.7%)	18,092 (25.3%)
Tyrone	142,665	79,051 (55.4%)	63,650 (44.6%)
Belfast C.B.	386,947	93,243 (24.1%)	293,704 (75.9%)
Londonderry C.B.	40,780	22,923 (56.2%)	17,857 (43.8%)

The distinctiveness of Ulster was re-inforced by the influence the Scots had on many aspects of life. Large areas of Antrim and Down had been settled by Scots several decades before the Ulster plantation proper; there was a notable Scottish element among the planters; and many of the colonists' losses sustained in seventeenth-century insurrections were replenished from Scotland. Ulster was, after all, the part of Ireland closest to Scotland. Although it is no longer possible to regard religious affiliation as an infallible guide to 'national' origin, the dominant Scottish influence among the settlers was reflected in the fact that Presbyterians became the largest single Protestant denomination. With 421,410 members in 1911, they were strongest in Counties Down and Antrim through to Co. Londonderry and the east of Donegal and in Co. Monaghan. They easily outnumbered the 366,773 members of the former established church, the Church of Ireland (more numerous than Presbyterians in the Lagan valley and Counties Armagh, except the extreme south, Fermanagh and Tyrone), the 48,816 Methodists and the membership of the myriad small evangelical sects which were a constant feature of Ulster Protestantism.

This influx of settlers from England and Scotland had hardly been welcomed by the Gaelic and Catholic host community, deprived of its traditions and often its land — certainly its best land. Whereas the Gaelic Irish resented and remembered the foreign occupation, Ulster Protestants long recalled with horror attempts to massacre and expel them. It was not until the end of the seventeenth century that doubts about the future of Protestants in Ireland were resolved, as Irish Protestants sided with the Protestant William of Orange in his successful attempt to wrest the English throne from the Catholic James II. Ulster Protestants' resistance to James centred upon Enniskillen and Londonderry, where they withstood a three months' siege, thus giving William time to land in Ireland and fight on Tuesday 1 July 1690 (12 July by the new calendar) the decisive battle of modern Ireland, the Battle of the Boyne. Thenceforth, the Protestant minority ruled Ireland. The Protestants in the North dominated Ulster. For this reason the Battle of the Boyne was and is celebrated each year by Ulster Protestants as the charter of their civil and religious liberties.

History was one divisive force. Religion was another. It was partly a

3

question of numbers, most of Ireland being Catholic and parts of Ulster overwhelmingly Protestant, but it was mainly a matter of the nature of religious commitment. The predominant trends in Ulster Protestantism and Irish Catholicism were mutually antagonistic. Since the 1850s Irish Catholicism had had a strong ultramontane streak and in the 1880s it experienced a new access of enthusiasm, emphasising devotion to the Sacred Heart and even developing a fundamental hostility towards the North. By contrast, Ulster Protestantism, the predominant strain in which was Presbyterianism, had since the 1830s been characterised by a narrow fundamental evangelicalism, believing that the Bible was the literal word of God and that the soul should be free to commune directly with its Maker. It was thus the spiritual aspect of Catholicism, the placing of the priest between man and God, that exercised Ulster Protestants as much as the demonstrable influence of the Catholic clergy on Irish life and politics. 'Popery is something more than a religious system,' claimed one Orangeman in 1869. 'It is a political system also. It is a religio-political system for the enslavement of the body and soul of man.'[2]

Moreover, Irish Catholicism from the early nineteenth century onwards always appeared a gigantic monolith compared to Ulster Protestantism. Catholics were the largest single denomination not only in Ireland but also in the North, were always united at least publicly on doctrine and had an impressive hierarchical and parochial organisation backed by the universal church headed by the Pope. By contrast, Ulster Protestantism was dispersed and riven with doctrinal and other disputes. There were numerous small, fiercely independent sects; neither the hierarchical structure of the Church of Ireland nor the Presbyterian General Assembly could rival the administrative and organisational coherence of the Catholic Church; and, anyway, Episcopalians and Presbyterians were separated by considerable theological and historical differences, for Presbyterianism had for long been just as much the religion of the under-privileged as Catholicism, both being outside the pale of the established church. Indeed, Ulster Protestants experienced unity only in opposition to Catholicism. Confident in their faith, Catholics felt able to ignore the existence of Protestantism, but the Catholic Church was a constant source of morbid fascination and speculation and generations of Protestant children were taught of the tyranny of Rome.

The religious divide was not a matter of mere theology but affected all aspects of life. Children of different denominations were usually educated in different schools controlled by their own clergymen, while social life revolved round the churches and associated organisations, thanks partly to the stiflingly gloomy Protestant conscience which discouraged the provision of public recreation and entertainment. The Catholic Church was particularly inventive in keeping its young together and ordering the temporal as well as the spiritual life of its members, while Protestants had in addition to their churches the Orange Order. Dedicated to maintaining

4

the Protestant religion and the Protestant ascendancy, the Order had originated in the rural tensions of North Armagh in the 1790s but had quickly become an integral part of political and social life in Ulster. By the twentieth century it embraced some two-thirds of the adult male Protestants organised hierarchically into lodges, and gave colour and cohesion to Protestantism and Unionism there. Its marches, sashes, banners, bands and thudding, evocative Lambeg drums lent excitement and drama, especially on the annual 12 July demonstrations celebrating the Battle of the Boyne. The Orange Halls provided social centres for Protestants, especially in the countryside, while the fact that all Protestants regardless of denomination or class could enter it on the same basis of equality enabled the Order to act as a link between different sections of society. Indeed, the Orange Order acted both as a social emollient and a stimulus to patriotic emotion, giving a sense of unity and purpose to Protestants but at the same time dividing them from their Catholic fellow-countrymen.

Ireland was also economically divided. The industrial development of the North-East marked it off from the rest of the country and helped to heighten the Ulster Protestant's sense of solidarity. Ulster as a whole was predominantly agricultural: even the six counties that eventually made up Northern Ireland were at first almost evenly balanced between town and country and for long agriculture remained the largest single employer of male labour. Nevertheless, the North-East was the only part of Ireland to industrialise in the nineteenth century, a process most obvious in Belfast which by the twentieth century had become the world's major linen centre and the home of two flourishing shipyards, Harland and Wolff and Workman Clark & Co (the 'wee yard'), producing some of the world's largest ships, including the ill-fated *Titanic*. Their success stimulated other developments in engineering and rope-making, while Belfast's transformation from an indifferent anchorage into a thriving port enabled its major industries to flourish, largely as exporting concerns, and to provide the core of the city's industrial prosperity before the First World War.

The industrial revolution in the North-East, which gradually spread out into a thirty or more mile radius around Belfast, had at least two consequences for Irish and Ulster politics. Most obviously, it separated Ulster from the rest of Ireland, for the North-East relied mainly on Britain and abroad for markets and raw materials and its industrial structure was inextricably bound up with that of Britain. The result was that Ulster hardly ever looked southwards and had more in common with Merseyside and Clydeside than with the rest of Ireland. Less obviously, but equally importantly, the nature of industrialisation helped to produce cohesion among Ulster Protestants, particularly those engaged in industry. The owners and management of most industrial and commercial concerns were Protestants as were the bulk of the workforce and the skilled trades. They comprised 93 per cent of Belfast's skilled working class in 1901, while Catholics, although constituting 24 per cent of the city's population, provided the remaining 7 per cent. The paternalism that characterised industrial relations in linen and the more cosmopolitan outlook of the aristocracy of labour in shipbuilding and engineering meant that the Protestant working classes were willing to accept the political leadership of their employers in order to maintain full employment. As one successful candidate, Belfast's most successful linen baron, told shipyard workers in 1880: 'I come to you with a desire to serve you. Your interests and mine are identical. You are working men, and so am I.'[3]

History, religion and economic development thus combined to divide Irishmen and to produce two distinct communities. How far they produced two nations is a matter for debate. Certainly, the validity of Irish nationalism has long been accepted, but it is doubtful whether Ulster Protestants constituted a separate nation, despite the sense of community and common interest that enabled them to combine in a mass movement of opposition to Irish nationalism. If anything, they resembled colonists in other parts of the world, such as Algeria or Rhodesia, where settlers formed a compact and dominant minority determined in face of local nationalisms to preserve their ascendancy, traditions and feeling of community which defied glib characterisation. Ulster Protestants had only a very hazy sense of nationality. They neither felt themselves truly British, which is probably why they identified so strongly with the Empire instead of Britain the nation state. Nor could they reject their Irishness. Their confusion was summed up by one clergyman who remarked in 1914 that 'If in one sense, Ulstermen are Irishmen first and Britishers afterwards, in another sense they are Ulstermen first and Irishmen afterwards.'[4]

Yet, however uncertain they may have been of their national identity, Ulster Protestants were absolutely certain that they were different from the Catholic majority of Ireland. If there were not two nations, there surely were, according to one leader, two Irelands — one 'Loyal', the other 'Disloyal' — both professing to have 'the welfare of their country as their dearest wish, but seeking to secure it by entirely different means'. 'Disloyal Ireland' sought by 'intimidation, by murder, by threats of revolt and separation' to extort 'from English fear that which England's reason refuses to concede'. 'Loyal Ireland', on the other hand, strove 'for their country's welfare by every lawful method within the lines of the Constitution of the Empire'.[5]

II

The modern phrase of the struggle between 'Loyal Ireland' and 'Disloyal Ireland', and the British pledges to both, dated from the late nineteenth century. Until then there had been only spasmodic and ineffectual demands for the repeal of the Act of Union and the restoration of self-government to Ireland. In the 1880s, however, Irish politics were transformed by the development of a powerful democratic and constitutional nationalist movement, which demanded not independence but a limited form of self-government within the British Empire, home rule as it was known. Drawing its strength from the Catholic tenant farmers and Catholic Church throughout the South of Ireland, the new movement was for many years powerfully led by Charles Stewart Parnell, mobilised through such organisations as the Irish National Land League and the Irish National League, and represented in parliament at Westminster by the Irish Parliamentary Party (IPP). The success of the movement, in the South at least, was evident in the 1885 general election. Outside Eastern Ulster and Trinity College, Dublin, no candidate other than pledge-bound IPP members succeeded in securing election so that home rulers won 85 of Ireland's 103 parliamentary seats.

The results of the 1885 general election highlighted the strengths and weaknesses of the home rule movement. Virtually unchallenged throughout most of Catholic Ireland, it made no headway in the predominantly Protestant areas of Ulster. With the eventual help of an energetic Northern 'boss', Joseph Devlin, the Catholic clergy and the Ancient Order of Hibernians, often regarded as the Northern Catholic equivalent to the Orange Order, the IPP won and retained the votes and loyalty of the Catholics of Ulster but it never succeeded in converting more than a handful of Protestants to home rule. Despite its failures in Ulster, the IPP dominated Irish politics and parliamentary representation for over thirty years, and under Parnell and later leaders, such as John Redmond, made British opinion uncomfortably aware of the changing aspirations of most Irishmen. Most notably, it succeeded in converting William Ewart Gladstone, leader of the Liberal Party and four times British Prime Minister, to home rule as early as 1885-6.

Gladstone's Home Rule Bills of 1886 and 1893, giving Ireland limited self-government within the Empire, were defeated in the House of Commons and House of Lords respectively. Conservatives and Unionists in Britain, as well as those in Ireland, completely rejected the notion of home rule, partly on narrow party grounds and partly on grounds of principle. They feared that any such concession at a time when other European states were accumulating overseas empires would spark off a chain reaction and lead to the eventual break-up of the British Empire. They also feared that home rule would jeopardise the prosperity and even the lives of members of Irish minorities loyal to Britain. Nevertheless, there grew in Britain a gradual recognition of the justice of the nationalist case and the obstacles to home rule were slowly eliminated. In particular, the passing of the Parliament Act in 1911 meant that the House of Lords, the barrier to home rule in 1893, could no longer reject outright but could only delay for up to two years any measure passed by the House of Commons.

Accordingly, in April 1912 Herbert Henry Asquith's Liberal government confidently introduced the Third Home Rule Bill bestowing a limited form of home rule on a Dublin parliament. It was warmly welcomed by Redmond, the leader of the IPP and prospective Prime Minister of Ireland, as a final settlement of the Irish question which would transform Ireland into a peaceful, prosperous and loyal part of the British Empire. Redmond had good reason for optimism, because thanks to the votes of his party Asquith's government had a large majority in the House of Commons, which soon endorsed the bill. Equally quickly, however, such optimism proved to be misplaced. The opponents of home rule in Britain and Ireland not only exploited the delaying powers left to the Lords and condemned the bill to complete three parliamentary circuits under the provisions of the Parliament Act; they also launched such a fierce agitation as to bring the United Kingdom to the verge of civil war by the time the bill was nearing the end of its protracted parliamentary odyssey in the middle of 1914.

III

The Irish Unionists, opponents of home rule, were largely responsible for the failure of the Third Home Rule Bill. In the mid-1880s an Irish Unionist movement had emerged among Irish Protestants to oppose Parnellism and maintain the legislative union with Britain. Despite initial attempts to hold together all Irish opponents of home rule in a single movement, Irish Unionists quickly divided into Southern Unionists, basically the Protestant ascendancy in the three provinces of Leinster, Munster and Connaught, and the Ulster Unionists, the Protestants of the northern province, maintaining separate organisations and developing different and sometimes competing policies and aims. In the long run Southern Unionism represented a lesser threat to Irish nationalism. The Southern Unionists were a small and scattered minority, representing at best some 10 per cent of the population of the South, and their strength lay in their connections with fickle British governing circles. In Ulster, on the other hand, there developed a mass movement in opposition to home rule, as landowners, tenant farmers, businessmen, artisans and labourers all combined in a movement which cut across class barriers. Often dismissed by opponents as an artificially contrived movement based on the deliberate exploitation of religious bigotry by landowners and employers, Ulster Unionism did, nevertheless, reflect and draw its strength from the regionalism of the North and its distinctive Protestant community.

Ulster Unionists would have no truck with 'Disloyal Ireland'. They scathingly denied that Ireland had ever been a separate and historic nation or that any genuine nationalist movement existed in the late nineteenth century, attributing the support given to the IPP to intimidation by priests and agitators enflamed by bad whiskey. Furthermore, they rejected nationalist criticisms of the harmful effects of British rule and retorted instead that British intervention had brought untold benefits to Ireland, turning Ulster from an economically backward 'sink of murder, misery and vice' into a 'land of smiling prosperity'.[6] Ulster Unionists were particularly attached to the constitutional and political arrangements established by the Act of Union. They enjoyed being part of the Protestant majority of the United Kingdom and believed that Ireland generally and the North-East in particular had prospered under the Union. Moreover, they were convinced that they would suffer sorely at the hands of an Irish parliament dominated by nationalists, Catholics and agriculturalists, which, through incompetence or malevolence, would put a swift end to Protestant ascendancy and Ulster's prosperity. Many Ulster Protestants did really believe that home rule meant Rome rule and all certainly declared that home rule would result in social and economic chaos and the abrogation of civil and religious liberties.

Such intransigent opposition to home rule and the claims of Irish nationalism is sometimes attributed to a 'siege mentality' and hostile commentators 'give the impression of a Kafka-like situation, in which the population behaves as if a siege were in progress, but no one refers to, or knows anything of, any besieging army'.[7] A siege mentality does, however, require besiegers and besiegers there were for Ulster Unionists in the late nineteenth and early twentieth centuries.

The main besiegers were, of course, Nationalists and Catholics who made no attempt to assuage their opponents' fears and convince them of the benefits of home rule. Like all nationalist movements, Irish nationalism was concerned with territorial unity, the integrity of what was seen as the national territory, rather than Irish brotherhood and did little to develop a political culture capable of uniting the population of the island. Indeed, quite the reverse happened with the Gaelic revival in the later nineteenth century, as the Gaelic Athletic Association (GAA), 1887, and the Gaelic League, 1893, sought to emphasise the uniqueness of the Gaelic Irish and to de-Anglicise Ireland. Sport was particularly divisive. Few Protestants participated in the Gaelic football, hurling and camogie organised by the GAA, which until 1970 banned its members from participating in such 'foreign' games as rugby, soccer, hockey and cricket and refused to permit members of the British armed forces or the police to participate in its sports. Generally, too, Nationalists were embarrassingly inept and misinformed on the preoccupations and achievements of the North, although this did not prevent the IPP from interfering with Belfast Corporation affairs at Westminster. What made this interference irksome to Ulster Unionists was the fact that Nationalist MPs dealt with Belfast affairs not on their merits but in order to win political and other concessions for Belfast Catholics, thus increasing the Protestant suspicion that 'ethnicity and not ability would determine the social stratification of Home Rule'[8] Ireland.

Neither did developments in the Catholic Church, locally and universally, do anything to calm Ulster Unionist fears. Ulster 'corruptive materialism, lust for wealth, and degrading urbanisation were the antithesis

9

of all that was holy, peasant and Catholic',[9] and to many Southern priests Ulster Protestants were not to be conciliated but converted. The possible effects of any crusade of conversion were seen in the promulgation in 1908 of a papal decree, *Ne Temere,* which tried to put an end to marriages between Catholics and Protestants. Much controversy was aroused in 1910 by its application to a case in Belfast, where one Alexander McCann, instigated it was alleged by his priest, left his Protestant wife and took away the children. Such 'encroachments of the Papal power in the United Kingdom'[10] alarmed Ulster Protestants and confirmed many in their belief that under an Irish parliament they would be reduced to the position of hewers of wood and drawers of water for their Catholic masters.

So determined were Ulster Unionists not to have home rule that they were prepared to resist by force of arms if necessary the authority of a Dublin parliament. However, in the first instance, they preferred constitutional methods and tried to fight the home rule movement by contesting elections in Ireland and by trying to persuade the British parliament and electorate of the folly of weakening the Union. To spearhead their battle they devised a series of organisations which held them together for over eighty years.

The first Ulster Unionist organisations developed in 1886, in response to Gladstone's conversion to home rule, but it was not until 1904-05 that the most comprehensive and effective organisation, the Ulster Unionist Council (UUC), was formed. It centralised Unionist forces in Ulster, determined policy and represented Ulster Unionist interests in Britain. It thus sought to be democratic and wholly representative of Ulster Unionism with a central council, the supreme governing body, of 200 representatives — 100 nominated by local Unionist associations, fifty by the Orange Grand Lodges, and the remaining fifty divided among MP, peers and *ex officio* members. These arrangements, which could be and were to be easily modified to enlarge the central council, ensured the representation of a wide range of opinion. Nevertheless, real control lay in the hands of a few landowners and professional and business men, for the day-to-day work was carried out by the permanent staff and a small elective standing committee. Within a short space of time the UUC became an effective political machine and the directing power of Ulster Unionism.

Electorally, the province was finely balanced between supporters and opponents of home rule and Unionists had their work cut out to secure a majority of its thirty-three parliamentary seats. Sometimes they and sometimes their opponents won seventeen seats. In Britain, they both worked through their parliamentary representatives and carried on, usually in conjunction with the Southern Unionists, a vigorous and extensive anti-home rule campaign in the constituencies, operating largely through local Conservative and Unionist associations. All this work was beset by difficulties. In Ulster, class tensions between town and country, landowners and farmers, industrial employers and employees and political divisions

10

between Liberals and Conservatives were often in danger of undermining cohesion, while the success of the appeal to Britain was by no means guaranteed. The Protestantism and imperialism of Ulster may have struck a response among Protestants and imperialists in Britain, especially in the Conservative and Unionist Party, but the Ulster Unionist case was often jeopardised by the tactlessness of its politicians and by the Ulster Protestant reputation for extremism and bigotry, especially when manifested in the sectarian rioting that had long been a feature of life in Belfast. The prolonged crisis over the Third Home Rule Bill, 1912-14, intensified these problems and provided a stern test of Ulster Unionists' determination, cohesion and discipline.

Admittedly, changes in the Conservative and Unionist Party in Britain did ease relations with the opposition. In November 1911 Arthur Balfour, unsympathetic to 'noisy Irish Protestants',[11] was replaced as leader by Andrew Bonar Law, a Scots-Presbyterian of Ulster descent who claimed to care about only two things in politics — tariff reform and Ulster. Moreover, the party at large, frustrated at continued exclusion from power and incensed at the clipping of the powers of the Lords, was the more inclined to endorse any stand taken by Ulster Unionists to thwart the Liberal government. Ulster Unionists did exploit this potential support by adopting an even more vigorous campaign in Britain, helping Conservative candidates in by-elections and concentrating money and men in marginal seats.

In the last analysis, however, Ulster Unionists were prepared to stand alone, for they had little confidence in Westminster's ability or willingness to protect them from Irish nationalism. Most leading politicians in England looked upon Ulster Unionists with something approaching contempt and this sentiment was heartily reciprocated by Ulstermen who felt that the English could not even see and look after their own interests let alone those of the British Empire. Much thought was thus given to the mobilisation of Unionist forces in Ulster. With the financial backing of the business community, the UUC laid down plans of opposition to the Third Home Rule Bill. It was agreed that a provisional government should be set up in the event of the bill becoming law and on 25 September 1911 a commission of five was appointed to draw up a constitution. Meantime, great efforts were to be made to sustain Unionist energies in Ulster and to convince the British electorate of their determination not to have home rule.

This campaign was dominated by two leaders whose names are often regarded as synonymous with Ulster Unionism — Sir Edward, later Baron, Carson, and James Craig, later Sir James and then Viscount Craigavon. A vain, hatchet-faced, hypochondriacal but talented lawyer with a penchant for histrionics, Carson was a fervent Unionist from Dublin who had a good standing in Britain as a successful barrister and a member of the last Conservative administration. Carson was the public face of Ulster Unionism in these years, but the mastermind behind the campaign was Craig, a

11

Presbyterian, the son of a whiskey millionaire and since 1906 MP for East Down. The future and first Prime Minister of Northern Ireland, Craig was a big, bluff, kindly-looking man with a large, red craggy face. Born with no sense of mission or great personal or intellectual gifts, he proved a competent backbench opposition MP, but the crisis over the Third Home Rule Bill enabled him to develop his one outstanding talent — the power of organisation. In those years as a potential rebel leader he showed prodigious energy and ingenuity in promoting the Ulster Unionist cause. His stability and geniality complemented Carson's mercurial temperament and powers of imagination. Each had what the other lacked, and pooling their resources 'they became a third and undeniable person. Effective apart, they were irresistible together.'[12]

At first, the method of agitation was by peaceful but massive demonstrations, culminating in the signing of the Solemn League and Covenant. A pledge by Ulster Unionists to use 'all means which may be found necessary to defeat the present conspiracy to set up a Home Rule Parliament in Ireland',[13] the Covenant acted both as a safety valve for popular emotion and as evidence to the world of the solidarity, determination and self-discipline of the movement. Covenant day, or Ulster Day, 28 September 1912, was declared a public holiday by the UUC, when 237,368 men signed the Covenant and 234,046 women signed a parallel declaration. Yet, in view of the scoffing of Irish nationalists and English Liberals at such 'Orangeade', something more than demonstrations was needed to underline the resolve of Ulster Unionists and maintain the movement's momentum. Thus at the end of 1912 a private volunteer army, the Ulster Volunteer Force (UVF), was organised. A distinguished Indian army officer was appointed commander of the force which eventually enrolled 90,000 men, organised into regiments and battalions with a number of supporting corps — Medical, Motor Car, Nursing, and Signalling and Despatch Riders.

Moreover, by the end of April 1914 the UVF was almost fully armed. Following increasing discontent among volunteers at having to parade with wooden rifles, the leadership of the UUC hesitantly decided to defy a recently-imposed ban on the importation of arms and authorised a Belfast businessman, Major 'Fred' Crawford, who had been gun-running for years, to buy arms and ammunition in Germany. The project, surrounded by secrecy and alarums, was dramatically and successfully concluded on the night of 24-25 April 1914, when the *Clydevalley* landed 35,000 rifles and 5 million rounds of ammunition at Larne harbour, which were speedily and efficiently distributed throughout the province by the carefully-briefed Motor Car Corps. It was a brilliant and novel piece of staff work, but Ulster Unionists' jubilation was not allowed to undermine discipline. Strict orders sent out from headquarters to ensure that the new arms would be well safeguarded and not misused were re-inforced by local commanders who instructed their men not to mix themselves up with riots or Street fights unless to protect themselves or other Protestants, who may be assaulted, or when called on by the Police to assist them . . .

No Rifles or Revolvers are to be used until the last extremity.[14]

The result of all these efforts was that by the summer of 1914, when the Home Rule Bill had completed its parliamentary circuits, Ulster Unionists were fully prepared to resist its implementation in their province and were in a position to form their own provisional government protected by an armed and disciplined volunteer force.

It was ironic that men who professed to be loyal to the Crown and staunch upholders of the constitution should threaten armed resistance to an act of parliament. The prospect did give some Ulster Unionists pause for thought, but in the last analysis they were convinced that resistance was justifiable, even a duty. They contended that the home rule policy violated the convention that parliamentary democracy must depend on respect for the convictions of minorities; and they further argued that the constitution was in suspense, since the Parliament Act prevented the House of Lords from submitting the question to the electorate. 'The Government,' Craig told the Commons, 'is not to be treated as a Government, but as a caucus, led by rebels.'[15] Such defiance was fully in keeping with the Presbyterian tradition which had done much to shape Ulster Unionism. That tradition was characterised by political radicalism, anti-establishment feeling, experience of persecution, intransigence and even (for example, in 1798) rebellion. Indeed, political thinking among Ulster Protestants had scarcely developed since the covenanting days of the seventeenth century, when contractual theories of government had been in vogue. The result was that Ulster Protestants and Unionists maintained that citizens owed only conditional allegiance to the government and that rebellion was perfectly justifiable should any government be deemed to be failing in its duty towards its subjects or any part of them. 'It is incompetent,' declared the UUC in 1912, 'for any authority, party or people to appoint as our rulers a government dominated by men disloyal to the Empire and to whom our faith and traditions are hateful.'[16]

IV

This campaign of defiance did not succeed in its original object of killing home rule once and for all. It did, however, focus attention on the Ulster question and generated in Britain a good deal of sympathy for the objections of Ulster Unionists. It was increasingly felt that while it would be unfair to allow Ulster Unionists to deprive the rest of Ireland of home rule, it would be equally unjust to force home rule and a Dublin parliament on an unwilling Ulster. It might also have been militarily impossible, for there was considerable support for the Ulstermen among some officers of the British army, as was dramatically manifested in March 1914 by the so-called Curragh mutiny. Under the mistaken impression that they were about to be ordered to take action against the Ulster Unionists, fifty-eight officers of the 3rd Cavalary Regiment stationed at the Curragh, the army's headquarters in Ireland, said that they would rather be dismissed than move against the North. The matter was soon glossed over, but Ulster Unionists benefited from the attendant publicity and found support in Britain growing almost daily.

The miners of North-East Derby, who had believed that Ulster was a town, were glad to have their ignorance corrected by Ulster Unionist canvassers equipped with an instructive industrial map of Ireland, while at the other end of the social scale a British Covenant movement was launched. Its first signatories included Field Marshal Lord Roberts, Rudyard Kipling and Sir Edward Elgar, and the motto of its magazine, *Covenanter,* was 'Put your trust in God and keep your powder dry'.[17] By the end of July nearly two million people were supposed to have signed the British covenant. Admittedly, the British support was less for Ulster than for what Ulster represented – a bastion of the Empire: 'The appeal for readiness and, if need be, resistance, was directed to Ulster but it was not for Ulster. It was for the integrity of the Empire that Ulster was to fight.'[18] Nevertheless, such support made impossible the coercion of Ulster before the First World War.

Such support gradually forced the Liberal government and the IPP to take Ulster Unionism seriously and to consider some amendment to accommodate it rather than risk violence and losing the Home Rule Bill altogether. Discussions began in the autumn of 1913, but it was not until following spring, as the bill was about to begin its final circuit, that serious attempts were made to reconcile the apprehensions of Ulster Unionists with the aspirations of Irish nationalists. The dilemma stimulated a good deal of ingenious political discussion but most attention was devoted to three broad lines of solution: the federal re-organisation of the United Kingdom; home rule within home rule; and the exclusion of Ulster from the jurisdiction of a Dublin parliament.

Advocates of federalism envisaged the devolution of power throughout the United Kingdom and the establishment of a number of regional parliaments, including two in Ireland, one for Ulster and the other for the remaining three provinces, all of which would send representatives to a central federal parliament in London. Such a scheme of 'home rule-all-round' would ensure that Ulster was governed, as Ulster Unionists demanded, in the same constitutional manner as the rest of the United Kingdom, and yet provide a parliament in Dublin for Irish nationalists. Moreover, it had the added attraction of safeguarding the integrity of the United Kingdom. As one among several, the Southern Irish parliament could never rival the imperial parliament at Westminster. It was an ingenious scheme, but too complicated to execute completely and speedily, although it did influence the eventual solution of Britain's Irish dilemma.

'Home rule within home rule', by contrast, involved the establishment of a parliament in Dublin to govern the whole of Ireland under a constitution which contained substantial safeguards for minorities. There might be extra representation for Ulster and/or a special committee to deal with matters affecting the North. Nationalists preferred this solution, because it respected the integrity of Ireland which was important to them ideologically and economically. Apart from believing that Ireland was one nation in a seamless garment, they also regarded Ulster's wealth and industry as essential to keep a self-governing Ireland solvent if not prosperous. Ulster Unionists, on the other hand, would have nothing to do with such a scheme. They refused to acknowledge the authority of any Dublin parliament however constituted and thought that the proposed safeguards would be valueless and unworkable. On the whole, British opinion agreed. A single parliament with an Ulster committee to monitor legislation would allow the committee to block and stultify the work of the Irish government without enabling it to develop Ulster itself; and it was doubted whether the artificial over-representation of Ulster Unionist areas was compatible with modern democratic notions.

The third suggestion, partition, the exclusion of Ulster from the jurisdiction of a Dublin parliament, appealed to most Ulster Unionist and British opinion. It had the obvious advantage of separating the two opposing sides. If ways could not be devised to enable them to live together, then Irish nationalists and Ulster Unionists had to be kept apart. The trouble was that partition not only offended nationalist susceptibilities but also raised at least three awkward questions. Should exclusion be permanent or temporary, with a time limit set by Westminster? What should be the status of the excluded area: should it be ruled directly from Westminster, or should it have some form of subordinate regional administration of its own? And which parts of Ulster should be excluded: the whole province, which had only a small Protestant majority, or simply the predominantly Protestant districts? Indeed, the drawing of a border raised a host of poignant conflicts between political wishes and geographical and economic reality, particularly for nationalists and Catholics. Political inclinations led one way, geography and economic self-interest the other, as for the large Catholic and Nationalist majority in the town of Newry. Its future as a port seemed to depend on the import of coal for distribution to the rest of Ulster, and its linen industry was bound up with Belfast and Britain. Moreover, a network of river valleys gave easy access to the North, whereas communications to the south and west were obstructed by a barrier of hills.

Of the three solutions, the idea of partition took the firmest root. In order to expedite the establishment of the long awaited Dublin parliament, the IPP reluctantly agreed to accept the temporary exclusion of part of Ulster from the jurisdiction of that parliament. This suspended death sentence, as they put it, was unacceptable to Ulstermen who wanted the permanent exclusion of all or most of the province. This difference of opinion contributed largely to the breakdown of a conference of party leaders summoned by King George V at Buckingham Palace in July 1914 so that the Irish question remained unsettled before the outbreak of war on 4 August. Nonetheless, the position of Ulster Unionists had been secured. When the Third Home Rule Bill finally went on the Statute Book in September 1914, its operation was suspended until the end of the war and Asquith dismissed as 'absolutely unthinkable'[19] any suggestion of the coercion of Ulster, pledging instead the introduction of an amending bill to meet the objections of Ulster Unionists to Irish home rule. By demonstrating the incompatability of Ulster Unionism and Irish nationalism, the crisis over the Third Home Rule Bill paved the way for the partition of Ireland.

Chapter 2
PARTITION AND DEVOLUTION

The idea of partition was almost overtaken by dramatic changes in Irish politics during and after the First World War. The rise of Republicanism and the eclipse of the IPP once more threw open the whole debate over Irish self-government and minority safeguards and for a time the favoured solution, except among Ulster Unionists, became 'home rule within home rule'. However, when the Irish question was seriously taken up by the British government, Lloyd George's Liberal and Conservative coalition, after the war, Ulster's separate position was secured. The 1920 Government of Ireland Act partitioned Ireland and set up not one but two devolved governments and parliaments, one for Southern Ireland, the other for Northern Ireland. An ill-conceived and inadequately thought-out measure, it was quickly superseded in the South but for fifty-one years remained the constitution of Northern Ireland.

I

The failure to win even a limited form of home rule before the war discredited the IPP and led to its eclipse by a new generation of nationalists inspired by an uncompromising sense of nationalism and committed to both the establishment of an Irish Republic and the maintenance of Irish unity. There had been signs of a changing mood before the war, such as the formation by Arthur Griffith in 1905 of Sinn Fein (Ourselves) and the success of the two organisations dedicated to the Gaelic revival, the GAA and Gaelic League. But it was not until the middle of the war that the Republicans showed their mettle and willingness to use violence to achieve their ends.

The initial excursion into the field, the Easter Rising of April 1916, was a military failure but as a blood sacrifice it re-awakened Irishmen to a sense of their nationality and, with good organisation and the help of British ineptitude, put the Irish republican movement on its feet. In the general election of 1918, held after the ending of the First World War, the IPP was swept aside, winning only six seats to the 73 won by the more uncompromising nationalists. Having ousted the home rulers in the South but not the Unionists in the North-East, the Republicans then tried to force the British out of Ireland and secure the Republic which had been declared during the Rising. Abroad they sought international recognition and in Ireland they tried both passive and armed resistance. They attempted to supplant existing British institutions at national and local levels. The victorious

17

Sinn Fein candidates in the 1918 general election refused to take their seats at Westminster and instead established Dail Eireann in Dublin. On 21 January 1919 the Dail pledged itself to the Irish Republic; it elected Eamon de Valera, the senior surviving officer of the Rising, President with Griffith as his deputy; and it set up various departments of state. On the other hand, an armed campaign was inaugurated. Also on 21 January 1919 the first shot was fired in 'The Troubles', otherwise known as the Anglo-Irish War or the War of Independence. The Republican forces, efficiently organised by Michael Collins who took command of what came to be known as the Irish Republican Army (IRA), waged guerrilla warfare against the British government. The latter was reluctant to deploy the regular army and preferred to retaliate with such controversial *ad hoc* forces as the Black and Tans and Auxiliaries, which were hastily recruited to re-inforce the severely under-manned and increasingly demoralised regular police, the Royal Irish Constabulary (RIC).

The Republic the new nationalists demanded was to rule the whole of Ireland. They were contemptuous of the IPP's readiness to compromise by contemplating even temporary partition, for, as Griffith once put it, 'Ireland cannot shift her frontiers. The Almighty traced them beyond the cunning of man to modify.'[1] Undeterred by the fact that Sinn Fein had made little headway in Ulster in the 1918 election, they dismissed the Ulster question as, de Valera told an American audience, 'a thing of the mind only, non-existent in the world of reality'[2] and attributed the agitation of Ulster Unionists to the machinations of the British government or 'a number of men ... who think that by keeping up the bogey of the Pope and the Boyne they can keep the industrial population quiet'.[3] By the middle of 1921 most of the new leaders recognised the intractability of the Ulster question and advocated accommodation, but until then they were uncompromisingly opposed to claims for special treatment. De Valera successively suggested that expulsion, coercion or assimilation into an Irish-Ireland should be the fate of Ulster Unionists.

Many people in Britain, even Conservative and Unionists, held Ulster Unionists at least partly responsible for this deterioration in Anglo-Irish relations, which first jeopardised the war effort and then threatened to blacken Britain's name throughout the civilised world. This feeling was all the stronger after Ulster Unionists had rejected a plan for an all-Ireland parliament put forward in the Irish Convention, convened by the British government in 1917-18 to shore up the IPP, outflank Republicans and Irish-Americans and encourage America to enter the war on the Allied side. Changing circumstances meant that many shared *The Observer's* view that 'the former unyielding exclusionist position of Ulster ... has become absolutely untenable'.[4] However, when Ulster Unionists remained adamantly committed to exclusion, Lloyd George's coalition government honoured earlier pledges with the Government of Ireland Act which superseded the 1914 Home Rule Act. Introduced in February 1920 and passed in the following December, it divided Ireland and answered the three questions long raised by discussions over exclusion and partition: the status, extent and duration of the area excluded from the jurisdiction of the Dublin parliament.

It decided that the excluded area should be ruled not directly from Westminster but on the same basis as the rest of Ireland. Thus two devolved governments, two subordinate administrations, were set up, one for Northern Ireland, consisting of the six counties of Antrim, Armagh, Down, Fermanagh, Londonderry and Tyrone plus the county boroughs of Belfast and Londonderry; the other for the remaining twenty-six counties of Southern Ireland. Both parts were given bi-cameral legislatures, a Commons elected by Proportional Representation (PR) and a Senate, elected on a high property qualification in the South to secure adequate representation of minority interests, but in the North mainly elected by PR by members of the Commons. Both parliaments were given almost complete power over most internal matters, such as law and order, local government, representation, education, social services, agriculture, industry and internal trade, but they had little control over revenue. Few taxes were transferred to them and the most important taxes – customs and excise and income tax and surtax – were reserved to Westminster which was to impose and collect them and dole out the revenue to both parts of Ireland in accordance with an agreed formula. In addition to these reserved services, which also included the Post Office, Savings Banks, land purchase and the Supreme Court, Westminster also retained power over 'excepted services', on which uniformity was essential throughout the United Kingdom, such as the Crown, the armed forces, external trade, coinage etc. Above all, ultimate sovereignty was reserved to the Westminster parliament, in which Irish representation was retained but drastically reduced.

The re-establishment of a parliament in Dublin represented a triumph, albeit a qualified one, for Irish nationalism, but the establishment of a parliament in Belfast was by no means an unqualified victory for Ulster Unionists. It was ironic that they, the most determined opponents of home rule, should themselves be given a form of home rule. They had never sought a parliament of their own and had agitated only to be governed as the rest of the United Kingdom. Nevertheless, the British government decided that they should have a separate parliament in order to facilitate the settlement of the Irish question. The obvious alternative – simple exclusion of the North with direct rule from Westminster – was unacceptable to Lloyd George's government because it would have kept Britain directly and openly embroiled in Irish affairs, enabling, so decided the cabinet's Irish subcommittee, 'opponents of Great Britain ... to say either that Great Britain is ruling nationalist majorities against their will, or that it is giving its active support to Ulster in its refusal to unite with the rest of Ireland'.[5] Seeing which way the wind was blowing, Ulster Unionists decided to make a sacrifice, as they put it, in the interest of peace, and accept their own regional administration. Self-preservation as much as patriotism prompted this decision, for a parliament of their own offered better security against rule by Dublin. They fully realised that there was little sympathy and affection for them in Britain and feared that Westminster might try to force them into the South. They, therefore, saw safety in

> Having a Parliament of our own, for we believe that once a Parliament is set up and working well . . . we should fear no one, and we feel that we would then be in a position of absolute security . . . and therefore I say that we prefer to have a Parliament, although we do not want one of our own.[6]

The decision to erect a six-counties border did, however, represent a triumph for the Ulster Unionist viewpoint. It was the largest area with the safest Unionist majority. Nationalists had wanted the exclusion of the smallest possible area, probably only the four counties of Antrim, Armagh, Down and Londonderry, while there were those of all political persuasions who advocated the exclusion of the whole historic province of Ulster as a geographic, economic and historic entity, a view which attracted the Lloyd George government. Any boundary line would have raised serious problems, but, in the event, the wisdom of Solomon was not required, because the six-counties border was the only one acceptable to the majority of Ulster Unionists. Despite cries of betrayal from fellow Covenanters in Cavan, Donegal and Monaghan, leading Ulsters Unionists decided to sacrifice these three counties in the interests of the stability of Northern Ireland.

A nine-counties Northern Ireland would contain only a small, 56 per cent, Protestant majority, 890,880 non-Catholics to 690,816 Catholics, and it was feared that even this slim majority would be jeopardised by the growth of the Labour vote in and around Belfast. The Unionist majority in a nine-counties parliament would, therefore, be so slender that 'no sane man would undertake to carry on a Parliament with it. . . . A couple of Members sick, or two or three Members absent for some accidental reason, might in one evening hand over the entire Ulster Parliament and the entire Ulster position' to the South. 'A dreadful thing to contemplate,' said one of their parliamentary spokesman.[7] On the other hand, a six-counties Northern Ireland with a 66 per cent Protestant majority, 820,370 non-Catholics to 430,161 Catholics, would be safe for Protestantism and Unionism. Indeed, with the rise of Republicanism it was held to be more in keeping with the letter and spirit of the Covenant than a nine-counties split, since it would provide an imperial base in Ireland to protect the southern minority and the Empire's strategic interests.

Finally, partition was not meant to be permanent. No time limit was set, but the whole of the 1920 act was framed on the assumption that Irish unity was both desirable and attainable and various inducements were offered to the two Irish parliaments to ensure that partition would be only temporary. A Council of Ireland, representative of both parliaments, was to deal with matters of common concern, and if they decided to unite, then the British government would confer upon a united Ireland more significant accolades of statehood by transferring most of the crucial powers originally and deliberately withheld as an incentive to unity. Partition was, in fact, no deep-laid plot on the part of Britain to divide Irishmen and retain Ireland in its clutches. It was simply a recognition of reality. Irishmen were divided before partition: partition merely recognised, though ultimately accentuated, these divisions.

<h1 style="text-align:center">II</h1>

If partition was realistic and even inevitable, the way it was executed was not. The establishment of two Irish parliaments may have resolved Britain's immediate problem of withdrawing from Ireland while redeeming contradictory pledges, but it only stored up future trouble. The hope that it would foster Irish unity was based upon wishful thinking rather than serious calculation. The two parts of Ireland soon went their separate ways with very unequal parliaments and very different attitudes. In face of the dominance of Republicanism and the violence of the Anglo-Irish War, the 1920 act was stillborn in the South which shortly received the much wider powers of a dominion and gradually but inexorably detached itself from the Empire and Commonwealth as well. Thus the 1920 act became effective only in Northern Ireland where it hardly made for good government and civic contentment. From the middle of 1921 Northern Ireland became a semi-autonomous region of the United Kingdom but operated under considerable handicaps. Ingenious though it was, the 1920 act was an ill-considered measure which failed to take account of the difficulties likely to face a six-counties administration and to provide satisfactory institutions of government, a satisfactory political and administrative structure.

Most notably, the distribution of power and responsibility was hardly conducive to prompt, efficient, disinterested and even fully representative government. In theory, Northern Ireland had wide power over its internal affairs – law and order, local government, representation, education, social services, industry, agriculture and internal trade (and eventually trade with other parts of the United Kingdom as well). In reality, the capacity to develop distinctive regional policies was highly circumscribed. The 1920 act prohibited the confiscation of property, religious discrimination and the endowment of any religion, while reserving ultimate sovereignty to Westminster (article 75). But more important than these constitutional restrictions were those imposed by administrative and financial practice.

Responsibility for the administration of transferred services was shared between the regional government and parliament and congeries of local authorities inherited from the Union. In the early twentieth century there were six county councils, two county borough councils, thirty-six borough councils, urban district councils and town commissions, thirty-two rural district councils and twenty-seven boards of guardians. Hardly models of civic responsibility, they had long been distinguished by their partisanship and extreme conservatism. They were first and foremost party political battlegrounds and sources of employment and patronage. They had no elevated or dynamic concept of their role in providing services to the community at large and preferred instead to keep rates as low as possible.

The way its finances were arranged also limited Northern Ireland's real power and capacity for independent action. It lacked control over its revenue, which was derived from three main sources: transferred revenue largely levied by its own parliament from such minor taxes as death and motor duties; special payments from the British Treasury; and reserved revenue, controlled by Westminster, including such major taxes as income tax, surtax and customs and excise. Transferred revenue comprised at most only 20 per cent of its income, the bulk of which was thus determined by Westminster, not in accordance with the needs of Northern Ireland but in accordance with those of the United Kingdom as a whole. In addition, Northern Ireland had little real control over its expenditure. In law it did, for the transferred services accounted for some 90 per cent of expenditure. In practice, however, the pace of spending was set by Britain, whose example Northern Ireland felt obliged to follow to ensure that Northern Irishmen received the same benefits as people in the rest of the United Kingdom. Ulstermen were, after all, paying the same taxes.

The inadequacy of such financial provisions was evident from the very beginning. Revenue proved much lower and expenditure much higher than original estimates had forecast. The forecasts had planned for a revenue of £16.5m (£1.8m transferred, £14.7m reserved) and expenditure of £6.3m (£4.1m on transferred services, £2.2m on reserved services). Of the surplus £10.2m, £7.9m was to provide Northern Ireland's contribution towards the cost of imperial services, with the remaining £2.25m as 'pocket money' for the new government. The reality, even in the first full financial year of 1922-3, was entirely different. Revenue was only £13.8m (£1.9m transferred, £11.9m reserved), but expenditure had risen to £6.9m (£5m transferred, £1.9m reserved), leaving a surplus of only £6.9m. Had the imperial contribution remained at £7.9m, Northern Ireland would have had not the promised bonus of £2.25m but a deficit of one million pounds. It was the same story in the following years. The amounts may have got larger, but revenue was always chasing expenditure, with the result that Northern Ireland was often on the verge of bankruptcy and always financially dependent on Britain. It was always able to balance its budget while expanding its services, but the price of repeated begging expeditions to the Treasury was the devaluation of representative institutions and a further restriction on regional autonomy. Policies on a wide range of transferred matters had to be trimmed to suit British notions of financial and economic propriety, while the complicated details of financial relations were settled in private by civil servants rather than elected representatives or the Joint Exchequer Board, the body responsible under the 1920 act for attributing revenue and determining Northern Ireland's imperial contribution. Not even the British Chancellor or his deputy, one cabinet minister commented in the late 1960s, 'knew the formula according to which the Northern Ireland Government gets its money. In all these years it has never been revealed to the politicians and I am longing to see whether now we shall get to the bottom of this very large, expensive secret.'[8]

While in most respects the form of devolution bestowed upon Northern Ireland restricted opportunities for regional development, in one crucial and ultimately fatal respect it allowed too much freedom: the working-out of sectarian rivalries. The 1920 act completely ignored the fact that Ulster society as well as Irish society at large had been rent by bitter divisions both historically and in the struggle over home rule, as Ulster Catholics and Nationalists fought against Ulster Protestants and Unionists and identified with their co-religionists in the rest of Ireland. It also overlooked the fact that the Ulster Unionists, who were to rule Northern Ireland, had not developed over the years of struggle any political philosophy to enable them to take responsibility for a government they had neither expected nor wanted. Lloyd George's government simply assumed that majority rule would operate as satisfactorily in Northern Ireland as it did in Britain, and thus the 1920 act offered no inducements to the minority to participate and failed to erect adequate safeguards to ensure just and impartial government. What safeguards there were (the retention of PR in parliamentary elections for three years and the prohibition of religious discrimination and the confiscation of property) were designed to help the scattered Southern minority, the Southern Unionists; and while the Southern Senate was so constituted as to involve the minority in the process of government, the Northern Senate was intended to reproduce the Unionist majority in the Commons, where it was argued, the minority would be strongly represented.

Nor did the fact that Northern Ireland remained an integral part of the United Kingdom act as a minority safeguard or a corrective to regional myopia. No thought was given to the question of the effective exercise of Westminster's ultimate sovereignty to iron out deficiencies in regional government. Britain had a considerable financial whiphand over Northern Ireland, but chose to make little use of this weapon to influence the general administration of transferred services, particularly in respect of relations between Protestants and Catholics.

In fact, the six-counties border, long and tortuous, aggravated this particular problem. It did give Unionists and Protestants a safe majority which hardly varied over the years, as the proportion of two-thirds non-Catholics to one-third Catholics remained roughly constant. However, the size of this majority did not engender a sense of confidence in Ulster Unionists. A substantial Catholic minority remained committed to nationalist traditions and ideals and was so distributed as to represent a major threat in some areas. The uneven distribution of Protestants and Catholics created both centres of power and sources of fear and resentment. The Protestant majority was strongest in the east, the Catholics in the south and west, but neither constituted a completely homogenous bloc. In the east the Protestantism of Belfast was compromised by the existence of a large Catholic community along and above the Falls Road, which comprised about one-quarter of the city's population and was hemmed in by two staunchly Protestant working-class districts, the Sandy Row and Shankill. The city of Londonderry contained a Catholic majority, but the surrounding countryside was largely Protestant. In the far west Protestant communities felt equally vulnerable. In West Tyrone they found the border to the west and to the east a large Catholic population cutting them off from the Protestant majority on the other side of the province. In Fermanagh Protestants formed a triangular wedge in the centre of the county with its base along the southern border. They thus lived on the doorstep of the dreaded South, and were completely isolated from their co-religionists elsewhere. In such areas many Protestants thought that they were well on the way to being absorbed into a Catholic-dominated state, and proximity to the South re-inforced that fear. What is more, Protestants worried about being outbred by Catholics who for long had a higher birth-rate – as much as 50 per cent higher – than Protestants as a whole, a rate of increase which could be enlarged by immigration from the South. A high rate of Catholic emigration kept the population balance, but speculating about the year in which Catholics would finally be in a majority in Northern Ireland became a titillatingly painful habit among Ulster Unionists, something akin to probing an aching tooth with the tongue.

III

All these defects in the 1920 settlement were enhanced by the circumstances in which regional government had to operate in Northern Ireland. First and foremost, was the political immaturity of Ulstermen. The size of a large English county but with a much smaller population, Northern Ireland lacked sufficient men of ability and vision to man the glut of representative bodies with which it had been blessed or cursed. There was a distressing amateurism about MPs who displayed both lack of information and a curious refusal to accept responsibility. The only issues on which they took a six-counties view were the most divisive ones of the constitution and religion: the maintenance or otherwise of partition; and the defence of either Protestantism or Catholicism. Otherwise, members preferred to look at questions, as one of them urged, 'not from the point of view of Belfast or the country districts, but from the point of view of what their local knowledge is'.[9] The dearth of political talent and unwillingness to take a broad view was as marked at the top. Leaders of all religious or political persuasions found difficulty in escaping from conventional grooves. Co-operation between political parties is never easy, but even within parties leaders were slow to subordinate personal and local interests in order to devise well-considered policies in the interests of Northern Ireland as a whole. It is not surprising that leaders of opposition parties, denied access to power, should find difficulty in devising comprehensive policies, but neither did the Unionist Party, the governing party, produce leaders capable of taking Ulstermen and their problems by the scruff of the neck.

The limitations of politicians were those of society at large. Home rule neither brought about a miraculous transformation nor fostered a sense of Ulster nationalism that looked to the community as a whole. Instead, society continued to be characterised by an intense conservatism and manifold divisions, with geographical, economic and class divisions sometimes cutting across the great religious divide. The division between the industrial and more prosperous east and the agricultural south and west was a constant source of complication. It was not simply, as is often said, a conflict between Protestant and Catholic areas, because the Protestant and Unionist minority in the south and west of the province was also exercised by the distinction and resented what it regarded as the undue attention given to the affairs of Belfast and its environs. Moreover, the east and west were themselves divided by highly localised loyalties to a particular townland, urban or rural district, or even part of working-class Belfast where community ties were particularly strong, such as the Protestant Shankill, where one survey in the late 1960s found that 82 per cent of all residents had relatives in the area and no fewer than 45 per cent of the men and 60 per cent of the women had lived there all their lives.

Some of these economic and geographical divisions reflected class differences, but such class differences were too muted to overcome the sectarian divide and bring about a re-alignment of parties and opinion. This was particularly true of the conflict between Capital and Labour. Employers were well organised into industrial and trade associations and chambers of trade and commerce, and the large industrial workforce in and around Belfast became one of the most unionised in Western Europe and maintained links with trade unionists in the South. The often opposing economic interests of the two sides of industry complicated but left fundamentally untouched the integrity of the conflict on constitutional and religious questions. Unlike their British counterparts, Northern Ireland unions failed to sponsor a party capable of surmounting the sectarian divide and challenging for political power on the basis of the reconstruction of the economy and society. Remaining a forum for workers of all religions only by avoiding contentious issues dividing society, they thus shared 'the problems of amorous eunuchs, well-intentioned and willing to take action, but unable by their nature to produce fruitful results'.[10]

Yet, although they had limited views, Ulstermen held them strongly and without reticence. Any and every issue could call forth some more or less representative pressure group demanding the ear and even the body and soul of public men. What is more, the size of the country and its informal social manners meant that they were assured of at least the ear of the object of their attention. Such accessibility was not without advantages, making sometimes for prompt and personal government and administration. Northern Ireland MPs were used much more frequently by their constituents than had been the case with Westminster MPs under the Union, while ease of access to ministers and government departments was even more appreciated, especially the way Prime Ministers could sweep 'red tape aside in a regal fashion' and utter their fiat 'let it be done from this day'.[11] However, the disadvantages of accessibility were even more obvious. Ministers and politicians generally lacked the prestige and mystique of their British counterparts and were unable to distance themselves psychologically and physically from problems and supporters.

Moreover, the position of political leaders was made the more difficult by the refusal of many Ulstermen to be bound by normal constitutional and political methods. The activities of extra-parliamentary groups in both Protestant and Catholic communities eventually rendered constitutional processes almost irrelevant, but even before then their very existence exercised a considerable influence on politicians who sometimes used the men of violence as instruments of policy but were more often than not their prisoners. Rather than providing an incentive for constitutionalists to unite, potential or actual violence usually polarised opinion still further. Quite apart from the very real threat of personal danger, politicians were often deterred from abandoning established positions lest they lost support to extreme elements ready to denounce any change as betrayal or surrender, while violence by one side merely hardened the attitude of the other instead of cowing it into submission. Like much else in Northern Ireland, the existence and activities of extra-constitutional groups was destructive of political initiative.

In fact, to be a politician in Northern Ireland was a very narrowing experience. Horizons which expanded during absences soon narrowed again on return to the six counties. Governments and politicians rarely led, but were at the mercy of so many pressures that calm political discussion and detached and efficient government became virtually impossible. The interests of the region or community as a whole often became obscured by, and were sometimes deemed to be identical with, sectional, private or party interests. The restricted nature of politics and political thinking was reflected in the fact that throughout most of Northern Ireland's separate existence there were only two consistently and properly organised political parties, the Northern Ireland Labour Party (NILP) and the Unionist Party. The former, which tried to cut across the sectarian divide and for long to ignore the constitutional question, met with little success. The latter enjoyed a long succession of resounding electoral victories largely because it remained unadventurous, Protestant and totally committed to maintaining the Protestant ascendancy and the status of Northern Ireland.

A second difficulty constantly dogging Northern Ireland's existence was an economic one – the decay of the traditional economy. Under the Union Ulstermen had boasted of their prosperity and it was ironic that the decline of the old staples, agriculture, linen and shipbuilding, should coincide with partition. Partition may have aggravated the problem by cutting up market areas and depriving Northern manufacturers and traders of their traditional markets in the South, but the basic cause of the decline was changing world economic conditions following the First World War. Agriculture was at first affected by a world-wide decline in the price of foodstuffs and by fierce and superior foreign competition in the British market. The over-expansion of world trade and later changing requirements caused a fall in demand for the types of vessels in which the Belfast shipyards had long specialised. The decline in the linen industry was also permanent, brought about by the introduction of new fibres, high tariffs in the United States (the best customer) and the development of the industry overseas where production costs were lower. The consequent problem of unemployment was increased by people's insistence on reproducing themselves more often and eventually living longer than those in the rest of the United Kingdom and thus, despite a high rate of emigration, annually swelling the number of those seeking work.

The problem was made more intractable by the fact that unemployment affected some areas and communities more than others. It was more severe in agricultural than industrial areas, that is, it was worse in the largely Catholic south and west, where there were fewer alternative occupations to compensate for contracting agricultural employment. Still further complications were created by the fact that dramatically high percentages of unemployment in areas with small populations did not necessarily mean the existence of a substantial enough potential workforce to attract modern industries, while the 'employment mix' often led to higher male than female unemployment.

Attempts to re-invigorate the economy and provide employment either by the revival of existing or the attraction of new industries faced daunting obstacles. Despite formal responsibility for agriculture, internal trade and industry, Northern Ireland lacked real power to regulate its economic life. Economically, it did not constitute a separate economy, but was part of a single economic system embracing the whole of the United Kingdom and its industries, trades and unions were organised on this basis of economic interdependence, if not outright dependence. Moreover, Northern Ireland was the most disadvantaged part of the United Kingdom economy. The existence of a reasonably docile workforce with a good industrial tradition and a responsive regional administration were undoubted advantages, but they were largely offset by the disadvantages of geographical location, lack of natural resources, a small internal market and liability to political crisis, all of which put Northern Ireland at a disadvantage compared with other areas, particularly in the rest of the United Kingdom, which were competing for new industries. These 'natural' economic constraints were reinforced by constitutional and financial ones, for Northern Ireland lacked adequate powers of economic and financial manipulation. It could not offer protective barriers to existing and incoming enterprises, for these matters depended on Westminster. Nor could it give significant financial aid without British sanction.

Attempts to resolve these problems were as much a cause of controversy as of congratulaton, as in the case of aid to existing industries. Fundamental weaknesses of the farming and linen industries were high costs of production and inefficiency caused by the small scale of the operations conducted by the small family firms which dominated these industries. In such circumstances, subsidies either propped up some very inefficient and uneconomic concerns, largely in the interests of owners, or actually reduced employment, for effective rationalisation meant the elimination of many enterprises with the consequent loss of jobs. On the other hand, incentives offered to incoming enterprises were resented not only by existing businessmen but also by those concerned about the cost of creating jobs to line the pockets of interlopers with no permanent interest in the country. This financial aspect lent further fuel to a bitter controversy over the location of new industries, most of which opted for the existing industrial complex centred on Belfast, as the entrepreneur's tendency to gravitate towards established centres of industry and communications may have been re-inforced by doubts about the stability and future of the border areas. Whatever the cause, many, and not only Catholics and nationalists, were willing to believe that it was part of a deep-laid Unionist plot to further depopulate the Catholic areas by depriving them of sorely needed opportunities for industrial employment.

The weaknesses of its economy meant that Northern Ireland became the poorest part of the United Kingdom. Its rate of unemployment was usually the highest in the kingdom and people earned less in Northern Ireland than in Britain. High unemployment and low incomes further accentuated historic divisions, particularly between Catholics and Protestants. Violence tended to vary with the level of economic distress, and in times of political crisis rioting was more severe in those towns or parts of towns which constituted areas of greatest social need. Even in 'normal' times economic conflict was not far from the surface and in times of severe depression the question of employment became a passionate and divisive issue. Catholics complained of discrimination against them, while Protestants were concerned that too many Catholics were being employed at their expense. In fact, the problem of the decaying economy was not a problem of economics alone but had repercussions throughout an already divided society.

The operation of government and politics in Northern Ireland was yet further affected by the existence of the 'Irish dimension' — the continued nationalist commitment to Irish unity reinforced by the existence of an independent Southern state claiming sovereignty over the North. Initially, before a settlement was reached in the South, the Irish dimension threatened the very existence of Northern Ireland as part of the United Kingdom. Once a settlement between Britain and the South was achieved, most Southern Irishmen quickly abandoned the idea of coercion, not simply because of the determination of Ulster Unionists to maintain partition, but also because the happy vision of a united Ireland was somewhat marred by the reflection that an influx of a large number of Northern Protestants, impatient with the South's Gaelic and Catholic traditions, would overnight turn an overwhelmingly Catholic state into a mixed religious society with a strong, compact and scarcely amenable Protestant minority. Moreover, the economic and financial consequences of re-unification became yearly more daunting with the decline of the North's once prosperous industries and then the establishment and extension of the welfare state in Britain. Indeed, it became increasingly clear that any scheme of Irish unity would have to be heavily subsidised from outside sources.

Such obstacles explain why Dublin took no decisive action to bring down the North, but they did not stop many leading politicians, especially the long-lived de Valera, from frequently stomping around the world condemning partition. In times of crisis Southern governments and politicians claimed the right to intervene in the North's affairs and were quick to attribute all troubles to partition. Moreover, despite repeated disavowals of force and assertions that unity could be achieved only by peaceful means, there was no consistent effort to win over the Northern majority by offering inducements to unity. On the contrary, Southern policy and attitudes often seemed calculated to confirm Ulster Unionists' worst fears of Dublin rule, for on a wide range of issues little account was taken of their susceptibilities. Economic policy began to show some sensitivity in the 1960s, but not until the 1970s was there serious discussion in the South as to how far its constitution and laws were repugnant to Ulster Unionists and Protestants and what amendments were needed to make them more palatable. In fact, Southern policies were determined by Southern economic and political needs with scant regard for their impact on the North or their ultimate consequences for the cause of Irish unity, especially as changes to ease the path of relations with the North could be easily denounced as betrayals of Catholicism and nationalism.

The attitude of the South accentuated and gave an added edge of bitterness and fear to the already grave difficulties under which Northern Ireland had to labour. In particular, it was largely responsible for the importance attached to the constitutional question, which was discussed not in a vacuum but in the knowledge that there was on its borders a sovereign state convinced of its right to rule the whole of Ireland. Nationalists were deterred from fully participating in and regarding Northern Ireland as their own state. There always seemed the prospect of Irish unity and nationalists, especially in the border areas, were readily seduced by the anti-partitionist rhetoric of men like de Valera. Moreover, the insistence of Southern governments and politicians on dabbling in the North's internal affairs undermined both the unity and credibility of local Catholic and nationalist leaders. Similarly, Southern claims to and intervention in the North made real and kept alive Protestant and Unionist fears of being engulfed by Irish nationalism and Catholicism and created an unhealthy sense of insecurity among Unionist politicians alarmed that they might be outdone if not overrun by the South. The greater independence of the South, with its wider powers of economic and financial management, in the early years often threw into stark relief the helplessness of the North, prompting some Londonderry Unionists to ask in 1926, 'What is the use of staying under a Government that either don't care a d——n for our interests, or at any rate can't protect them?'[12]

VI

In face of all these difficulties — a ramshackle political structure, a dearth of political talent, a divided society, a decaying economy and an irridentist neighbour — the wonder is not that the 1920 settlement eventually collapsed in violence in 1972 but that it lasted so long. To that extent Lloyd George's dual plan of partition and devolution was a success. It extricated Britain from its debilitating Irish dilemma and for over fifty years removed the storm centre of Irish politics from Westminster. But the price of Westminster's relief was paid by Northern Ireland which became the most disadvantaged part of the United Kingdom with an unenviable reputation for sectarianism, bigotry and violence.

30

Chapter 3

STRUGGLE FOR SURVIVAL

Unwanted creation that it was, the new government of Northern Ireland had to fight for survival in the early months of its existence, 1921-2. Not only did it have to face the normal problems associated with the foundation of any new state, such as the erection of governmental machinery and the establishment of credibility in the eyes of its citizens, but it was also confronted in their most virulent form with all the special difficulties that were to characterise its subsequent history — confused lines of responsibility, economic distress, shortage of cash and, above all, attacks from within and without. There was constant pressure on Ulster Unionists to surrender their new-found security and submit to Dublin rule; nationalist and Catholic opinion throughout Ireland remained hostile and aloof; and a combination of communal violence and IRA assaults brought Northern Ireland to the verge of anarchy. Thanks largely to the efforts and temperament of its first Prime Minister, James Craig, Northern Ireland survived, but only at a price. What chance it had of becoming a united and loyal, if not prosperous, part of the United Kingdom was ruined by the events of 1921-2 which deepened existing divisions and laid the foundations of Northern Ireland's reputation for unjust and partisan government.

I

Craig gave up a promising career in British politics to become Northern Ireland's first Prime Minister. Since leading the Ulster revolt of 1912-14, he had enjoyed a reasonably successful career as a junior minister in various government departments and there was even talk of cabinet office. Yet, although he returned to Northern Ireland out of a sense of duty rather than hope of personal fulfilment, he looked forward to a bright future in Northern Ireland. His government would be, he pledged, 'at the disposal of the people of Northern Ireland' and would only have in view their welfare. Its duty and privilege would be 'to look to the people as a whole, to set ourselves to probe to the bottom those problems that have retarded progress in the past, to do everything that lies in our power to help forward developments in town and country. . . . We will be cautious in our legislation. We will be absolutely honest and fair in administering the law.'[1] Craig had qualities that made him the more fitting midwife to Northern Ireland than the ageing, ill and administratively incompetent Carson. Apart from his organisational and administrative abilities, Craig had huge energy and a massive calm which defused crises and deflated

31

ranting opponents. Admittedly, his lack of imagination and his touching confidence in the abilities and fair-mindedness of his Ulster Unionist supporters turned out to be serious defects in his leadership, but his patient determination steered Northern Ireland through many of its initial difficulties.

The most immediate problem, the creation of an apparatus of state, was completed in the first part of 1921. Under the Union the powers of government had been distributed among some thirty different departments, and the problem was how to group these powers most efficiently in Northern Ireland without producing too many office holders in parliament. After administrative convenience had been weighed against political expediency, the scheme of government announced towards the end of May 1921 contained seven departments: the Prime Minister's, which was to co-ordinate activities in Northern Ireland and act as a channel of communication with the imperial government, and the Ministries of Finance, Home Affairs, Education, Labour, Agriculture and Commerce.

The choice of ministers to head these departments reflected no long-term political programme or vision of the future. Rather it reflected Craig's desire to secure a respectable cabinet, to reward past services to Ulster Unionism and to balance the various geographical and sectional interests of the province. The Minister of Home Affairs, Sir Richard Dawson Bates, a solicitor, had been since 1905 honorary secretary to the UUC and had thus been closely involved in the organisation of resistance to home rule. The conscientious, energetic and humane John Miller Andrews, a linen manufacturer and chairman of the Ulster Unionist Labour Association (UULA), became Minister of Labour, while Hugh McDowell Pollock, a flour importer with a fine mind and the Ulster Unionists' leading financial expert, was appointed Minister of Finance. The east of the province was represented by the Minister of Education, the 7th Marquess of Londonderry, who owned much land in Co. Down, had held junior office at Westminster and was later to attain cabinet rank there: he may have stood too much on his dignity and spent too much time in England, but he was respected and had broader views than most Ulstermen. The west was represented by a man from an old Co. Fermanagh family, Edward Mervyn Archdale, who initially took charge of the Ministries of Agriculture and Commerce. He was not bearing his sixty-eight years well and had difficulty in reaching Belfast, but his long experience as a Westminster MP enabled him to preside decently over his ministries.

Most of these were good initial appointments, lending dignity, weight and talent to the government. The exception was Bates's appointment as Minister of Home Affairs. His was a key ministry, involving responsibility for some of the most controversial questions in Northern Ireland, such as electoral affairs, local government and law and order, but Bates, a small man physically and intellectually, was unable to give such questions the careful and sympathetic handling they so urgently required, particularly since he looked upon all Catholics as nationalists and all nationalists not just as political enemies but as traitors. Moreover, the attitude of his subordinates did little to mitigate his partisanship or broaden his outlook. His first Parliamentary Secretary, Richard Dick Megaw, a barrister, could be the most uncompromising of Unionists, while experience of Dublin Castle methods had given his first Permanent Secretary, Samuel Watt, a less than disinterested attitude on questions affecting law and order.

The first senior civil servants were drawn either from Dublin or Westminster, while a number of experienced officials were borrowed for short periods from various British departments to help get the Northern Ireland departments off the ground. For the rest it had been hoped to transfer civil servants from Dublin, but officials were slow to apply for Northern postings. Thus, despite frequently reiterated complaints that it was manned by Southerners and Englishmen at the expense of Ulstermen, the bulk of the civil service was from the start recruited locally. There were a number of political appointments, but the majority were recruited by a specially established Selection Board which tried to apply the entrance criteria of the imperial civil service, particularly loyalty and competence. Since competence did not necessarily imply experience, the early years of the Northern Ireland civil service were something of an adventure.

The size and powers of the parliament were laid down by the Government of Ireland Act. The House of Commons of fifty-two members, all representing territorial constituencies, was to be elected by PR on the single-transferable vote system. The Senate was half the size, consisting of two *ex-officio* and twenty-four members elected, also by PR, by the House of Commons. The first elections to the Commons took place on Empire Day, 24 May, and was both the first general election in Northern Ireland and the first general election in the United Kingdom to be held under PR. The campaign revolved entirely around the question of partition. The remnants of the old IPP condemned partition as a violation of Ireland's historic unity; de Valera on behalf of Sinn Fein urged that 'Ireland one is Ireland peaceful, prosperous and happy'; but Craig exhorted Unionists to 'Rally round me that I may shatter your enemies and their hopes of a Republic flag. The Union Jack must sweep the polls.'[2] The Union Jack did sweep the polls. Eighty-nine per cent of the electorate voted, and when the poll was declared on 27 May it was a triumph for official Unionism. Every Unionist candidate who stood was elected. Having expected to win only 32 or 36 seats, Unionists actually took 40, the remaining 12 being equally divided between Nationalists and Sinn Fein. The size of their majority of 28 obscured the facts that Unionists won only two of the four Co. Armagh seats and that in the large combined constituency of Fermanagh and Tyrone 57 per cent of the electorate had voted against partition and had returned four anti-partition candidates.

The government and parliament were eventually housed in the imposing Parliament Buildings at Stormont, a district near Belfast, hence the use of the term Stormont to describe the regime and parliament. A long time in the construction, the new buildings were not formally opened until November 1932 so that at first a variety of temporary accommodation had to be found. Parliament first met on 7 June 1921 when the cabinet was sworn in and the Senate was elected in the image of the Commons, but the formal opening by King George V took place in the Belfast City Hall on 22 June. The occasion, planned with great care down to the last detail of plaiting with red, white and blue ribbon the straw edging of the stalls for the royal horses, was considered an outstanding success by Ulster Unionists. Craig's wife recorded in her diary:

> The King said to J[ames] when he was saying good-bye on the yacht, 'I can't tell you how glad I am I came, but you know my entourage were very much against it.' J[ames] replied, 'Sir, you are surrounded by pessimists; we are all optimists over here.'[3]

Despite the buoyant optimism of the 22 June, Northern Ireland's continued existence was by no means assured in the following twelve months. It faced serious challenges within and without and these challenges were the more difficult to handle since they were all interconnected and could not readily be isolated. One problem had little to do with politics and would have daunted any government. A slump had such serious effects on Northern Ireland's hitherto prosperous linen and shipbuilding industries that in October 1921, 78,000 insured persons were unemployed in the six counties and a further 25,000 were working short-time. In Belfast alone 45,000 were totally unemployed with 12,000 on short-time. The other problems were, however, closely connected and all stemmed from the state of Anglo-Irish politics after the First World War.

At first the government lacked authority and finance. Although the regional executive and parliament had been established in May–June 1921, few of the powers assigned to Northern Ireland under the 1920 act were actually transferred by Westerminster until the end of the year and the beginning of 1922. The government of Northern Ireland was anxious to secure the speedy transfer of powers, not merely to gain credibility in the North, but also to safeguard the position of Northern Ireland. The more entrenched it was, the harder it would be to dismantle. Moreover, the unrealistic financial provisions of the 1920 act meant that by the end of 1921 it was clear that Northern Ireland was heading for a budget deficit, a mortal sin according to the financial orthodoxy of the period.

A further problem arose from the continued conflict between Irish nationalism and British imperialism and attempts to end the Anglo-Irish war. The 1920 act had proved unacceptable to the Republicans, less on account of partition than the subordinate status accorded to the South. Nevertheless, Northern Ireland became embroiled in attempts to reach a settlement in the South. Nationalists were inclined to use Northern Ireland's status or performance as sticks with which to beat the British government and extract recognition of the South's status as a republic completely independent of Britain and the Empire. For its part, the British government, desperate for peace yet equally anxious to secure the Crown in Ireland and Ireland within the Empire, increasingly saw Northern Ireland as a troublesome obstacle to an Irish settlement. It thus felt unable to accord full and enthusiastic support to the new government of Northern Ireland and was even willing to hand it over to the South. The North had few friends in British official circles and among Lloyd George's ministers only Winston Churchill, the Colonial Secretary and in 1922 the minister responsible for Irish affairs, and, to a lesser extent, Balfour, then Lord President of the Council, appreciated that Northern Ireland's special problems merited sympathetic handling.

Yet another problem was a boycott of the new government and parliament by Northern Catholics and nationalists. The twelve anti-partition MPs elected in May 1921 refused to take their seats, while twenty-one nationalist-controlled local authorities declined to acknowledge the new government and parliament and instead pledged allegiance to Dail Eireann. The Catholic clergy fully endorsed this boycott. The Cardinal Archbishop of Armagh and Primate of all Ireland, Michael Logue, declined Craig's invitation to attend the opening of the Northern Ireland parliament on the grounds that he had a previous engagement. He also refused in the most truculent manner to participate in a government inquiry into the educational system, and a large number of Catholic schoolteachers and managers refused to co-operate with the Northern Ministry of Education and, like the local authorities, looked instead to Dublin.

Finally, violence threatened to engulf the six counties, which were hardly handed over to the new regime in good order. Until the middle of 1920 it had seemed as though the North would escape the worst of the Anglo-Irish war, but a series of IRA attacks at the beginning of June ended that immunity. The consequent problem of maintaining law and order was complicated by outbursts of communal violence, particularly in the cities of Belfast and Londonderry, where rival groups of Protestants and Catholics attacked each other, often with fatal results. In Belfast, too, many Catholics were expelled from their jobs, especially in the shipyards. In some respects violence in the North developed its own momentum, but the close connection with events in the South was underlined by the Southern boycott of Belfast goods, at first imposed simultaneously in the summer by some local authorities but later endorsed by Dail Eireann. Protestant fears were to some extent assuaged in the autumn of 1920 with the formation of the Ulster Special Constabulary (USC), an auxiliary police force to supplement the regular Crown forces, the Northern equivalent of the Black and Tans and Auxiliaries. But the formation of this overwhelmingly Protestant force only enhanced Catholic and nationalist anxieties. Conflict thus continued throughout the first half of 1921 with the result that from the start Northern Ireland was faced with two related problems of law and order:

the suppression of violence aimed at its overthrow or immobilisation, and the ending of communal violence. It was unfortunate that the distinction between these two problems was often obscured by the hostile attitude of the Catholic/nationalist minority to the state.

The response to these problems rendered even more inauspicious Northern Ireland's introduction to regional government. What Northern Ireland sorely needed in these traumatic early months was responsive but responsible government, calmly implementing well-considered policies. What it got was policies hastily improvised with scant regard for longer-term or wider consequences. Feelings were running too high and too many interests were involved but too few of them were concerned with the long-term fate of Northern Ireland. In the resulting bitter confusion neither policies of coercion or conciliation were consistently pursued, as the Unionist siege mentality was re-inforced and Catholics and nationalists were confirmed in their initial rejection of the new regime.

II

From the very start Northern Ireland's interests were subordinated to those of Britain and the need for a settlement in the South. Simultaneously with the agreement of the truce which ended the Anglo-Irish war, Lloyd George tried to involve the two parts of Ireland in negotiations. It was an unrealistic attempt, because on the 5 May previously Craig had visited de Valera outside Dublin, not, as was later rumoured in Dublin, to ask de Valera to become Prime Minister of a united Ireland, but to see if the two parts of the country could live in peace. The tense meeting only under-lined the differences between North and South. Nevertheless, despite these unhopeful signs, on 24 June the ever optimistic Lloyd George invited de Valera and Craig to talks in London. De Valera accepted the invitation on behalf of the Irish nation and much offended Craig by trying to speak for the North as well. Craig refused to take part in tripartite discussions on the grounds that as Northern Ireland's position had been fully secured by the 1920 act, the conflict was now between Britain and the South. Although logical and consistent this attitude did make difficult the defence of Northern Ireland's interests when partition became a crucial issue in the negotiations between Sinn Fein and Britain which began in earnest in the following October. The most the British were prepared to offer the South was dominion status, to keep the South within the Empire, but the re-sponse of the Irish negotiators was a clever one. Their ultimate aim was an Irish republic, but they expressed a willingness to accept 'free partnership with the other states associated within the British Commonwealth',[4] pro-vided that Ireland was united. During the negotiations the Irish also spent much time and energy dilating on the illogicality and injustice of parti-tion. This largely tactical emphasis on the Ulster question put the British government in an embarrassing position. It was confident of public support if talks broke down on the issue of Irish allegiance to the Crown and membership of the Empire. On the other hand, as Austen Chamberlain, the Conservative leader in the coalition, explained to his wife, partition

> would be the worst ground to fight on that one can imagine; for the six counties was a compromise, and like all compromises, is illogical and indefensible, and you could not raise an army in England to fight for *that* as we could for Crown and empire.[5]

The need or desire to play down the Ulster question had at least two consequences for Northern Ireland. In the first place, the British government was unwilling to take decisive action in the North in order to consolidate the new government's position. This was most evident in its response to continued violence. Despite the fact that many people in Northern Ireland looked to the new government to maintain law and order, responsibility remained with Westminster almost until the end of the year. The trouble was that Westminster's security policy was conditioned by the letter and spirit of the truce concluded between the IRA and the British army in the south, as a result of which the security forces were even more hamstrung than before.

The truce gave official recognition to the IRA, establishing liaison officers to sort out details at a local level, and emasculated the Crown forces. The USC was immobilised; the army withdrew from peace-keeping activities and ceased to exercise its emergency powers under the Restoration of Order in Ireland Act (ROIA), 1919, and the freedom of the RIC was severely curtailed. The truce thus made almost impossible any decisive response to threats to security throughout the six counties and particularly in Belfast. The result was that the IRA re-grouped and drilled openly in many places. Protestants and Unionists organised for self-protection and even attack, as attempts were made to revive the UVF and initially respectable defence associations, such as the Ulster Protestant Association (UPA), degenerated into murder gangs. Above all, the impotent infant government became almost demoralised and certainly forfeited respect and prestige, for, the Cabinet Secretary complained,

> Nothing can be more disastrous to any community than to allow the rank and file to imagine that Civil Authority has broken down. The people cannot understand why, having elected a Parliament, and the Government having been set up, that Government is not functioning.[6]

Moreover, in the following November matters were made even worse when considerable pressure was put on Northern Ireland and its Prime Minister to make some sacrifice in the interests of peace. The sacrifice suggested was that, while retaining its powers under the 1920 act, Northern Ireland should switch allegiance from Westminster to Dublin and accept legislative subordination to an all-Ireland parliament. Craig refused. He correctly pointed out that Ulster Unionists had already made a sacrifice by accepting their own parliament and that inclusion in a Dublin parliament was 'precisely what Ulster has for many years resisted by all the means at her disposal'.[7] If Ulster was to be thrown out of the United Kingdom, he added as a rhetorical flourish, she would leave only with the more financially advantageous status of a British dominion. Craig's refusal to budge brought down a shower of unfavourable press comment and even outright abuse on Ulster Unionists. Ulster, it was said, must sacrifice herself in the interests of peace and the Empire or 'be guilty of the greatest political crime in history'.[8]

Nevertheless, because Ulster Unionists still had considerable support in British Conservative circles, Lloyd George had to stop short of physical coercion. Thus the Anglo-Irish Treaty, which was signed on 6 December 1921, was a compromise between the ideal of Irish unity and the reality of Northern Ireland's position. It set up the Irish Free State with dominion status and with formal authority over the whole of Ireland. On the other hand, it also enabled Northern Ireland to opt out of the Free State and maintain its powers and status under the 1920 act. In that inevitable event, a Boundary Commission would be set up to examine and adjust the frontiers between the two parts of Ireland, not only in accordance with the wishes of inhabitants but also in the light of economic and geographical conditions. Despite this last qualification, all shades of nationalist opinion confidently expected that the Commission would so reduce the area of Northern Ireland as to make its continued existence impossible. Altogether the Treaty gave the appearance of Irish unity without actually changing the status of Northern Ireland and without giving Sinn Fein the opportunity of staging a break on Ulster.

Hailed in Britain and in many other parts of the world as a triumph of English statesmanship, the Treaty was bitterly denounced by Ulster Unionists. It is true that the Treaty made provision for the continued existence of Northern Ireland as part of the United Kingdom, but Craig and his government regarded its general tenor as a gross violation of the pledge given at the time of the 1920 act that the Ulster Unionist position had been secured. The declared intention to place Northern Ireland automatically in the Free State was, Craig told Lloyd George on 14 December 1921, 'a complete reversal' of the declared policy that 'Ulster should remain out until she chose of her free will to enter an all-Ireland Parliament'. It was in this letter that Craig anticipated the value of Northern Ireland's ports to the Empire during the Second World War, prophesying that 'In years to come the British nation will realise the advantage in having in Northern Ireland a population which is determined to remain loyal to British traditions and citizenship.'[9]

III

Ulster Unionists were right to be angry at the terms of the Treaty. Article 12, providing for the Boundary Commission, may have been a masterstroke in preventing negotiations breaking down on the Ulster question, but it served only to intensify the problems facing Northern Ireland. The result was that, whereas in 1921 the dominant question had been the constitutional status of Northern Ireland, in 1922 the whole concept of civilised government was thrown into question by mounting tension and violence which reached a peak towards the end of May.

The Treaty heightened apprehensions among Unionists, particularly those living in border areas, who were alarmed to the point of panic at the possibility of being transferred to the Free State. It also created among nationalists in the North and South an expectation that Northern Ireland would soon disappear and a notion that its territory was a legitimate target for seizure. These difficulties were further accentuated by a split in the South over the terms of the Treaty. The supporters of the Treaty, largely led by Collins, formed a Provisional Government, but critics, led by de Valera, took an increasingly hostile stance against those who had betrayed the Republic, and the rift culminated in civil war. The IRA, which had never ceased to operate in the North, received a new impetus from the split, as pro- and anti-Treaty volunteers co-operated in a campaign against the North and the Northern divisions were re-organised and armed by Collins both to protect the Northern minority and prevent the new government from establishing control. In 1922, therefore, law and order had to be maintained within Northern Ireland, which involved resistance to subversion and keeping Protestant and Catholic apart, and the long and tortuous border had to be secured against attack from without.

The government was in a better position to cope with these challenges than it had been in the previous year. It had assumed responsibility for law and order towards the end of the previous November, and other powers were being gradually transferred so that in the first part of 1922 the government became a really working concern. Nevertheless, it still lacked the basic necessity of any administration – money. The cost of unemployment insurance and of maintaining law and order was far higher than had been contemplated by the framers of the 1920 act so that Northern Ireland could escape a deficit only by obtaining special grants from Britain and by seeking a reduction of its contribution towards the cost of imperial services, which was a first, fixed and exorbitant charge on revenue. The need to go cap in hand to Britain meant that policy continued to be influenced, even dominated, by outside pressures and events.

Events in the North were used by opponents of the Treaty in the South to assail the Provisional Government; Collins, in turn, constantly appealed to the British government that the extermination of Northern Catholics, as he put it, was undermining both his position and the Treaty in the South. Such representations seriously worried the British government lest it should become tarred with the same brush as Ulster Unionism and the South be given an excuse to renege on the Treaty. Once again, therefore, in 1922 as in 1921, great pressure was brought to bear on the government of Northern

Ireland, not to enter a Dublin parliament but to mend its ways and so, Lloyd George hoped, 'eliminate the Ulster issue and leave a clean issue of "Republic versus British Empire" '.[10] Indeed, Churchill and Balfour apart, there was a general feeling in Britain that Northern Ireland did not merit assistance, since events there were in danger of upsetting the Treaty.

At one time it looked as if the government would quickly try to stamp its authority on the country. In February Craig invited Field Marshal Sir Henry Wilson, the recently retired Chief of the Imperial General Staff and from 21 February MP for North Down at Westminster, to advise on security matters; and in the following April a flamboyant English major-general with grandiose ideas, Arthur Solly-Flood, was appointed full-time Military Adviser with control over security matters. The main instruments with which to shape and implement a forward security policy were the Civil Authorities (Special Powers) Act, hurriedly passed in the spring of 1922 and an enlarged and partially reformed USC.

Foreshadowed in the King's Speech on 14 March 1922, the Special Powers Act speedily completed its parliamentary progress and became law on 7 April. It was intended to equip the government of Northern Ireland with frankly despotic powers similar to those contained in the ROIA, which the British army had been so reluctant to apply since the previous July. Such a measure had long been urged on Craig by the army and doubts in British official circles about its wisdom and legality were overborne by the reflection that the alternative was continued recourse to the ROIA. Although it eventually became permanent, the act was originally intended to last for only one year. Basically, it transferred many of the powers for preserving peace and maintaining order from the judiciary to the executive. Three features gave it particular bite. The act itself and some regulations scheduled in it were wide-ranging and laid down stiff penalities for certain offences – execution for throwing bombs and flogging for carrying arms without authority. Wide discretionary powers were bestowed upon the civil authority, defined as the Minister of Home Affairs, who was empowered 'to take all such steps and issue all such orders as may be necessary for preserving the peace',[11] including the issuing of regulations under the act. Finally, the minister could delegate all or any of his powers under the act to his junior minister or to any police officer. Indeed, according to one Unionist backbencher, the bill required only one section: 'The Home Secretary shall have power to do what he likes, or else let somebody else do what he likes for him.'[12]

The measure was greeted with howls of outrage by critics of Northern Ireland throughout the British Isles, but even stronger words were used about the USC. A product of the Anglo-Irish war, the USC had arisen out of the UVF which had been revived in July 1920 as a means of loyalist self-defence. It was re-formed with the tacit approval of the British government, not, as in 1912-14, as a highly centralised and disciplined body, but as a decentralised and localised force to assist the regular Crown forces in the protection of life and property. The experiment was not very successful, partly because of the unsympathetic attitude of the army authorities in Ireland towards the arming of what the Commander-in-Chief regarded as Orange bigots, and partly because of the onerous night-time duties imposed upon an unpaid and part-time force. These difficulties led the Ulster Unionist leadership to press for the UVF to be put on an official footing. Otherwise, it was feared or threatened, anarchy would result and the loyalist rank and file would take matters into their own hands. After some hesitation the British government agreed and the result was the formation of the USC.

Details of the scheme were published on 22 October 1920. The new force was to consist of three classes of constables. Class A were to be whole-time men enlisted to serve in the regular RIC but only within the divisional area where they were recruited. Class B were to be part-timers, organised under their own officers who, in turn, would be subject to the police authorities in the area in which they were serving. They were to do occasional duty, usually one evening a week, exclusive of training drills, but could occasionally be called on for day-time duties. These services were to be unpaid but various allowances were offered, and the force was not to be fully uniformed or necessarily fully armed, the arms and equipment being determined by the county authority. Class C was to be a reserve force, drawing no pay or allowances and doing only occasional drills. The cost of maintaining and equipping the new force was to be borne by the British government, whose caution and parsimony accounted in the early months for the inadequate uniforms and equipment of the B Specials, who looked more like members of the Salvation Army than auxiliary policemen.

Despite some initial effort to prevent the force from becoming a sectarian one, and despite the early enrolment of a few Catholics, the USC rapidly became identified with Orangeism and Unionism. Indeed, many Orangemen considered it their duty to join the force, for

> The more Orangemen we have in that force, the better it will be for the Protestant interests and the success of the Orange body itself. This seems perfectly patent. We must remember the old adage 'He who is not with me is against me'. Orangemen must come out now or be very sorry later that they have been neutrals, when they see nationalists filling the ranks of an *armed* force where they might have been.[13]

Undoubtedly, members of such a force could perform some peace-keeping role within their own communities, for, as one commandant's wife remarked, the B Class 'have more influence over these young hotheads than either police or military, for they patrol their own districts, & know the boys by name'.[14] Nevertheless, its Protestant nature meant that the USC could have only a limited value as a police force. Hasty recruitment, inadequate training and a very loose chain of command meant that too many unsuitable people were allowed to join the force, that most Specials had no wider conception of their role and duties, and that many local units were allowed to act as private local armies. Many of the specific complaints against, if not the blanket condemnations of, the force by Catholics and nationalists were probably justified.

Despite its weaknesses, the USC was taken over by the government of Northern Ireland in 1921-2 and became its main peace-keeping force. It became so almost by default, as a result of the British government's determination to disband the old RIC and reluctance to use the army as a police force in the North. At its peak in the early summer of 1922, the military presence in the six counties amounted to sixteen battalions, but many of these consisted of raw recruits, were below strength and were usually kept in reserve rather than used actively. The regular police force, on the other hand, was in a state of flux. The old RIC, already considered demoralised by its experiences in the Anglo-Irish war, was in the process of disbandment as part of the British withdrawal from Ireland. Its strength, under 2,400 and almost 400 below establishment at the beginning of 1922, consistently dwindled down to its disbandment on 31 May, when it was replaced in the North by a new police force, the Royal Ulster Constabulary (RUC). Great hopes were pinned on the RUC for it was intended to recruit one-third of the force from among Catholics, preference being given to former members of the RIC. Armed and modelled on its predecessor, the RUC was ultimately intended to have an establishment of 3,000 men, but by mid-summer only 1,100 had been taken on.

Solly-Flood was fully aware of the deficiencies of the USC, especially the B Specials who, he once said, 'are not only a sedentary force but their ability is greatly impaired by the lack of commanders, discipline and training'.[15] His plans to render the force more mobile by turning it into a territorial army complete with tanks and planes were blocked by the Colonial and War Offices, while his efforts to improve image, discipline and the chain of command were thwarted by vested interests in the force which enjoyed local freedom and would brook no interference, especially from a prying Englishman. It was thus an enlarged rather than a reformed USC that bore the brunt of security work in Northern Ireland in 1922. By the mid-summer, apart from a large but unestimated number of the old Class C (mainly elderly men used in a static role close to their homes), the USC's establishment was 42,250 and its strength 32,000 (5,500 Class A; 19,000 Class B; and 7,500 of a new Class C1, akin to a territorial army). Such a rapid enlargement of both numbers and role accentuated all the defects inherent in the force, but since it was the only force readily available, the government's response to well-founded criticism was not to reform the force but to praise and exalt it.

Though armed with a draconian Special Powers Act and a sizeable police force, the government of Northern Ireland was still reluctant to adopt an uncompromisingly coercive policy. Controversial though it was, the Special Powers Act did not go as far as the ROIA, for it did not include any equivalent of courts martial, since it was feared that 'the establishment of special Courts would have a bad effect in England where it would not be understood'.[16] This desire not to appear provocative also stopped the cabinet from authorising preventative action in the middle of April, when urged by the police and Ministry of Home Affairs to use the Special Powers Act to forestall an anticipated IRA onslaught.

Such reluctance to act stemmed partly from the need to carry along British opinion with security policy. Northern Ireland relied on Britain to finance the cost of maintaining law and order, particularly the mounting cost of the USC, but that money had to be fought and manoeuvred for in face of considerable hostility especially from leading civil servants. Treasury officials, who thought that Northern Ireland should stand on its own financial feet and not sponge off the British taxpayer, disliked Craig's informal methods of conducting business and his demand that the British government should spend millions of pounds on the USC, a transferred service over which it had no control. Moreover, officials at the Cabinet and Colonial Offices suspected that Northern Ireland was acting *ultra vires* in trying to build up what was in effect a military organisation with British money, thus laying the British government open to charges of breach of faith and departing from the spirit of the bargain with the South.

Yet it was not simply a question of tactics, for Craig did always hope that tension could be dissolved by discussion. Attempts were made to secure the minority's recognition of Northern Ireland, and from time to time Craig had talks with various Northern Catholic and Nationalist leaders. On 9 March he had a long talk in London with Devlin, the leader of the Northern Nationalists, and from the beginning of April he and the Cabinet Secretariat carried on a series of meetings with some respected but unrepresentative Belfast Catholics, said to be in touch with the local bishop. More dramatic and highly publicised were Craig's meetings with Collins on 24 January, 2 February and 30 March. His colleagues were unenthusiastic about such encounters, but, Craig told his wife, 'No stone ought to be left unturned to try and stop the murdering that is going on in Ireland.'[17]

On 24 January 1922 Craig had a three-hour meeting with Collins in London to see if agreement could be reached on the border. It was a hopeful meeting, for, according to Craig, Collins 'made it clear that he wanted a real peace and that he had so many troubles in Southern Ireland, that he was prepared to establish cordial relations with Northern Ireland, and to abandon all attempts to coercion, but hoping to coax her into a union later'.[18] Agreement was reached on a number of questions, including the lifting of the Southern boycott, the restoration to their jobs of Catholics expelled from work, a review of the cases of certain nationalists imprisoned or charged with political offences and co-operation on railways. Above all, it was decided to dispense with the dreaded Boundary Commission and to settle the question of the border directly between the two Irish governments.

Optimism quickly evaporated when Craig visited Dublin on 2 February to iron out the details of a border settlement. It transpired that the January accord had been based upon a misunderstanding. Craig had been assured by Lloyd George that only minor modifications to the boundary had been contemplated, whereas Collins and his colleagues had assumed that substantial tracts of Northern Ireland would be transferred to the South. Moreover, a few days later tension along the border was brought almost to fever pitch by the kidnapping of loyalists as hostages for the release of IRA prisoners in the North, and by a fatal armed clash between Specials and the IRA at Clones station, a few hundred yards on the Southern side of the border. There was parallel violence within the six counties. Belfast was the main centre of disturbance and on the night of 12 February fighting was renewed in several parts of the city and continued for several days with heavy losses in dead and wounded. By the middle of March parts of the North were virtually in a state of civil war and North and South were to all intents and purposes at open war.

At the end of March, therefore, a further round of discussions was inevitably called by Churchill. Craig met Churchill, Griffith and Collins at the Colonial Office in London and the result was the Craig-Collins pact, the so-called peace pact, of 30 March. Countersigned by Churchill and others on behalf of the British government, the agreement began: 'PEACE IS TODAY DECLARED.'[19] The pact provided for the enrolment, with the help of a new committee, of a proportion of Catholics in the Northern police forces; the compulsory wearing of uniforms by and the numbering of all policemen in the North; the proper control of arms and ammunition; a specially constituted court for trial without jury; and a joint committee of Catholics and Protestants to investigate complaints of intimidation and outrage. IRA activities in Northern Ireland were to cease, for Collins boasted absolute control over the IRA. Political prisoners were to be released by agreement, and expelled persons re-admitted to their homes and jobs. The British government was to allow the Northern Ministry of Labour £500,000 for relief works, one-third for the benefit of Catholics, two-thirds for Protestants.

However well-intentioned, the peace pact took too little account of reality. Indeed, such dramatic discussions and declarations were probably counter-productive and served to harden rather than reconcile opinion. Any discussion of the border simply underlined the gap between Unionism and nationalism. Talk about the return of Catholics expelled from the shipyards or their homes was unrealistic at a time of high unemployment and a housing shortage, and merely provided occasion for future recriminations when expectations were not realised. On the other hand, Unionist fears and resentments were increased, since such proposals as the numbering and disarming of the police seemed simply to invite identification and assassination.

Moreover, no Irish leader was capable of delivering the support of his so-called followers for any agreement. Northern nationalists were divided into supporters of the old IPP and those of Sinn Fein. The former were stronger in the North, especially in Belfast, Devlin's hunting ground, and some were inclined to co-operate with the government, especially if concessions, largely financial, were made on Catholic education. On the other hand, they were reluctant to air their views publicly on account of the strength of Sinn Fein in the rest of Ireland, the Republican resort to violence, and the prestige conferred on Collins's supporters in the North by the fact that he seemed to be recognised by the British and Northern governments as the spokesman for the Northern minority. After all, Devlin had been eclipsed and it was Collins they negotiated with and who was asked to make nominations to the various committees proposed under the peace pact. Collins, for his part, was unable to look at events in the North dispassionately, since they played into the hands of his critics in the South. His interest in the North's affairs was spasmodic and even hysterical and certainly took little account of the differences among the Northern minority and still less account of the likely impact of his actions on Unionist opinion.

The inability of Catholic and Nationalist leaders to develop an agreed and consistent policy weakened the position and will of the few Unionist advocates of conciliation, such as Craig. He needed encouragement from the South, because he was unable to convince even his own subordinates of the value of conciliation. The peace pact was unpopular with the police authorities, and ministers and officials connected with the administration of law and order showed no urgency, imagination or generosity in implementing it. On the contrary, the Junior Minister of Home Affairs and the Attorney-General both threatened to resign, and the Ministry of Home Affairs displayed a contemptuous rather than an accommodating attitude to the minority.

Not surprisingly, therefore, the peace pact proved as abortive as the earlier Craig-Collins agreement. Only one part was successfully implemented — the distribution of money for relief works. Otherwise, the pact did nothing to reconcile the two sections of the community. Protestants and Unionists were if anything more hostile and suspicious, while Catholics and nationalists were confirmed in their boycott of the state, not simply because of 'some deep-seated ideological attitude' but rather because of 'a specific conjuncture of events'[20] including the unhelpful attitude of the Ministry of Home Affairs and the government's inability to restore Catholics to their home and work. Nor did the pact prevent mounting violence from reaching a climax at the end of May and the beginning of June, when a renewed IRA assault provoked fierce Protestant retaliation.

Belfast continued to be the main centre of disturbance. On the weekend of 22 May fourteen deaths, described by the press as callous, deliberate murders, occurred, including that of Councillor William John Twaddell, the Unionist MP for West Belfast, shot in the street on his way to his tailor's shop by men armed with revolvers. Nor did the country or border areas escape and the most dramatic incident outside Belfast occurred on the Fermanagh-Donegal border. Members of the IRA entered the village of Belleek in Co. Fermanagh and fired on a party of Specials in neighbouring Pettigo, a village divided by the border and partly in Co. Fermanagh and partly in Co. Donegal. They failed to kill any of the Specials but, it was reported six months later, reduced the Unionists of Belleek 'to a state of nerves comparable only . . . to the panic among the better class of inhabitants of villages which the Bolsheviks have once held and threaten to revisit'.[21]

Such events were the climax of a long period of violence in Northern Ireland, which between 21 June 1920 and 18 June 1922 claimed over 2,000 victims – 1,766 wounded and 428 killed. This violence has often been represented as part of a deliberate attempt by Protestant and loyalist forces, official and unofficial, to exterminate Catholics. Certainly, more Catholics were killed than Protestants, but such a simplistic view takes little account of IRA activity in the North and the number of Protestant casualties. There was some disagreement about the casualty figures for the first six months after the Northern Ireland government assumed responsibility for law and order; yet even the most pessimistic statistics covering Belfast in the period 6 December 1921 to 31 May 1922 underlined both the extent and the impossibility of any glib explanation of the violence facing Northern Ireland in its early days. In that period 236 people were killed and 346 injured. Of those killed, 16 were members of the Crown forces, including five Catholics; 73 were Protestants; and 147 were Catholics, many of whom may have been killed by indiscriminate IRA firing in their own areas. Of the wounded, 37 belonged to the Crown forces; 143 were Protestants; and 166 were Catholics.

IV

The May violence finally compelled the government to assert itself and to take full advantage of the powers and forces at its disposal. Action was required, not empty words and abortive agreements. The alternative was anarchy, for in that month alone ninety murders were committed in Belfast and, as the Minister of Home Affairs later told the Commons, 'Not a man was brought to justice. The people knew who committed those murders, but no one had the courage to come forward and give evidence.'[22] Moreover, an electoral pact between Collins and de Valera towards the end of May was seen by Ulster Unionists as a prelude to a concerted attack on the North.

Such circumstances explain the actions taken by the government at the end of May and the beginning of June. On 24 May the IRA and several of its brother organisations were declared illegal and internment was introduced. The police, both regular and special, arrested 500 people within twenty-four hours of the proclamation and those arrested were interned in a wooden hulk, the *Argenta,* a prison ship anchored in Belfast Lough. One or two Protestants and loyalists may have been among the first internees, but the overwhelming majority of the 728 men interned between May 1922 and 24 December 1924, when the first bout of internment came to an end, were Catholics and nationalists, such as Cahir Healy, later a Westminster and Northern Ireland MP, detained between May 1922 and February 1924 as a 'cunning and clever organiser'[23] and Sinn Fein intelligence officer in Co. Fermanagh. The great round-up was followed by other measures. On 1 June a curfew was imposed over the whole six counties and rigorously enforced. Moreover, the movement of individuals was further restricted by an exclusion regulation, which enabled the civil authority to exclude a person from certain areas of Northern Ireland and confine him to a specified area under penalty of committing an offence. The security forces also increased the number of searches to ferret out persons, arms and ammunition.

The judiciary, too, began to take a harder line with offenders. Flogging had been an optional extra under the 1916 Larceny Act, but the Special Powers Act had, without any clear idea of its effect, extended its use, and some judges began to take advantage of the enlarged power of flogging. Between 26 April and 17 July 1922 twenty-one prisoners were sentenced to both long terms of imprisonment and lashes of either the cat or the birch. The first person sentenced to flogging was a Presbyterian, but of the twenty-one so sentenced only three were Protestants (all Presbyterians), the rest Catholics. By mid-summer two of the Presbyterians and two of the Catholics had actually been flogged, and appeals for clemency in the other cases had been rejected. Later considerable pressure was put on the North by the British and Provisional governments to remit the outstanding sentences on nationalist prisoners, but, although Craig was inclined to be lenient, he was overruled by the Ministry of Home Affairs, which insisted that the law should take its course.

These stern measures provoked a storm of criticism in the South and in Britain, particularly since they coincided with delicate negotiations over the Free State constitution which raised once more the question of the South's place in the Empire. During these discussions, Lloyd George reported to his cabinet that Collins and Griffith were 'more anxious about the North-East than anything else'. Talking of the 'extermination of Catholics',[24] they argued that since it was paying for the police in Northern Ireland and had handed over law and order to the Northern government, the responsibility rested with the British government. This conversation alarmed most ministers, dissatisfied as they were with the draft constitution submitted by the Provisional Government, which they held was simply a thinly veneered republic. As in 1921, they feared that the South might try to stage a break on Ulster and make it impossible to enforce the Treaty settlement. Ulster was once again in danger of confusing and obscuring the

47

issue of Crown and Empire versus republicanism and there was strong talk of martial law and putting Northern Ireland in the dock with a judicial inquiry. Craig wavered on the latter, but his colleagues were adamantly opposed to both and insisted on full backing against what they saw as 'a great conspiracy' to destroy Ulster and stir up hatred between Catholics and Protestants. 'The whole of the rebellion organisation of the South, which had been engaged in resisting the British forces, having nothing further to do in the South, had immigrated to the North where they were concentrating all their machinery and were making the utmost trouble.'[25]

In the face of such strong representations, the British government confined itself to warning words and the appointment of an ineffectual, one-man private enquiry. It even eventually responded to Craig's demands for the removal of the IRA from the Belleek-Pettigo area. Lloyd George and his advisers were anxious to avoid any direct confrontation between British and Free State troops, but Churchill insisted on taking action 'to retain the confidence of the Ulster people' and to reassure the Westminster parliament that 'a British village' was safe.[26] As he told Collins, 'It must not be supposed that any part of the border can be kept in a continuous state of disorder and alarm either by raids or by fire directed from your territory.'[27]

The process of stabilisation effected by these stern measures was also assisted by events in the South. The civil war that had been threatening finally flared into the open when on 28 June the Provisional Government, prompted by British reaction to the assassination in London of Sir Henry Wilson, bombarded the Four Courts in Dublin, which had been occupied by Republicans since the previous April. Hostilities lasted until May 1923 and encouraged members of the IRA to drift from the North to the South. The power struggle in the South took the pressure off the North, and at the end of June Collins enunciated a new, more conciliatory policy towards the North:

> There can be no question of forcing Ulster into union with the Twenty-six Counties. I am absolutely against coercion of this kind. If Ulster is going to join us it must be voluntary. Union is our final goal, that is all.[28]

The result was that by the summer of 1922 comparative peace had been restored to Northern Ireland. Police reports, which had hitherto been catalogues of death and outrage, were by September commenting favourably on a new spirit affecting most parts of the country, as all sections of the community began to co-operate with the Crown forces in maintaining law and order.

The assertion of the government's authority was the most significant achievement during the first twelve months of Northern Ireland's existence. That done, it enabled attention to be given to other fundamental problems, notably the question of finance. For most of 1922 Craig had successfully negotiated various grants from the British government, brushing aside Treasury criticism by retorting that Britain virtually owed Northern Ireland a living. Ulster Unionists had not sought a government of their own and had accepted one only to assist the British government resolve the Irish question; Northern Ireland had been handed over in a deplorable and disorderly condition, with an uneasy neighbour to the South; and, anyway, Northern Ireland remained an integral part of the United Kingdom. Britain was thus morally and even legally obliged to repair the damage and help maintain the North. That, at any rate, was Craig's view, for, he told Churchill on 26 May 1922, 'In helping us in the generous way you are doing you are only carrying out British traditions. . . . In coming to our rescue — as you put it — you are only doing what would be done if one of the eastern counties was threatened by an enemy from without.'[29]

These arguments and British reluctance to become directly involved in its affairs ensured a stream of grants to Northern Ireland, but in the autumn of 1922 the government made a determined effort to put its finances on a permanently sound footing. Craig's first detailed proposals for a revision of the financial provisions of the 1920 act were contemptuously dismissed by the Treasury as 'incredible if they were not in black and white'.[30] Nevertheless, Bonar Law's Conservative government, which had succeeded Lloyd George's coalition on 25 October, agreed to submit the question to an arbitration committee headed by Lord Colwyn. The committee's interim decisions alleviated Northern Ireland's immediate financial problems, while the final award, known as the Colwyn Award, gave the North a few years of much needed financial stability. Described by the disgruntled Treasury as a spendthrift's charter, the award made domestic expenditure instead of a crippling imperial contribution the first charge on Northern Ireland's revenue.

It was thus as a going concern that at the end of 1922 Northern Ireland confirmed its status within the United Kingdom and cut its formal links with the South. Admittedly, the threat of the Boundary Commission hung like a pall over the border districts, but on 7 December parliament submitted a petition to King George V, formally opting out of the Irish Free State. As Craig said in moving this humble address:

> We . . . feel safe and sure whilst we remain under the Imperial Parliament. . . . We have our right there, we have our say there on those affairs which affect the country and the Empire as a whole, and we have our own institution here with our Senate and our Commons, and I pray God as long as I have anything to do with it we shall remain steadfast in the true faith.[31]

V

Northern Ireland's survival as a semi-autonomous and integral part of the United Kingdom was a considerable achievement but one purchased at a price. Some pressing problems had been overcome, not least the onslaught of violence and the equivocal and often hostile attitude of the British government, but some basic problems remained unresolved and even accentuated. Considering its origins, it was always likely that Northern Ireland would be divided and that its government would operate largely in the interests of one section of the community. The traumatic early months turned likelihood into certainty.

The community emerged more divided than ever. The minority became convinced that it was persecuted and victimised. It was said that between 1920 and 1922 8,750 Catholics were driven from their employment and some 23,000 from their homes, while two-thirds of those killed were Catholics, some in horrific circumstances. Moreover, the minority's aliena-tion from the new regime was confirmed by the belief that many of the outrages had been perpetrated by appointed agents of the new regime, particularly the USC. The denunciations of the Specials were constant and vivid and rhetoric came to represent reality, for their behaviour seemed to confirm early forecasts that:

> These Special Constables will be nothing more and nothing less than the dregs of the Orange lodges, armed and equipped to wreak their ven-geance on the liberty-loving, tolerant and generous Catholic and Nation-alist people of the most Christian and democratic country in the world.[32]

Whereas Northern nationalists and Catholics saw themselves as an oppressed minority, Ulster Unionists and Protestants emerged from the trauma not as a confident and generous majority but feeling more be-leaguered and misunderstood. They too had their victims, and what in-creased their resentment and strengthened their determination to go their own way was pressure and criticism from Britain and the South. The abuse and cajoling during the Treaty negotiations and the Treaty itself particu-larly heightened the Ulster Unionists' sense of isolation and betrayal, which was as ever reflected in comments on British leaders. Chamberlain, the mildest of men, was a 'renegade and a disgrace to his father, a liar and accessory to the murder of hundreds of innocent people'. Lloyd George was almost unspeakable and the politest thing he was called was that 'little Welsh rabbit'.[33] The lack of sympathy in the South and in Britain for Protestant victims of violence, and the British inability to distinguish be-tween loyalty and rebellion, frequently exasperated Ulster Unionists, even the most patient of them, causing Craig to complain of the British press, 'If a cow died in Kerry, they would say it was Belfast or Ulster was the cause of it.'[34]

The early months also left their mark on the nature and processes of government. Most obviously, the minority's continued refusal to co-operate and the majority's wish to consolidate its position meant that discrimination became built into the system of government at a very early stage, particularly in respect of questions over which the regional govern-ment and parliament had real control — education, representation and law and order. On these matters policy was determined by the majority with scant regard for the interests and susceptibilities of the minority.

In 1922 the government was anxious that the law should be applied fearlessly without regard to outside pressures. Otherwise it feared that the North would sink to the depths of Ireland during the last years of the Union, when justice had been subordinated to political expediency and vacillation and ineptitude had characterised the administration of law and order. A crime was a crime, no matter what the political intentions of its perpetrator, against whom the law should be strictly enforced. That was the theory, but too often it was applied only to Catholic and nationalist offenders. Once Protestant law breakers were apprehended, and there was sufficient evidence to secure a conviction in the ordinary courts, the law did take its course. The trouble was that in 1922 prompt steps were not always taken to apprehend and punish Protestant offenders. Prejudice, a feeling in the Ministry of Home Affairs that exceptional legislation should apply only to 'disloyal and disaffected persons', not to those 'loyal to the Crown',[35] and fear of alienating Protestant opinion sometimes deterred responsible ministers and officials from making or carrying out decisions that were known to be just and proper.

The most striking of the early instances of this discrimination was the special treatment accorded to the UPA. In the crisis of May–June the government tried to tame this Protestant murder gang, not by interning its members under the Special Powers Act, but by enrolling them in the USC and enlisting their aid in the work of a newly established Secret Service! Indeed, considerable latitude was given to Protestant and Orange extremists in the police forces. In the earliest days of the RUC, fear of upsetting Belfast Orangemen stopped Bates from asserting his authority over a particularly partisan and insubordinate officer, John William Nixon, later an Independent Unionist MP, who thus, as Bates admitted, continued to encourage in his district the notion that 'there is only one law and that for the Protestants', thus allowing 'the Protestant hooligan . . . to interpret in his own fashion the law of the country'.[36] There was a similar brushing aside of problems relating to the USC, the most notorious example being the suppression of the report of an inquiry into the murder of a number of Catholics in Cushendall, Co. Antrim, in June 1922. The public version was that 'Cushendal was the ambush of A Specials on 23 June in which four IRA were killed.'[37] On the other hand, the secret report concluded:

> No one except the police and the military even fired at all . . . I am unable to accept the evidence of the Special Constabulary from Bally-mena. I am satisfied that they did not tell me all they knew about the circumstances in which three men died, and in view of the reports made by the military officers at the time and the evidence given by them before me, I do not believe that none of the police entered any of the houses.[38]

As regards education, the beginning of discrimination was facilitated by Catholics themselves. The refusal of the Catholic hierarchy to nominate representatives to the Lynn Committee, appointed in September 1921 to examine the education system, meant that the committee, which presented the most detailed articulation of the reform ideas that had been discussed by educationalists in Ulster since the end of the First World War, was dominated by Protestants. Although it claimed to have borne Catholic interests in mind, its educational assumptions were inevitably framed according to those of the Protestant churches. In local government, by contrast, the pressure for discrimination came from the Unionist rank and file. The first step in an attempt to make public boards safe for Unionism occurred in the summer of 1922 with the abolition of PR in local government elections.

PR had been introduced into Irish elections in 1919. Since it had required that in some areas hitherto segregated and smaller Protestant communities should form part of larger electoral areas with Catholic majorities, it had in Ulster resulted in substantial Unionist losses, particularly to nationalists. In the 1920 local elections nationalists had gained clear majorities in such traditionally marginal authorities as the Fermanagh and Tyrone County Councils and Londonderry Corporation. In addition, they had revelled in their triumph, much to the chagrin of Unionists who were usually the largest ratepayers and who resented subsidising disloyalty and having 'to sit there and listen to our King being insulted, to our government being derided'.[39] Unionists, especially those in the west, thus demanded that their own government and parliament should redress the balance by abolishing PR and redrawing electoral areas so as to put the 'natural rulers' back in control.

Whatever the drawbacks of PR, there was certainly a case for retaining it as a minority safeguard at a time when attempts were being made to persuade some Catholics and nationalists to abandon their boycott of the new regime. Nevertheless, with no consideration of the implications for minorities, the government introduced and, in the absence of nationalist MPs, parliament quickly passed unopposed by 5 July 1922 a bill abolishing PR, the Local Government Bill. Only when Collins persuaded the British government to delay for over two months the royal assent to the bill, did it dawn upon the government of Northern Ireland that there was more to PR than the satisfaction of Unionist demands for its abolition. Even then, realisation was tinged with disbelief, Craig arguing that PR had proved 'utterly useless' in securing the representation of minorities and asserting that Catholics would be better off under the 'old system'.[40]

The fact that the royal assent was eventually given to the Local Government Bill answered a question about government in Northern Ireland that had been in the air ever since 1921. Who really ruled the six counties? The devolution of power and the establishment of regional governments and parliaments always raises the troublesome question as to where real power

52

lies – with the regional government and parliament, or with the sovereign power. In the case of Northern Ireland in 1921-2, did effective power lie in Belfast, to whom certain powers had been transferred, or did it lie at Westminster, to whom ultimate sovereignty had been reserved under article 75 of the 1920 act? In 1921 the government and parliament of Northern Ireland had existed in name only, but even in 1922, when powers had been formally transferred, the regional government could scarcely operate without reference to Westminster. Westminster tried to supervise the regional administration and on one occasion, at the beginning of February, acted deliberately against the considered advice tendered by the cabinet of Northern Ireland by authorising the Lord Lieutenant to release certain nationalist prisoners and commute a death sentence. This particular use of the prerogative was, the *Northern Whig* claimed on 25 February 1922, 'A grave outrage has been committed against the Northern Parliament and against constitutional law – an outrage more suited to Stuart times than our own day.' Nevertheless, many British officials were prepared to argue that in the circumstances of 1922 Westminster had the right and even the duty to intervene in Northern Ireland's affairs, even on transferred matters, since it was pumping millions of pounds into the North to finance transferred services, particularly those relating to law and order. In addition, it could be and was argued that since events in the North had repercussions for British relations with the South, then the administration of Northern Ireland was of imperial and not merely local concern. This was certainly the line of argument pressed by Collins and his successors when urging the British government to block the Local Government Bill.

Northern Ireland ministers and officials were incensed at what they saw as yet another instance of the intolerable treatment meted out to them by the Lord Lieutenant at the behest of the British and Provisional governments. They maintained that the withholding of the royal assent was completely unconstitutional, since the Local Government Bill dealt with a purely local affair within the terms of the 1920 act and had been approved by an overwhelming majority of the people of Northern Ireland. More to the point, the government threatened to resign and hold an election on the issue. 'No Government could carry on in Northern Ireland,' Craig told the Permanent Secretary of the Colonial Office, 'if it knew that the powers of the Parliament . . . were to be abrogated.' To allow the creation of such a precedent would, his ministers agreed, 'warrant the interference by the Imperial Government in almost every Act introduced in Northern Ireland'.[41] Most ministers and officials would have welcomed a showdown with the British government, but no showdown was necessary because, as Craig had forecast, the British government backed down rather than risk 'complete disorganisation in Ulster at the moment'.[42] Quite simply, the British government quailed before the prospect of Craig's resignation over the Local Government Bill. Resignation would mean a general election in the North, which, in view of the built-in Unionist majority and the widespread

Unionist dislike of PR, would endorse Craig's action. Since there would be no alternative to Craig's administration, the British government would be faced with two equally unpalatable options. Either it would have to climb down or take on responsibility for governing the six counties – the latter being the very thing the 1920 act had been so carefully designed to avoid.

The climbdown by the British government over the Local Government Bill determined that effective power in Northern Ireland lay with the regional government and the Ulster Unionist majority. In theory, Westminster had the legal power and the moral duty to iron out any marked deficiencies in the regional government and administration and this power and duty could have been exercised with effect, particularly to correct the imbalance created in the state by the minority's opting out. However, as the dispute over the Local Government Bill demonstrated, short of sweeping aside the regional government and parliament and imposing direct British rule, Westminster lacked effective political power to influence decisively legislation and administration in Northern Ireland in face of the large in-built Unionist majority and the lack of an alternative administration.

Westminster's lack of effective political power and total reluctance to assume direct responsibility meant that no brake was put on the emergent tendencies in the government of Northern Ireland towards sectarianism and discrimination. The early months of struggle for survival left indelible marks and by the end of 1922 Northern Ireland was well on its way to becoming a Protestant state for a Protestant people.

Chapter 4

A PROTESTANT STATE

The years between 1922 and the outbreak of the Second World War in 1939 constituted a critical period in the development of Northern Ireland. In those years its ultimate fate was sealed. The violence and bloodshed over, it was open to Irishmen to create a new spirit, if not of unity then of harmony within Northern Ireland and friendly competition between North and South. The opportunity was not seized. There was no new departure, no new sense of brotherhood or even mutual respect. Instead, the divisive pattern of government and politics sketched out in the angry early months were confirmed and became even more deeply entrenched in the inter-war years. Northern Ireland maintained its status and territory and its separation from the South became even more marked in an atmosphere of cold war. It also remained politically divided and the divisions fossilised so that, just as the South could vaunt its Catholicism, so Craig could say in 1934, 'All I boast of is that we are a Protestant Parliament and a Protestant State.'[1] It was not, however, a prosperous state. As the price for the security of a separate existence, it was condemned to years of economic and social stagnation as the most disadvantaged part of the United Kingdom.

I

In the 1920s an optimist might have found grounds for believing that a new departure was possible in Northern Ireland. Even if there was an inbuilt majority determined to uphold partition, the two parts of Ireland might have lived in friendly competition. The new parliament might have provided a meeting ground for all shades of political opinion to concentrate on exploiting Northern Ireland's resources and to develop well-considered policies in the interests of the six counties as a whole.

One hopeful sign was the confirmation of Northern Ireland's boundaries and an agreement with the Free State. For the first four years the provision in the Anglo-Irish Treaty for a Boundary Commission was a source of considerable uncertainty and unrest, but it was eventually rendered harmless by some astute political manoeuvering and legal argument by the government of Northern Ireland and its legal advisers. The Commission spent most of 1925 collecting evidence and perambulating the border, and its final report, leaked to the press on 7 November 1925, recommended relatively insignificant exchanges of territory between North and South. The North would have lost such recurrent trouble spots as Crossmaglen in South Armagh, but the changes were too minor for the

South and so the report was suppressed. Instead, the existing border was confirmed by a tripartite agreement signed on 3 December 1925 by the British, Free State and Northern Ireland governments, which also tied up other loose ends and finally disposed of the Council of Ireland. It was a hopeful sign, since the three governments 'united in amity ... resolved to aid one another in a spirit of neighbourly comradeship.'[2]

Within Northern Ireland, too, there were indications that the government was anxious to act responsibly and on behalf of the whole community. All internees were released by December 1924 and all political prisoners by January 1926. PR had been speedily abolished in local elections, but it was retained for the 1925 parliamentary election, despite the fact that after three years it was within Northern Ireland's power to abolish it. There was also a rash of parliamentary enquiries into education, natural resources, the cost of living and the like, all of which testified to the initial willingness and enthusiasm of the new government and parliament to probe to the depths, as Craig had promised in 1921, and create a new sort of society. There was, too, a serious attempt to bridge old divisions in the vital sphere of education, the first major task of reconstruction undertaken by the government.

The first Minister of Education, Londonderry, had a happy vision of children of all denominations being educated together and his 1923 Education Act aimed to create an efficient system of non-sectarian schools under public control to replace the old and divisive system of inadequate and clerically controlled schools which had grown up under the Union. Public elementary schools were to be controlled by county and county borough councils acting through regional education committees, and were to be open to children of all religious denominations for combined literary and moral instruction, with religious teaching being given to the different denominations outside the hours of compulsory attendance. Under the new scheme no school was entirely without public money, but a graduated scale was adopted to encourage the building of new schools by local authorities and the transfer of church schools to public control.

Schools which wanted to keep their voluntary status and control over religious instruction received least public money. They lost the 60 per cent building and reconstruction grants they had received under the Union, but the Ministry of Education paid teachers' salaries and the local education authorities paid half the cost of lighting, heating and cleaning. An intermediate status was partial public control by a school management committee of four members nominated by the school manager and two by the education authority. Voluntary schools accepting the 'two and four committees' were entitled to more public money than purely voluntary schools. In addition to the grants given to the latter, they received from the Ministry of Education half the cost of repair and general upkeep, and had the prospect of further money from the local authorities to defray half the cost of repairs and general upkeep. Finally, new schools provided by education authorities or schools transferred to them were financed fully by public money. Local education authorities were forbidden to require teachers to belong to any particular church or denomination or to provide religious instruction, although they had to afford opportunities outside the hours of compulsory attendance for any religious teaching to which parents did not object. Though to the liking of none of the churches, Protestant or Catholic, the act was endorsed by parliament, for, commented one MP, 'sectarianism and denominationalism' are 'two things that we are particularly anxious to avoid here in the North of Ireland'.[3]

It also looked as though a variety of viewpoints would be introduced into the Commons. Owing to the atmosphere of the first general election and the nationalist boycott, only official Unionists actually sat in the first parliament, but the 1925 general election, the first 'peacetime' election under PR, introduced two new elements – Independents and Labour. The latter sought to be a mass political party, cutting across the sectarian divide to provide a political platform for both Protestant and Catholic workingmen on social and economic issues. Called the Labour Party, Northern Ireland, until 1949, it had been formed in 1923-4 by Northern trade unionists and socialists who had been members of the Belfast Labour Party and the Irish political labour movement active since the late nineteenth century but non-commital on the 'national' question. It adopted a programme similar to that of the British Labour Party, seeking to promote working-class interests by the gradual reconstruction of society on socialist lines. It put forward three candidates in Belfast in 1925, all of whom were elected, one even topping the poll in East Belfast and ousting the sitting Unionist, a Protestant trade unionist. In Belfast, too, four Independent Unionists, acting as individuals, were returned, while in Co. Antrim a tenant farmers' candidate edged out the Junior Minister of Home Affairs. All these successful candidates were Protestants and their gains were made at the expense of official Unionists, showing that, at least in areas away from the border, the electorate was capable of encompassing issues other than the religious and constitutional ones. In Belfast in the 1920s unemployment was of as much concern as the border, and in Co. Antrim the fate of land purchase worried many farmers.

Moreover, the Nationalists, the heirs of the old IPP, the constitutionalists among anti-partitionists, decided on 21 March to contest the 1925 election and that successful candidates unaffected by the Boundary Commission, then in progress, should take their seats. Eleven candidates were nominated. The success of ten of them and the failure of Republicans to win more than two seats showed the minority's support for constitutional politics. It was realised that Northern Ireland would not be whittled away by the Commission, while Catholic bishops were becoming alarmed that their educational interests were being overlooked in the absence of any formal parliamentary opposition to Protestant agitation on educational issues. Devlin and the member for Antrim took their seats on 28 April

1925. Others slowly followed, the border MPs being the most reluctant but they were finally influenced by de Valera's decision in 1927 to accept the role of constitutional opposition in the South. By 1927 Devlin was the leader of a party of ten in the Commons and some effort was made to give the parliamentary party a wide organisational base and a programme with the formation in 1928 of the National League of the North, complete with local branches, an annual conference and an elected council. Its programme was threefold: a united Ireland; defence of Catholic interests; and economic and social reform. Its election manifesto in 1929 contained a fairly radical policy for its time, calling for an end to unemployment, public works, raising of the school-leaving age, earlier and higher old age pensions, town planning and slum clearance. According to Devlin, politics should be about social and economic issues, not religion and 'instead of having Protestant and Catholic have democrat and Tory'.[4]

II

No such transformation occurred either within Northern Ireland or in relations between North and South. Despite the 1925 agreement, it was not for another forty years that leaders met across the conference table. In place of a 'spirit of neighbourly relations', there developed a state of cold war which along the border could become very warm indeed, especially after de Valera came to power in the Free State in 1932. His Catholic and anti-partitionist rhetoric and his winning the Stormont seat of South Down in 1933 inspired considerable alarm among Unionists and hope among nationalists in the North. Catholic and Republican Ireland did seem to be on the march, as de Valera used the occasion of the 1932 Eucharistic Congress in Dublin, a spectacular demonstration of Catholic devotion and power, to insult the Crown's representative in the Free State; engaged in an economic war with Britain, eventually extracting considerable financial and other concessions; and in 1937 promulgated a new constitution, turning the Free State into Eire and claiming sovereignty over the whole of Ireland. The question of partition was kept alive as part of a continuous power battle in the South, not because there was any serious possibility of unity. Even the Eire constitution accepted the de facto position of Northern Ireland and most Southerners realised that partition had become firmly entrenched in the inter-war years, as the differences between the two parts of Ireland became increasingly pronounced, the one remaining emphatically British, imperial and Protestant, the other developing into a Catholic state with a Gaelic veneer and impatient with the British connection.

The Free State proved a very restless dominion. The Crown was by degrees taken out of the South, which gradually moved out of the Commonwealth, a process confirmed in the 1937 constitution which made Eire a republic in all but name. The distinctiveness of the South was further reinforced from the outset by the emphasis given to Gaelic culture and language in an attempt to realise Patrick Pearse's dictum 'Ireland . . . not free merely, but Gaelic as well'.[5] The South did not become a theocratic state after independence, but it was 95 per cent Catholic and the influence of the Catholic Church was all pervasive, even before the liberal and secular Free State constitution was replaced by the strongly Catholic Eire one. The latter not only recognised 'the special position of the Holy Catholic Apostolic and Roman Church as the guardian of the Faith professed by the great majority of Irishmen',[6] but also used Catholic social and moral teaching as the basis of law in crucial areas of personal and family life – outlawing birth control and divorce. Such provisions Ulster Protestants regarded as infringing on personal liberty at the behest of Rome, the more so since for various reasons the Protestant population of the South declined rapidly after independence and the Catholic Church, consolidating the position gained under the Union, carved out for itself more extensive control over education than in any other country in the world. Furthermore, the increasing pursuit of economic nationalism after 1924, which by the 1930s turned the South into one of the most highly protected countries in the world, affected both Northern businessmen and farmers, especially along the border, and emphasised the different interests of North and South.

The extent to which the South was prepared to accept the existence of Northern Ireland was underlined by the increasing isolation of the most militant Republicans. Having experienced many splits since its heyday in the Anglo-Irish war, the IRA was reduced by the 1930s to an underground rump totally dedicated to ending partition by force and uninterested in 'politics', although it did have in Sinn Fein, much changed since Griffith's day, a political wing with a militantly nationalist and a 'confused distributist social policy'.[7] Its nucleus of supporters in North and South was never sufficient to pose a serious threat to Northern Ireland. Its border raids and bombing campaign in Britain in 1939 had no popular support and 'only brought the wrath of three governments down on the IRA's head, leaving them with men in prison in Britain and both parts of Ireland'.[8]

III

Internally, no new spirit prevailed. On the contrary, the divisions of the early months became even more firmly entrenched and the new government and parliament failed to win or even make a sustained effort to seek general acceptance. The dominant issue remained the constitutional one – the very existence of Northern Ireland, to which was added the equally divisive religious question – the defence of Protestantism or Catholicism. Parties, groups or movements which tried to cut across these divides received short shrift. Protestants and Unionists were determined to

59

share power and privilege with no-one and the government became the instrument of the Unionist Party. The minority, on the other hand, despite the Nationalists' much heralded entry into parliament and Devlin's populist rhetoric, virtually opted out of the state, retreating almost into a ghetto.

The completeness of Unionist domination was summed up by the fact that in the inter-war years Northern Ireland had only one Prime Minister, Craig, who remained premier until his death in November 1940. There was, too, very little turnover of cabinet ministers, as all but one of the members of the original cabinet remained in the same offices until the 1930s and two soldiered on, one with a different department, until the early 1940s. Moreover, the government was always supported by a large majority in parliament. In successive general elections in 1921, 1925, 1929, 1933 and 1938, the number of official Unionists returned to the House of Commons was 40, 32, 37, 36 and 39 respectively, giving overall and docile majorities of 28, 12, 22, 20 and 26.

It was the same pattern with other elective bodies. Unionists dominated Northern Ireland's representation at Westminster, and more vitally, they controlled a disproportionate number of local authorities. In the 1920s Unionists represented at most some 66 per cent of the population but controlled 84.6 per cent of all local authorities, including many in areas with large Catholic and nationalist populations, all six county councils and the two county boroughs. Belfast was, of course, nearly three-quarters Protestant, but Londonderry was two-thirds Catholic and it was always a source of pride to Unionists that after partition they maintained the integrity of the Maiden City. The opponents of Unionism were by contrast left in control of only two councils of any consequence — Newry and Strabane.

The domination of public life by Protestants and Unionists was partly to be expected in view of the origins of the new region and its built-in Protestant and Unionist majority. However, it was by no means a foregone conclusion that the single-minded Unionist alliance which had fought against home rule would hold together after partition. Ulster Unionists had themselves long been divided and had found coherence only in opposition to nationalism and Catholicism. During the fight against home rule, these differences had been obscured, but the granting of regional autonomy potentially broadened the field of political debate and was always in danger of bringing out these conflicting interests.

Traditional rhetoric continued to provide a useful cement as did party organisation. The central co-ordinating body remained the UUC, employing a full-time professional organisation, and continuing to act as an umbrella for a wide range of representative individuals, such as MPs, and associations organised locally or regionally or on the basis of age, interest or sex, such as the Ulster Unionist Women's Council, the UULA and, most influentially, the constituency associations and the Orange Order. The nature and structure of the latter prevented it from becoming involved in sustained and constructive political action, but its numerous lodges and capacity for mobilising its large membership in massive demonstrations enabled it to exercise a strong if negative influence on the party and the government. The constituency associations enjoyed considerable autonomy, particularly in relation to the admission of members and the selection of candidates, a freedom which combined with the influence of the Orange Order to ensure that the Unionist Party remained almost exclusively Protestant. The few Catholic Unionists were never permitted to rise in the party ranks or selected as Unionist parliamentary candidates. In addition, maintenance of unity was assisted by emphasis on a very narrow programme. Economic and social thought was vague and even negative, characterised as it was by a hatred of socialism and 'Socialist Red Flaggers . . . destructive of the State and the individual';[9] a major preoccupation was the defence of Protestantism against the encroachments of the Catholic Church; and the overriding concern was to maintain Northern Ireland and the link with Britain.

Above all, it was the use of government power that gave Unionism its cohesion and stranglehold on public life after partition. Since parties and majorities require tangible rewards and individual satisfaction as well as words and organisation, the whole government machinery became geared to ensuring the contentment and continued support of the different sections of the party. Discrimination became built into the processes of government and administration, as the government pandered to Protestant and Unionist whims large or small — whether they concerned the upkeep of a particular piece of road, the educational interests of the Protestant Churches or the local defence of Unionism. Moreover, the completeness of the domination of both the Unionist Party and the constitutional issue was ensured by legislation designed to relieve two constant concerns of Unionists: the dread of being outnumbered and outvoted on public bodies by a Catholic population ever enlarged by a higher birth-rate and an influx of immigrants from the South — a preoccupation particularly pronounced in border areas — and the fear that other issues might arise to obscure the constitutional question and thus confuse Protestant voters into returning representatives committed to uniting Ireland.

Some of the measures adopted to make public bodies safe for Unionism, such as long residential requirements for welfare benefits, were not directly connected with representation. Other legislation concerned the attitude of elected representatives, requiring oaths of allegiance to the government of Northern Ireland as well as the Crown and eventually outlawing abstentionism. The most controversial measures, however, regulated the franchise and distribution of voters, particularly the abolition of PR in local and parliamentary elections and the return to the 'first past the post system' of voting with single constituencies being decided by simple majorities. The usual arguments against PR — expense, inconvenience caused to voters, candidates and members by large constituencies, the confusion created by a multiplicity of candidates and potential government instability — were all adduced to support abolition, but these arguments were hardly conclusive in Northern Ireland and were, in any case, irrelevant. The basic reason for the abolition of PR was that the system was deemed to weaken Unionism. PR had been abolished in local elections in 1922 at the behest of Unionists in the west, anxious to regain control of councils lost in 1920. It was abolished in parliamentary elections in 1929 to bring the constitutional question back to the centre of politics. It sought to prevent a repetition of the Unionist losses in Belfast in 1925 and restore a straight fight between Unionists and Nationalists, between 'men who are for the Union on the one hand or who are against it and want to go into a Dublin Parliament on the other'.[10]

The return to single-member constituencies enabled voters to be distributed in a way to favour Unionists. Had the rank and file had their own way, local electoral boundaries and parliamentary constituencies would have been so drawn that none of their opponents would have sat on local authorities or in parliament, but their suggestions were watered down by the government anxious to satisfy its supporters but also to avoid, as Bates put it, any suggestion of 'indecent gerrymandering'.[11] Following the abolition of PR in local elections, electoral areas in hotly contested districts were re-drawn in 1923 largely on the basis of schemes composed by local Unionists but modified by a government commissioner, Judge John Leech, and the Ministry of Home Affairs, the process of ensuring Unionist control being assisted by a provision in the 1922 Local Government Act that valuation as well as population should be taken into account in determining electoral areas. Subsequent changes were carried out by the ministry, sometimes after a public enquiry, as with the famous or infamous case of the gerrymandering of Londonderry Corporation in 1936 to maintain the Unionists' control of the city in which they were in a minority. Forced after a public enquiry to reject an outlandish scheme proposed by the city's Unionists, the Ministry of Home Affairs nevertheless produced its own scheme, later endorsed by the cabinet, to give Londonderry Unionists the substance of what they wanted. The Corporation was reduced from forty to twenty members and the electorate was arranged into three wards, two safely Unionist and the third, much larger, containing the majority of Nationalist voters. The result was that whereas 9,961 nationalist electors returned eight councillors, 7,444 Unionist voters returned twelve. This majority of four was still not good enough for leading Londonderry Unionists and they were mollified only when Craig promised another bite of the cherry if the scheme 'does not realise our hopes. You may rest assured,' he told the city's MP, 'that all of us have the one aim in view, and that is to maintain the integrity of the Maiden City.'[12]

Seven years earlier the government had itself accepted full responsibility for re-drawing parliamentary boundaries in an effort to restore the original balance of 40 Unionists and 12 nationalists returned in 1921. The government intended to be fair to the minority but any difficulties created by the uneven distribution of Protestants and Catholics were resolved in favour of the former. No provision was made to retain a Nationalist MP in Co. Antrim and one of the seats assigned to Nationalists in Belfast was always likely to be marginal; but Unionists were given Londonderry city and a disproportionate share of the representation of Counties Armagh and Fermanagh. The 55.6 per cent Protestant population of Co. Armagh was given 75 per cent of the representation, while the 56 per cent Catholic population of Co. Fermanagh had to be content with only 33 per cent of the county's seats.

Whereas the abolition of PR and the return to single-member constituencies brought Northern Ireland into line with Britain, other franchise legislation took the two parts of the United Kingdom out of step. The local government franchise began to differ in 1923 when a higher and more closely defined property qualification was introduced in Northern Ireland to end abuses and increase the influence of property. The extension in 1928 of the vote to all adult women aroused alarm that temporary female farm, domestic and other workers from the Free State might swell the Catholic electorate and jeopardise Unionist control in the border areas. Two precautions were, therefore, taken: the introduction of long residential requirements for voters — three years later extended to seven; and a limited company franchise, giving extra votes to individuals nominated by such companies. In sum, legislation and administrative action made the Unionist hold on public life almost absolute.

Public servants were mainly Protestants and Unionists. Long before partition it had been the practice of local authorities in Ireland to employ their own kind, and this practice continued afterwards so that those local authorities controlled by Unionists — the vast majority — tended to employ Protestants. It was the same with the Northern Ireland civil service. During the early years the already small number of Catholics dwindled so that by the Second World War the lower ranks were some 90 per cent Protestant and the senior ranks almost entirely so. The administrative class and analagous technical grades consisted in 1943 of 597 Protestants and 37 Catholics, 94.2 and 5.8 per cent respectively, while the fifty-five highest officers in the civil service were all Protestants. Recruitment was largely on the same basis as that for the civil service in the rest of the United Kingdom, but the minority's reluctance to serve a 'foreign' government and the attitude of the government ensured that the civil service would not be representative of society at large. Unionists but not Nationalist MPs were involved in selection procedures, while life was made difficult for serving Catholics, liable as they were to repeated attacks from the ever vigilant Orange Order on grounds of sedition and depriving loyal Protestants of jobs. What is more, ministers such as Bates and later Andrews shared these views, and Craig's habit of treating allegations seriously eventually led the permanent head of the service to expostulate:

63

If the Prime Minister is dissatisfied with our present system [of recruitment], I think the only course would be for the Government to come out in the open and to say that only Protestants are admitted to our Service. I should greatly regret such a course, and am quite convinced . . . that we are getting loyal service from all those who have entered our Service.[13]

Likewise, the maintenance of law and order and the administration of justice failed to win that general confidence so necessary in any state and especially in Northern Ireland after the turmoil and bitterness of the early months, 1921-2. Although the first Lord Chief Justice was a Catholic, the judiciary was hardly representative of the population. For very good reasons the judicial powers of lay magistrates, the Justices of the Peace, were clipped in 1932, so that the dispensing of justice lay entirely in the hands of professionals. Most were appointed by the government of Northern Ireland, nearly all were Protestant, and many were closely identified with the Unionist Party.

The RUC, the regular police force, usually fluctuated somewhat below its statutory establishment of 3,000 and never succeeded in establishing for itself an image as the servant of the whole community, the impartial enforcer of impartial law. Unlike forces in the rest of the United Kingdom, it was controlled by the government and retained its semi-military character, being armed and headed not by a Chief Constable but by an Inspector-General responsible to the Minister of Home Affairs. There was a fatal incompatibility in its dual role as an ordinary police and a security force, which often meant that police stations were permanently locked and barred and that at the first hint of trouble normal police behaviour was suppressed as the RUC became a paramilitary force. Moreover, the original intention that one-third of the force should be Catholic was never realised. As with the civil service, the number and proportion of Catholics fell in the early years, from 535 Catholics in 1924 to 488 twelve years later, when the total force was 82.9 per cent and the higher ranks 83.6 per cent Protestant.

The failure to recruit Catholics owed something to the minority's refusal to endorse the force and to the political influence to which the force was subjected. Once more, Orange charges against Catholic policemen, however vague and far-fetched, resulted in internal inquiries which in 1924 prompted the first Inspector-General to complain that such efforts 'to bring unfair influence to bear on the detriment of R.C. members of the Force' militated against 'efficiency as it tends to undermine the confidence of the men in their superiors'.[14] Moreover, in matters affecting Protestants or Orangemen, it was always possible that for political reasons advice would be set aside or cases not pushed to their legal conclusion, as happened in 1932 when the Law Officers took steps to ensure that leniency was shown towards Protestants arrested for attacking Catholics on their way to the

Eucharistic Congress in Dublin. 'I do not want,' Bates reported to Craig, 'when the New Parliament House is opened, or when . . . we are engaged in very violent disturbances in connection with the Free State, to have the Government handicapped by having 70 or 80 young fellows in gaol.'[15]

The auxiliary police force, the USC, remained unrepentantly and even triumphantly Protestant. There were in the early 1920s attempts to disband the force on grounds of economy and wider policy in view of its controversial nature. However, the USC had become an important political force in its own right, especially the part-time B class, capable of standing up to the government and justifying itself as the saviour of Ulster and a restraining influence on loyalists. Moreover, it was preferable to have a relatively cheap force under regional control than to rely on the army, an excepted and impartial service under Westminster's control, to defend the land boundary with the South, strictly an imperial duty. The USC was thus not disbanded but reorganised and cut back to leave in effect after 1926 only the part-time B class with reduced allowances and a smaller permanent staff. Its function was primarily a military one — guarding installations and manning road blocks, but it was often used to reinforce the usually under-strength RUC, particularly its 'fire-fighting' Reserve Force, and carry out such duties as riot control for which it was ill-equipped by training and personnel. Its formal establishment and conditions of service were varied from time to time, and its actual strength (12,317 in the middle of 1927, 12,150 in 1931) and state of mobilisation depended on the state of the country. During the 1939 IRA campaign, for example, the whole force was placed in the 'Active Patrol' category on the grounds that 'the best anti-dote was irregular offensive patrolling'.[16]

Furthermore, where it differed from that in Britain, the law in Northern Ireland usually reflected the distinctive morality and political preoccupations of the Protestant and Unionist majority. Most dramatically, the legal armoury of the forces of law and order included the formidable Special Powers Act. Although initially intended only as a temporary and exceptional measure, the act was renewed annually without trouble until the Nationalists' entry into parliament turned the procedure into an occasion for unedifying mutual recrimination. To avoid this annual slanging match the act was not abandoned but renewed for five years in 1928, after which, in 1933, it was made permanent. It is doubtful whether such wide powers were really necessary to cope with outbreaks of political violence after the early 1920s, which, according to some legal authorities, should not have been beyond the ordinary resources of the law and were of insufficient proportions 'to require running the risk of oppressing the innocent'.[17] The government realised that the act was provocative and admitted, in private, that powers of internment and arrest on suspicion both of having committed an act prejudicial to law and order and of being about to do so, were very drastic as part of a permanent enactment. Nevertheless, there was never any serious suggestion of abandoning the Special Powers Act, for the police and Ministry of Home Affairs felt more comfortable with exceptional powers behind them and maintained that the very existence of the act served as a deterrent to potential rebels and evidence of the government's determination to stamp out outrage and sedition. The act continued to be applied against Catholics and nationalists rather than Protestants and Unionists, although not as frequently or as promiscuously as is sometimes alleged. It was, however, used too much for Catholics and too little for Protestants, who in the early years would have liked to have used it even to ban the playing of Gaelic games on the Sabbath!

IV

Such Unionist and Protestant domination of public life was also facilitated by the attitude of the Catholic and nationalist minority. The latter's exclusion from power and public employment came to constitute a major grievance, but it is often overlooked that this exclusion was in part self-imposed. The boycott of public bodies may have begun to break down in the mid-1920s, but the change of policy was scarcely wholehearted. Catholic and nationalist leaders could never escape the claims of Irish unity or rise above their positions of power and influence within the Catholic community.

Although the largest opposition party, the Nationalists refused to endorse the regime by acting as the official opposition in parliament and were prepared to revert to the policy of abstention. Nor did Catholics and nationalists organise themselves for effective political agitation outside parliament. Internal divisions were partly responsible, as the rift between Nationalists and Republicans was complicated by the latter's split over the Treaty. Yet even among the dominant constitutionalists there was never a coherent Nationalist Party complete with its own headquarters and full-time organisers on the lines of the UUC. There were merely loose alliances between local notables – the clergy and the small-town middle class – which produced only ephemeral organisations. The National League, despite its confident inauguration, expired shortly after the 1929 general election, and even more transient was the Irish Union Association, formed in Belfast in 1936 with financial support from Dublin in the hope of bringing the gap between the various shades of nationalist opinion. Moreover, the prime focus of these organisations was not the development of Northern Ireland as a whole but the achievement of Irish unity and, in the meantime, the defence of Catholic interests. Devlin constantly denied that he led a Catholic party, but there was never a sustained effort to reach beyond the Catholic community and challenge for power on the basis of an economic and social programme, for, declared one of the members for Belfast in 1930, 'It is our duty in parliament . . . to look after the interests of the faith to which I am proud to belong.'[18]

66

This order of priorities reflected the flourishing position of the Catholic Church in Northern Ireland after partition, especially in the diocese of Down and Connor. Three of the best-known and most effective Catholic organisations in modern Ireland had their origins there: the Catholic Truth Society, the Pioneer Association of the Sacred Heart and the Apostolic Work Society. Many other Catholic associations were introduced into the North, such as the Legion of Mary and the Catholic Young Men's Society which came to Belfast in 1927, while the ideals of Catholic Action were fully implemented in one city parish, which began to help the unemployed in the years of depression by organising lectures, plays and outings and even sending a number of pilgrims to Rome in the Holy Year of 1933. Indeed, the Catholic Church became the focus of much of life as 'Catholic men and women found outlets for their abilities in the service of their neighbours in the fellowship of the Church. The nature and scope of these activities, their impact on the Catholic community, the administrative ability of those who run them, show what Catholics can do when working as a coordinated unit.'[19]

This retreat in on itself and refusal to play a full role in public life did, however, rebound upon the minority. It confirmed the identification of Catholicism with hostility both to the state and the Protestant majority, especially when in 1931 Cardinal Archbishop Joseph MacRory of Armagh declared that the Protestant Church in Ireland 'is not even a part of the Church of Christ'.[20] It detracted from the effectiveness of even valid criticisms of the Unionist regime, because they could plausibly be dismissed as purely destructive attempts to discredit Northern Ireland in the interests of Irish unity. Furthermore, it tended to develop a spirit of mutual admiration and complacency that made difficult any *rapprochement* with Unionists and the government. Indeed, Catholics helped Unionists to put them into the position of second-class citizens by refusing to participate and challenge for positions in official life.

V

The official Unionists' monopoly of power and the inability or unwillingness of the minority to mount an effective challenge meant that politics became fossilised and the new parliament never really struck roots. The abolition of PR in parliamentary elections, the return to carefully devised single-member constituencies, and the determination of established leaders to brook no opposition, soon frustrated the Labour and Independent challenges mounted in 1925 and restored a virtual straight fight between Unionism and Nationalism, Protestantism and Catholicism. Politics became so predictable that many parliamentary seats ceased to be contested. In 1929, following the abolition of PR, Independent Unionist representation was reduced by one, as only three of the ten Independent Unionist candidates were returned, while the Labour Party's representation was reduced to only one, as four of its five candidates were defeated. On the other hand, 37 official Unionists and 11 Nationalists were returned and 22 of the 52 seats – 42.3 per cent – were uncontested. Five years later no fewer than 33 or 63.5 per cent of members were returned unopposed, including 27 of the 36 official Unionists and 6 of the 11 Nationalists.

The Independent Unionist MPs represented no real threat to the official party and injected no new ideas into political debate. They were individualists and, the independent member for Queen's University apart, they were usually the most uncompromising of Orangemen. The longest-serving, Thomas Henderson, house painter and MP from 1925 until 1953, distinguished himself by becoming one of the most muddled and certainly the most long-winded member of the House, once undertaking a nine-hour filibuster. Protestant temperance reformers, basically prohibitionists, were always a source of irritation to the official party and in the 1929 general election launched their biggest attack on the government and its relatively moderate licensing policy, threatening to split the Unionist vote to let Republicans in. However, the low poll in the three seats they eventually contested proved that they had no real popular backing. The nearest approach to an organised and coherent Unionist opposition to the official party occurred in the late 1930s with the formation of the Progressive Unionist Party by the Belfast millionaire Unionist MP for the Westminster constituency of South Belfast, William John Stewart. The new party combined a call for more government initiative on housing with a demand for less government intervention in agriculture, but, although it helped to lower the percentage of uncontested seats to 40.4 per cent, it did not survive the general election called in February 1938, ostensibly as a riposte to the claims of the new Eire constitution over the North but in reality to crush the 'wreckers',[21] as Craig called Stewart and his party.

While the various unofficial Unionist groups worked only within the Protestant community, the Labour Party tried to win votes from both Protestants and Catholics. But, despite the existence of a large working class, a high degree of unionisation among skilled workers and the demonstrable need for social reform in the depressed inter-war years, the party never had a safe parliamentary seat, even in Belfast. What little success it did have in the 1930s, when it secured only one or two seats, it achieved 'not by uninhibited and uncluttered advocacy of social and economic reforms' but by the manipulation of the sectarian balance in a few constituencies and 'by being different things to different men, or by coming forward on a compromise platform'.[22] Part of this weakness was a failure of leadership. What few leaders or MPs the party produced either left Northern Ireland or quarrelled among themselves. In the 1930s and early 1940s there was a running and vitriolic battle between two Protestant trade unionist MPs, John Beattie and Henry Cassidy Midgley. The former was a passionate opponent of partition, the latter an equally impassioned opponent of the South, international fascism and its ally the Catholic Church. Both eventually formed their own parties in the 1940s, Midgley ending up as a Unionist and cabinet minister. Moreover, the party's appeal was limited by the government's policy of copying British social and industrial legislation, which meant that the battles of Northern Ireland's workingmen were largely fought out by the Labour movement in Britain. Finally, as the dispute between Beattie and Midgley underlined, the party could not overcome the problems posed by the religious and constitutional questions.

Until 1949 the Labour Party tried to avoid taking a stand on partition, leaving its members free to advocate what views they liked on the issue. This tactic only succeeded in exposing it to attack from both sides, while its socialism and the Protestantism of many of its leading members rendered it particularly suspect in Catholic eyes, as one Protestant candidate discovered to his cost in the 1929 general election. He and the other two Labour MPs had been co-operating with the Nationalists in the previous parliament but on the re-distribution of seats he was defeated in the Falls division of Belfast by a Catholic publican who had the full support of the clergy and such groups as the Catholic Union who stated that 'Catholic representation is required to defend Catholic interests especially on the education question'.[23] It is a moot question as to how far employers and political and religious leaders deliberately and consistently exploited the sectarian question to keep workers docile and malleable, but it is certain that political and religious sectarianism inhibited the development of an exclusive working-class consciousness impelling Catholics and Protestants to unite in bold political and industrial action. As one Belfast street orator complained in the 1930s:

If you took all the Orange sashes and all the Green sashes in Belfast and tied them round a ticket of loaves and threw them in the [River] Lagan, the gulls, the common, ordinary sea-gulls, they'd go for the bread, but the other gulls – yous ones – yous'd go for the sashes every time.[24]

Reflecting entrenched positions within the community at large, parliament never became an effective part of the decision-making or policy-making processes in Northern Ireland. MPs refused to take full advantage of what powers parliament did possess. Whatever their parties, they were socially unrepresentative, invariably middle-aged and older and so involved in their local communities that they had a very limited perception of their role and saw themselves primarily as representing their immediate constituencies. While religion might divide them, most MPs shared both a pronounced distrust of state activity and expenditure and a fierce determination to defend local interests. The most common dividing line on many issues was between those MPs sitting for Belfast and those representing rural constituencies. Parliament had little to offer and it largely acted as a rubber stamp for decisions made elsewhere – between the government and interested parties outside parliament.

In fact, in the 1930s parliament became almost irrelevant to many sections of the community. In May 1932 the entire Nationalist Party walked out of parliament, partly as the result of frustration at both the Unionist refusal to share power and the limited powers of parliament. What occasioned the withdrawal was the Speaker's refusal to allow discussion of reserved services, which prompted Devlin to complain that 'It is obviously a sham and a farce being Members of Parliament elected by the people to discuss public expenditure . . . if our rights and liberties are to be so circumscribed that we are not permitted to discuss them.'[25] The Nationalist attitude was also influenced by de Valera's assumption of power in the Free State. At least one border MP preferred electioneering in the South, looking 'for guidance to the great leader of the Irish people',[26] to sitting in Stormont.

The entire party remained away for eighteen months, after which time abstention was on an individual and sporadic basis. It was more frequent among representatives from the west, where Republican-abstentionist feeling was strongest and where public transport links with Belfast were poor. By the end of 1937 only two Belfast members, including Thomas James Campbell, barrister, journalist and party leader, continued to attend parliament regularly. Such a boycott was less a political tactic than a 'gesture of apathy and despair'. No effort was made to set up an alternative assembly, to lead extra-parliamentary agitation or even to build up a strong political organisation. The Nationalist MPs 'just stayed at home and looked after their businesses, meeting occasionally to discuss important topics and issuing infrequent press statements'.[27]

As for working-class politics, there was more excitement and action on the streets than in parliament. On 30 September 1932, when parliament met for a formal sitting during a long summer recess, the Speaker refused to let Henderson, the Independent Unionist, and Beattie, then the only Labour member, raise the question of unemployment, then reaching almost record levels. Beattie lifted the mace and threw it at the Speaker, saying 'I absolutely refuse to sit in this House and indulge in hypocrisy while the people are starving outside.'[28] He then walked out, followed by Henderson, leaving the government with an opposition of two, one of the members for Queen's University and the other that most outspoken of Orangemen, Nixon, who had eventually been dismissed from the RUC for partisanship and insubordination.

With the high unemployment and mounting distress of the 1930s there was much talk of working-class solidarity and repeated threats by Labour orators to make Craig's knees knock 'like the bones in a jazz band'[29] and to dissolve the Belfast parliament the way Cromwell had dissolved the English one. No such revolution materialised. The most that did occur was the remarkable phenomenon of a non-sectarian riot in Belfast in

70

October 1932, caused by the refusal of the niggardly Belfast Board of Guardians to give relief to the unemployed on the same basis as in Britain. Under the auspices of the Belfast Outdoor Relief Workers' Committee and the Marxist Revolutionary Workers' Group (the forerunner of the Communist Party of Ireland), a movement of protest gathered momentum and crossed existing lines of political and religious division, drawing in Protestants and Catholics, Nationalists and Labour, socialists and communists and a few members of the IRA who were in a socialist phase. Alarmed by the state of feeling and the obvious distress in the city, the government put pressure on the Guardians, but when the protesters refused to accept concessions, the Special Powers Act was employed to ban a proposed march on parliament. Nevertheless, crowds of unemployed workers gathered on both the Falls and Shankill on 11 October and when the much re-inforced police batoned charged and fired over the heads of the crowds in the Falls, for the first time in history the Shankill crowd rioted in their support. Rioting lasted for two or three days and resulted in two deaths.

Although there was some co-operation between Protestant trade unionists and a socialist wing of the IRA during a bitter rail strike in the following year, the 1932 riot represented the fleeting peak of Orange-Green collaboration. Sectarian rioting in various towns was more common than ephemeral demonstrations of working-class solidarity, as the violent rhetoric of Labour orators was matched by the inflammatory and provocative slogans and rallies organised by the Ulster Protestant League, formed in 1931 to safeguard the employment of Protestants. Tension came to a head in Belfast on 12 July 1935. Bates at first banned all processions but then capitulated to the Orange Order's demand to exempt its processions. Rioting, sniping and arson lasted for three weeks in the Falls-Shankill area, during which the RUC was supported by the army and the USC. Eleven people were killed and 574 injured; there were 367 cases of malicious damage and 133 of arson; and over 300 families, mostly Catholic, were driven from their homes. The fierceness of the rioting, the worst since 1922, focussed unwelcome attention on Northern Ireland and its government. The RUC had done its best to keep the two sides apart and to assist people driven from their homes, but it was subsequently accused of discrimination by both Protestants and Catholics. The latter's demand for a British inquiry was supported by some 100 Westminster MPs, but the British Prime Minister, Stanley Baldwin, refused an inquiry on the grounds that responsibility for law and order lay with the government of Northern Ireland. An inquiry was, however, undertaken by the London-based National Council for Civil Liberties whose report constituted a scathing indictment of the Unionist regime, particularly the use of the Special Powers Act as begetting contempt for the representative institutions of government.

Like many other critics, the National Council for Civil Liberties overstated the faults of the government of Northern Ireland. Condemnations of the intolerable conditions under which Catholics laboured to uphold their faith in an atmosphere of privileged Protestantism were deliberately over-drawn to discredit and undermine Northern Ireland in the interests of Irish unity. The Unionist regime was neither as vindictive nor as oppressive as regimes elsewhere in the world with problems of compact or irridentist minorities. Moreover, most criticism ignored the difficulties of governing Northern Ireland and the extent to which the government mitigated the extremism of its supporters. Nevertheless, when all these qualifications have been made, the fact remains that, owing to local conditions, the power of the government was used in the interests of Unionists and Protestants, with scant regard for the interests of the region as a whole or for the claims and susceptibilities of the substantial minority. Whatever comparisons can be made with the rest of the world, standards of political behaviour and justice in the crucial formative years of Northern Ireland's existence developed out of line with those obtaining in the rest of the United Kingdom, of which the six counties were supposed to be an integral part.

Such a verdict prompts the question, why did Westminster, the sovereign power, not intervene to iron out the deficiencies of regional government in relation to such controversial transferred services as education, representation and law and order? There was certainly concern in official circles both in the Home Office, the ministry responsible for Northern Ireland, and in the Dominions Office, which dealt with the South, particularly over the close relationship between government and party in the North. Yet there was little to be done short of resuming control of the province, as the chastening experience of the 1922 Local Government Bill had shown the perils of trying to thwart the majority in Northern Ireland when no alternative government was available. Britain did have an increasingly powerful financial weapon to bring Ulstermen to heel and counter threats of resignation, but generally declined to use it except on strictly financial matters. In 1924-5 Labour and Conservative governments did finally resort to a little financial blackmail to secure the long-sought-after release of nationalist internees and political prisoners, but it was not until the late 1960s that such pressure was used again to achieve non-financial objectives. Between times, Westminster was concerned mainly to see that Northern Ireland did not enjoy higher standards at the expense of the British taxpayer and that the rights of the imperial parliament were not infringed. Otherwise, it did not monitor the North's internal administration and preferred to accept assurances from ministers and officials that all was well.

VI

Devolution condemned Northern Ireland to economic and social as well as political stagnation in the inter-war years. Before partition the six counties, like the rest of Ireland, had lacked much compared with the rest of the United Kingdom. Living standards were lower, as were the quality and range of services provided by the state and local authorities, but the prospect of radical change offered in the early 1920s never materialised. There was little consistent, let alone adventurous, imaginative or vigorous economic and social planning on a regional basis, and in many spheres standards deteriorated. What few improvements or successes there were emanated as much from Britain as within Northern Ireland.

Economically, the most pressing problem Northern Ireland faced was the decline of the old staples – agriculture, linen and shipbuilding – and the consequent high rate of unemployment and social distress. Yet the only real success story was the beginnings of the modernisation of agriculture. Farming remained conservative, but the efforts of the Ministry of Agriculture at least helped to restore it to a competitive position in its main market, Britain, after Northern Ireland farmers had fallen from grace for abusing their monopoly during the First World War by supplying inferior produce at inflated prices. Indeed, Northern Ireland led Britain and the Free State in efforts to improve standards of produce and marketing. The Live Stock Breeding Act of 1922 raised standards of breeding in the North's most prestigious agriculture pursuit, cattle, and preceded similar legislation in Britain and the Free State by nine and three years respectively. Compulsory marketing schemes ensuring minimum standards for eggs, potatoes, fruit, milk and butter were also distinctive features of agricultural policy in Northern Ireland, and in the 1930s Northern Ireland turned to good advantage the change in Britain from free trade to protection. Marketing schemes, to help United Kingdom producers fill the gap left by banned or reduced imports of foreign foodstuffs, were skilfully adapted to suit Northern Ireland conditions. Pig marketing measures, implemented under the 1933 Agricultural Marketing Act, expanded pig production and even helped to change the breed of pig to enable Northern Ireland to supply the south of England with the lean Wiltshire cure bacon previously bought from Denmark. The 1934 Milk Marketing Act, admired in Britain, enabled milk for human consumption to be sold in Northern Ireland more cheaply than elsewhere in the United Kingdom.

In other spheres of economic life there was gloom and despondency, particularly in face of government impotence to halt the decline in linen and shipbuilding. To have speeded up the rationalisation of the linen industry, which was beginning slowly to take place, would have created further unemployment, while the implementation of the other solution widely canvassed in the 1920s – the limitation of linen imports into the United Kingdom – was beyond the powers of the government of Northern Ireland and had to await Westminster's adoption of protection in the 1930s. To help shipbuilding Northern Ireland copied and then made more generous the British scheme for guaranteeing loans raised by shipowners ordering ships from the Belfast yards. The Loans Guarantees Acts, 1922-36, may have only slowed down the rate of decline, delaying the closure of the 'wee yard' until 1935, but it was more successful than attempts to persuade the British government to have naval vessels built in Belfast. Too many other struggling shipyards in Britain had prior claim to British assistance. The government was just as powerless to assist in any significant way smaller trades and industries, such as Londonderry's bakers and millers, who were sorely hit and even more sorely angry at the effects of Free State tariffs and other duties on their customary trade across the border.

Even in matters within its legal competence, the government found its initiatives thwarted, as in the failure of its attempts to rationalise the transport system by ending ruinous competition between road and rail and within road transport itself. Its Road and Railway Transport Act of 1935, which put most road transport under a Road Transport Board and required the board and railway companies to co-ordinate their services, was hailed outside Ireland as an honest attempt to grapple with a difficult and world-wide problem. It soon, however, broke down in face of the intransigence of the railway companies and their running battle with Northern Ireland farmers.

Nor was the government any more successful in attracting new industries. It did with some optimism give substantial subsidies to develop coal deposits in Coalisland, Co. Tyrone, but dreams of self-sufficiency in coal and flourishing heavy industries were soon dashed when it was discovered that coal could not be mined economically. In the 1930s new measures, the New Industries (Development) Acts of 1932 and July and December 1937, offered increasingly more but still limited incentives to bring industrialists to Northern Ireland — at first rent-free sites and relief of rates and later interest-free loans. The policy was not very imaginative in either conception or execution, generally following British schemes and trying to avoid stepping on the toes of local industrialists. The response was accordingly limited. The only large industry attracted in the inter-war years was an aircraft factory outside Belfast, Short and Harland, which probably would have been established there even without the annual government assistance of £2,709. More firms were given aid under the December 1937 act, and, although their output covered a wider range of products, they provided fewer jobs, and for women rather than men. Moreover, most of the new concerns settled in and around Belfast, and of the twenty-seven firms actually operating under new industries legislation by the middle of 1939, fifteen were situated in Belfast and a further three in the industrial complex centering on the city. Eventually the number of firms taking advantage of the new policy was only fifty-four, and even by 1955 they were providing employment for not more than 6,000 workers, mostly in Short and Harland. Neither in the short nor long terms did the 1930s new industries legislation do much to broaden Northern Ireland's industrial basis or alleviate unemployment.

The result was mounting distress as an increasing proportion of the labour force could not find work. In the inter-war years the rate of unemployment in shipbuilding never fell below 13.3 per cent (in February 1930) and was once as high as 64.5 per cent (in December 1932). In linen the rate of unemployment ranged between 6.2 per cent (in October 1927) and 56.3 per cent (in July 1938). Wales, with its dependence on the depressed coal industry, often had a higher rate of unemployment, but by the late 1930s Northern Ireland outstripped even Wales with 29.5 per cent unemployment compared with 23.8 in Wales and 12.8 for Britain as a whole. Not surprisingly, Northern Ireland became established as the poorest part of the United Kingdom, its people earning far less than those in Britain. In 1939 the average income per head in Northern Ireland was only 58.3 per cent of the United Kingdom average — £64.7 as against £111.

More success attended efforts to relieve distress as a result of the adoption of the 'step-by-step' policy of keeping pace with Britain in the provision of major cash social services. National insurance for unemployment and health had been introduced in Ireland in 1911 at the same time as Britain, and one of the first major decisions of the government of Northern Ireland was to keep national insurance on the same basis as the rest of the United Kingdom. The conditions (residence requirements apart from the 1930s) and levels of unemployment benefit followed those in Britain, and as the scope of British unemployment legislation expanded so did that in Northern Ireland with the result that in the 1930s National Assistance was added to unemployment insurance. Health insurance which had included, as in Britain, cash payments during sickness but not, unlike Britain, medical care, was brought into line in 1930. Similarly, old age pensions, out of step for a few months in 1924-5, were brought into step in 1925, after which pensions of all kinds, again residence qualifications excepted, were kept on a par with those in the rest of the United Kingdom.

Originally adopted almost unthinkingly in 1922, the step-by-step policy was subsequently justified on a number of grounds. The obvious argument was that since Northern Ireland paid the same taxes as the rest of the United Kingdom, it should enjoy the same benefits. This was buttressed by the political need to retain for Unionism the loyalty and support of Protestant working men who were organised on a United Kingdom basis and expected the same standards as their fellow trade unionists in Britain. Most importantly, to have abandoned the policy would have spelled financial disaster, since the concept of equal social standards was the cornerstone of Northern Ireland's complex financial relations with Britain. If Northern Ireland lagged behind Britain in any major reform, Craig told opponents of contributory old age pensions,

> The screw will be put on and we will be told that of our own initiative
> we refused to give the same benefits to people living in our area afforded
> to those [in Britain] ... and that as we had adopted that attitude

there was no necessity for our financial affairs to be so adjusted that we could live pari passu with the English and Scotch *in other directions.*[30]

There were, too, pressing social and humanitarian grounds for persevering with the policy. Otherwise, little might have been done to relieve the mounting distress caused by chronic unemployment in face of the tendency of agricultural and industrial employers and the traditional agencies for non-insured relief, the Poor Law Guardians, especially those in Belfast, to regard unemployment and the consequent distress as self-inflicted. The Belfast Guardians were quite willing to put people in the workhouse, but not to give outdoor relief, except on stringent and ungenerous conditions, and thus, as they said, subsidise sloth and fecklessness particularly among Catholics who married young and produced too many children.

Yet there were also drawbacks to step-by-step. The policy pre-empted a potentially invigorating field of political debate which concerned the whole community and cut across the sectarian divide. There were grounds for arguing that Northern Ireland should not blindly copy its more prosperous neighbour in the construction and expansion of a costly system of social services. Lower living standards, incomes and taxable capacity might have justified lower benefits, while Northern Ireland's special problems, such as chronic unemployment and high infant mortality, might have merited a different order of priorities, for example, applying the money spent on cash benefits for the unemployed and aged to the creation of employment and the improvement of health services. The step-by-step policy was also inimical to regional planning, since it came to mean that Northern Ireland should not lag behind in granting financial boons to its citizens. The result was that measures such as rate relief for agriculture and industry were often unthinkingly applied to Northern Ireland with little regard to their financial and other consequences. As a result, other services suffered, such as health and housing.

Housing policy in Northern Ireland differed from that in Britain in two crucial respects. The general level of subsidies was lower and more variable, and reliance was placed upon private builders rather than upon local authorities, partly because of the government's inordinate faith in the private entrepreneur who had successfully provided houses before the First World War, and partly because of its low expectations of local authorities. Thus proportionately fewer houses were built in Northern Ireland than in Britain during the inter-war years, and whereas extensive slum clearance was carried out in Britain, none was undertaken in Northern Ireland. What houses were built made no impression, as the Ministry of Home Affairs itself admitted in 1937, on 'the problem of providing accommodation for the poorer classes, mostly residing in houses more or less unfit for habitation'.[31]

Medical provision was also neglected. In the maternity service neglect was particularly conspicuous, and in 1938 an Ulsterwoman ran a greater risk of dying in childbirth than fifteen years before. Moreover, the failure

76

to devise plans to reduce deaths from the biggest killer disease, tuberculosis (in 1938 the cause of 46 per cent of all deaths between 15 and 25 years and 38 per cent of those between 25 and 35), afforded 'a striking example of incoherence in public administration. The death of a young parent could impoverish the family, making it not only a prey to further infection but a charge on public funds; and it made no sense to spend large sums on education if the citizens were to die when memories of schooldays were green.'[32]

Even the increasing amount spent on education was not necessarily used to best effect. The great ambitions of the 1923 Education Act were hardly realised. The new scheme and the spirit it implied did help to improve teacher training, school attendance and school buildings by the amalgamation of small schools and the construction of new ones, but educational provision generally remained patchy and sectarian.

Carefully devised as it was, the 1923 act completely underestimated the determination of the churches to maintain their control over education. Despite their theological differences and mutual detestation, Protestant and Catholic clergymen shared remarkably similar educational principles. Both believed that children should be taught by teachers of their own denomination; that children should attend schools with their co-religionists; and that religious instruction should be woven into the curriculum. They had bent the national system under the Union to suit their own ideas and were determined to preserve their position in Northern Ireland's educational system. They would have nothing to do with what they called Lord Londonderry's 'Godless' schools and successfully demanded instead both state money and independent control of teaching appointments to ensure sound denominational education.

The Protestants set the pace. The combined agitation of the Orange Order and the United Education Committee of the Protestant Churches virtually turned public elementary schools into Protestant establishments. They put pressure on the government when it was at its most vulnerable, just before the general elections of 1925 and 1929 and the annual Orange demonstrations in July 1925. Concessions made in 1925 proved insufficient to guarantee that only Protestant teachers would teach Protestant children and that the Bible would be read in all state schools, and thus further changes were sought. These proposals were vigorously opposed by officials of the Ministry of Education, by the new regional education committees and by teachers' unions as virtually restoring clerical control of schools. Nevertheless, the government bowed to the superior political clout of the Orange Order and the churches and in the 1930 Education Bill agreed to allow clerical representation on regional education committees; to give individual school management committees considerable influence on appointments; and to compel education authorities to provide and teachers to give simple Bible instruction in the hours of compulsory attendance if so petitioned by the parents of not less than ten children.

This concession to Protestantism solved one problem only to create others. In the first place, the changes could be construed as a contravention of the 1920 Government of Ireland Act as both endowing a religion and requiring religious tests; and the Home Office at Westminster threatened to refer the bill to the Judicial Committee of the Privy Council if there were sufficient representations in Northern Ireland against the proposals. In the second place, it played into the hands of the Catholic Church already alarmed at the mounting cost of education. Simple Bible instruction without denominational comment was anathema to the Catholic Church. The interpretation of the scripture by private judgment was the fundamental principle of Protestantism, whereas for Catholics the Bible was 'but a dead letter calling for a divine interpreter'.[33] Moreover, the government's policy on representation rebounded on it. Catholics argued that since partition they had even more reason not to put their schools under public control, as electoral changes had not only handed over most local authorities to Unionists but in doing so had shown scant regard for minority interests. To prevent a Catholic outcry, which in view of the Home Office's reservations could have jeopardised the agreement with Protestants, the government decided to buy off Catholic opposition. The 1930 Education Act, therefore, as well as implementing the clerical-Orange demands, also restored most of the grant withdrawn in 1923 and offered a 50 per cent building grant to voluntary schools. In so doing, it gave all voluntary schools a further reason for staying outside the state system, and marked the complete breakdown of the attempt to establish an integrated system of education. Instead of the single non-denominational system envisaged by Londonderry, a dual system became firmly established, as voluntary, denominational, schools flourished alongside those maintained entirely out of public funds. Protestant children attended the state schools and their own voluntary schools. Few Catholics went to state schools and were educated separately in schools run by their Church.

By 1938 more than half of all elementary schools with almost half the total number of pupils were voluntary. Whatever the effects on society at large, the consequence of continued sectarianism for education was lower standards, particularly in the provision of buildings and equipment. Added to this fundamental failure of the original scheme were other weaknesses. The volume of new building fell short of requirements. None of the education committees provided nursery schools; school services were inadequate and scholarship awards niggardly; books and stationery were bought for only one child in ten; and little was done to help feed or clothe needy children, who in rural areas often ate nothing but dry bread throughout the day. Even the two county boroughs failed to establish special schools or classes for mental defectives. Indeed, Northern Ireland was still a generation or more behind most of England and Wales.

In the inter-war years Northern Ireland developed not as 'a half-way house' with a united and contented population enjoying the advantages of responsive regional government, but as 'a lean-to',[34] a 'factory of grievances',[35] containing the most divided and disadvantaged people in the United Kingdom. Natural economic disadvantages, British indifference and the irridentism of the South all contributed, but the fundamental causes of this dismal performance were the provisions of the 1920 act and the political immaturity of Ulstermen.

The parliament of Northern Ireland never made much impact upon the intelligence and imagination of Ulstermen. Neither Unionists nor nationalists had ever demanded a separate legislature for the six counties and the one they were given was hamstrung by the key role assigned to local authorities and inadequate powers, especially of finance. Partition wrought no dramatic change in the attitudes of local authorities who continued to be bastions of partisanship and conservatism and slow to extend services for fear of increasing the burden of rates and demoralising and pauperising the population by reducing the necessity for individual endeavour. The inadequacies of the system were quickly realised by the new regional government but it lacked the confidence to undertake the drastic reform of such powerful and well-entrenched parts of local community life. Even though most local authorities were controlled by Unionists, the government's relations with them were characterised by perpetual wrangling over who should finance what, as was the case with the two county boroughs. Belfast Corporation liked to conduct its disputes in public and even in the mid-1930s unsuccessfully took the government to the highest court in the land, the Judicial Committee of the Privy Council, over the financing of education. Londonderry Corporation was more discreet but equally demanding and destructive of government initiative and planning. It could easily upset agreed lines of cabinet policy and extract money from the government by sending deputations to Belfast asking plaintively 'Is Londonderry worth to the Empire . . . £4,500?'[36] or even by telephoning ministers and implying mayhem unless money was given on the quiet. Such were only the most obvious instances of a crippling weakness in the governmental structure which often meant that decisions were delayed and lines of responsibility blurred.

The financial provisions of the 1920 act proved equally destructive of regional initiative and planning. In the inter-war years Northern Ireland was usually on the verge of bankruptcy and had to fight hard for whatever aid it received from Britain. Some relief was afforded by the Colwyn Award and the Unemployment Insurance Agreement of 1926. Under the former, domestic expenditure continued to be offset against the imperial contribution which dwindled annually. The latter agreement, while not amalgamating the two Unemployment Funds, as requested by Northern Ireland, did for a few years provide substantial British help towards the ever rising cost of unemployment benefits. These arrangements broke down in the early 1930s. The imperial contribution virtually disappeared and the complicated provisions of the Insurance Agreement meant that with increasing unemployment in Britain that source of income dried up and a new agreement was not finally negotiated until 1936. To retrieve the situation the government of Northern Ireland tried to invoke the concept of a 'minus' or 'negative' contribution, by which Britain should make good any deficit in the North's budget to ensure parity of services with the rest of the United Kingdom. The British government eventually accepted this principle, and made some concessions on agricultural subsidies, in the Simon declaration of 1938, as part of an attempt to buy off threatened Northern Ireland opposition to a series of Anglo-Eire agreements ending the economic war and supposedly reconciling the two nations. This came too late to have much effect before the outbreak of the Second World War, so that in the 1930s Northern Ireland's budget was balanced only by a series of what one senior Treasury official called 'fudges' and 'wangles' and 'dodges and devices' giving 'gifts and subventions within the ambit of the Government of Ireland Act so as to save the Northern Ireland Government from coming openly on the dole as Newfoundland did'.[37] Regional planning was thus inhibited by a shortage of money and the constant need to avoid, as Pollock said in 1927, 'irritating the Chancellor or making him think we want to oppose him in what he considers necessary'.[38] Fear of what the Treasury might say could easily determine the fate of policies.

The inadequacies of the governmental structure both re-inforced and were re-inforced by the political immaturity of Ulstermen. Their acute awareness of the constitutional and religious questions contrasted with their limited perceptions of economic and social issues, and they had little faith in state action to resolve what social and economic problems they did acknowledge. The myopic temperance movement apart, which liked to attribute all ills to the demon drink, there was no organised campaign or sustained movement of public opinion against poverty, unemployment, ill-health, poor housing, inadequate roads, indifferent education or the limitations imposed on the legislature. Still less were any solutions propounded. There was, for example, a striking contrast between the way economic policy was discussed in Northern Ireland and in Britain. In Britain economic problems were widely investigated and discussed by universities and private bodies as well as the government, but in Northern Ireland no such informed public existed from whom the government could seek advice and support.

Nor did party leaders educate their followers. Labour leaders were divided and indecisive. Devlin was past his best when he entered the Northern Ireland parliament. Frustrated and ill, oblivious to financial realities, 'his genuine sympathy for the poor appeared to hostile critics as windy verbiage'.[39] His successor and close associate, Campbell, was conservative and conscientious but no political heavyweight. Most vitally, the government lacked initiative and what drive it did have often came from civil servants rather than ministers. The latter lacked the self-confidence born of generations of governing to surmount their many difficulties and rise above party. The only one to attempt to do so in any significant way, Londonderry, soon returned to British politics after he and his educational policy had been thwarted and abused by what he regarded as noisy Presbyterians and Orangemen. Other ministers, born firmly in the nineteenth century and thrust unexpectedly into power, had little faith in the efficacy of government action; they preferred to rely upon private enterprise and Providence, and became even less active and open to new ideas as advancing years and ill-health sapped their energy.

In particular, Craig, who had done so much for Northern Ireland in 1921-2, had run out of steam by the end of the decade. In face of the country's problems and his own age and increasingly bad health, he abandoned the role of leader and tried instead to become a sort of benevolent and popular father-figure for the people of Northern Ireland, eminently approachable, handing out largesse and settling disputes with cups of tea served by his wife. It was a style that blurred the distinction between the government and the Unionist Party and which accentuated all the problems of the regional government. He increasingly mishandled relations with Britain, particularly over financial questions, while at home his policy of 'distributing bones', as he put it, created the impression that, as one disenchanted local official complained, 'The only way to get money from the Government is to make yourself unpleasant and then interview the Prime Minister.'[40] Indeed, in the 1930s Northern Ireland virtually became directionless so that by 1938 Spender, the permanent head of the civil service, was complaining of 'an entire absence of clear thought and co-ordination'. Craig was so unwell that he could do no more than an hour's concentrated work and preferred to make 'quick hasty decisions rather than go fully into a question with his colleagues'. Since, anyway, most of Craig's colleagues were absent, ill or dying, cabinet meetings seldom took place 'and very often the Ministers most concerned seem to be unaware of what is happening until an announcement is made in the Press'.[41]

Craig's achievement was that Northern Ireland struggled into existence as a semi-autonomous part of the United Kingdom, but during his long premiership he failed to create the conditions for its ultimate survival. Subsequent events were to show that devolution did not necessarily condemn Northern Ireland to economic and social stagnation, but the pattern of government and politics established in the formative years endured. It was a pattern based not upon the wholehearted consent of the entire community but upon the indifference of the minority and the determination of the majority to monopolise power. Northern Ireland really was a Protestant state.

Chapter 5

CHANGE WITHOUT CHANGE

The outbreak and aftermath of the Second World War presented both exciting and alarming possibilities for Northern Ireland. Apart from the dangers of a defeat of the Allies and a German invasion, which were never seriously contemplated, questions were raised about the status of Northern Ireland and the sort of society that should be reconstructed after the war. Changes did occur, almost justifying Northern Ireland's separate existence, as regional powers and a revolution in its finances were energetically exploited by new ministers and a reanimated civil service to transform at least some aspects of life so conspicuously neglected before the war. In the long run the successes and failures of social and economic reform helped to undermine the state, but until the 1960s much remained the same, especially the divisions within society and the Protestant and Unionist domination of official life.

I

Threatening for many months, the Second World War finally began in September 1939 and lasted in Europe until May 1945. 'We are King's men',[1] declared Craig, placing all Northern Ireland's resources at the disposal of the British government. Such instinctive loyalty embarrassed as much as gratified Westminster. Out of deference to and fear of nationalist opinion, the British government refused to apply conscription, an excepted service, to Northern Ireland and even contemplated the ending of partition in 1940 in an effort to persuade Eire to enter the war on the side of the Allies. How many Ulster Unionists would have responded to Eire's abandonment of its neutrality will never be known, for in face of Craig's intransigence and still more de Valera's refusal to commit himself to the war nothing came of these talks and Northern Ireland went on to prove its value to the Empire.

With its ports it stood as 'a faithful sentinel'[2] helping to protect the sea lanes between Britain and America, particularly the north-west approaches to Merseyside and Clydeside. As the war went on, its ports and bases served as shelter not only for British naval units but also for an increasing number of American forces. Agricultural production was stretched to the limit and industries assisted the war effort, as shipbuilding, engineering and aircraft concerns were transformed into veritable arsenals. Moreover, Northern Ireland suffered with the rest of the United Kingdom, sending volunteers to the front and being the victim of four air raids on Belfast in April and

May 1941, which brought fire-brigades hastening northwards from as far away as Dublin. The first air-raid, 15-16 April, demolished large areas of the city either by direct hits or fire and over 700 were killed and some 1,500 injured, many seriously. 'No other city in the United Kingdom, save London,' commented the official historian of those years, 'had lost so many of her citizens in one night's raid. No other city, except possibly Liverpool, ever did.'[3]

Northern Ireland reaped some immediate benefit from its participation in the war effort. The increased employment and prosperity generated by the heightened pace of industrial and agricultural production meant that income per head, which had been less than three-fifths of that in Britain before the war, rose by 1945 to three-quarters of the British figure. There were also prospects of longer-term changes, as some of the obstacles to more adventurous government were eliminated. In the first place, the British government became indebted to Northern Ireland and promised to transform its finances by conceding in 1942 the principle of 'leeway' by which Northern Ireland's services would be brought up to British standards. In the second place, attitudes and personnel changed within Northern Ireland. The war brought about an increasing awareness of just how under-developed Northern Ireland was in comparison with Britain. The air raids in particular revealed Belfast's low standards of hygiene and public health and for the first time brought the comfortable bourgeoisie into contact with the deprivations and habits of the slum dwellers. Moreover, a new generation of ministers came to power. In November 1940 Craig died and was succeeded by his Minister of Finance, Andrews, who, despite stabilising Northern Ireland's finances, proved both a partisan minister, over-responsive to the Orange Order, and insufficiently energetic for most Ulster Unionists in pursuing the war effort. Mounting backbench criticism in face of lost seats at Stormont and Westminster finally forced Andrews to resign in May 1943 and make way for new men.

His successor was Sir Basil Stanlake Brooke, the Minister of Commerce. Born in 1880, educated at Winchester and the Royal Military Academy, Sandhurst, he was a Co. Fermanagh landowner, a member of the Church of Ireland and an Orangeman long associated with Unionism as an organiser of the USC, a Senator, 1921-9, MP for Lisnaskea, 1929-68, Minister of Agriculture, 1933-40, when he became Minister of Commerce in Andrews' government. A lazy man of limited ability and considerable charm, his reputation as a minister had been built on the efforts of an energetic set of officials at the Ministry of Agriculture. His own strong suits were shooting and fishing in Fermanagh; according to his not unbiased successor, 'Those who met him imagined that he was relaxing away from his desk. What they didn't realise was that there was no desk.'[4] He remained Prime Minister until 1963, years which proved his limitations and his partisanship. Nevertheless, in 1943 he seemed the new broom the urgent war situation demanded. He replaced the older men with younger, untried and virtually unknown ministers and secured a solid vote of confidence on a threefold policy: to maintain the constitution; vigorously to assist the war effort; and prepare for post-war problems. The change of ministers gave increased scope to the more adventurous elements in the civil service, particularly the Ministries of Commerce and Education, previously curbed and discouraged by their political masters. Accordingly, a wide range of services was subjected to searching examination by a host of different enquiries, all of which eventually submitted proposals for post-war reconstruction.

Yet there were just as many signs that much would remain the same. Neither de Valera's continued firm action against the IRA in Eire, including the use of capital punishment, nor the despatch of fire engines from the South, could overcome the resentment felt by Ulster Unionists at Eire's neutrality, which served to confirm the partition of minds as well as the border. Nor was any radical change in community relations heralded by the petering out of IRA bombings and bank raids in 1940; nor by the lack of support given to a more sustained but still abortive campaign between 1942 and 1944, led by Hugh McAteer, the brother of the future leader of the Nationalist Party; nor by 'the spontaneous coming together of Catholic and Protestant in their hour of crisis when death fell on them impartially from the sky'.[5] Only two of the eight Nationalist MPs attended parliament throughout the war. The IRA campaign resulted in the hanging on 2 September 1942 of a volunteer for shooting a policeman, the first Republican to be executed in Northern Ireland, as black flags flew and sullen crowds gathered in the Catholic ghettos. IRA activities ensured the perpetuation of the USC and the Special Powers Act and also the continued resort in emergencies to flogging and internment. And a Unionist debate over the influx of war workers from Eire may have embarrassed the government but led one minister to remark that 'He was fully in sympathy with the view that unless some steps were taken to ensure the Protestant Ascendancy, the future of Northern Ireland was in jeopardy.'[6]

II

Precisely what Northern Ireland's future would be after the war, the precise effect of any new spirit or old resentments, was by no means a foregone conclusion, especially in view of events at first in Britain and then in Eire. In the British general election of July 1945 a Labour government led by Clement Attlee was returned to power, with an overall majority for the first time, and committed to the establishment of the welfare state and to increased state intervention in society and the economy. Moreover, the Labour Party had always been among the fiercest critics of Northern Ireland in Britain, and in 1945 some thirty Labour MPs of Irish extraction formed a group called 'Friends of Ireland', committed to both Irish unity and the remedying of the grievances of the Northern minority. The result was that Northern Ireland's status as part of the United Kingdom came under attack from both the minority and the majority in the six counties.

The majority, the Ulster Unionists, were determined to maintain partition, to have nothing to do with the South, but a significant section began to demand dominion status, virtual independence, to escape from the centralising tendencies and corruptive currents of socialism then sweeping Britain. The conversion of the Labour and Conservative parties, to, as one Northern Ireland minister put it, 'much tighter planning and control, irksome to Ulstermen used to "independence"' [7] seemed to threaten the North's autonomy, while the prospect of an expensive system of social services alarmed industrial and commercial circles already complaining that high taxation during and after the war was fatal to local enterprise. Resentment was further fuelled by the long-held belief that it was the feckless Catholics with their large families who swelled and reaped most benefit from state expenditure.

This debate within Unionism was short-circuited by renewed political vigour on the part of the Catholic/nationalist minority. The war had been fought in the name of democracy and new governments were being established throughout Europe, and these facts were given more point in Northern Ireland by the return of Attlee's government, which, it was assumed, would be sympathetic to the cause of the minority. Thus encouraged, the Nationalists abandoned their campaign of abstention and in July and August 1945 decided to take their seats at Stormont and Westminster. On 22 August the two MPs for Fermanagh and Tyrone, first elected in 1935, took their seats at Westminster for the first time in order, as the *Irish News* said, to do 'everything in their power to forward the claims of the Irish people for the unity and sovereignty of the Irish nation, unnaturally divided twenty years ago by the British government'.[8] Efforts were also made to provide effective party organisation with the formation in November of the Anti-Partition League (APL), equipped with full-time secretary, branches and regular meetings, to unite 'all those opposed to partition into a solid block'.[9] Its strength lay in the rural areas and it represented the Catholic small businessman. Of the fifteen MPs and Senators in the 1945 parliament five were lawyers, four were publicans, insurance agents or similar, three were farmers, two were editors of Nationalist newspapers. There was one company director and there were no industrial or manual workers.

It adopted a three-fold programme. It aimed to redress the political grievances of the minority. Its first set of resolutions condemned gerrymandering and demanded the release of all internees and political prisoners, while its earliest parliamentary battle was an unsuccessful fight to secure one man one vote. Like the old National League, it was determined to safeguard Catholic educational interests, for, as one MP said, 'We have a different concept of education probably from those who differ from us in religion . . . our concept of education has been expressed by the Pope in an encyclical.'[10] Most importantly, it wanted to end partition, to destroy rather than reform Northern Ireland.

The APL received no encouragement from the Labour government, but it was encouraged to persevere by the support of the Friends of Ireland and, more importantly, by events in Eire. There the various political parties were trying to 'out-republican' one another following the rapid growth of a new party, Clann na Poblachta, formed in 1946 and exploiting both the latent republicanism of the South and the social and economic grievances engendered during the stagnant war years. In February 1948 de Valera unsuccessfully tried to smash his critics in a general election which only resulted in his defeat and the return of a coalition of his opponents led by John A. Costello of Fine Gael, but also containing the new party. While the defeated de Valera, out of office for the first time in sixteen years, went off on a tour of Australia, New Zealand and the United States, denouncing partition, the new coalition, besides condemning partition, announced its intention of finally taking Eire out of the Commonwealth and turning it into a Republic on the symbolic date, Easter Monday 1949.

This new anti-partition campaign revealed the unreality of the Unionist debate over dominion status. The inescapable reality was that Britain remained Northern Ireland's sheet anchor morally and especially financially. Without British financial aid, Northern Ireland's living standards and social services would fall behind those in the rest of Britain and would result in the break-up of the Unionist alliance by alienating the Protestant working man. Ulster Unionists, therefore, remained determined both to maintain Northern Ireland's status under the 1920 act and to uphold the Protestant ascendancy in the same manner as before the war.

The link with Britain was tightened by a series of three agreements, which, capitalising on Britain's gratitude and war-time pledges, transformed Northern Ireland's finances and resolved many of the problems against which earlier governments had had to battle. The first agreement, concluded in 1946, laid down parity of services and taxation as the guiding principle of financial relations between Northern Ireland and Britain. In return Northern Ireland was required to submit to continued rigorous financial scrutiny by the Treasury. The other two agreements related to specific welfare services. The pre-war agreements on unemployment insurance had been so framed as to recognise the fact that social services were transferred services for which Northern Ireland was financially responsible, but in the post-war climate Britain was less anxious about constitutional niceties and more willing to advance the North's material welfare. By an arrangement made in 1951 but taking effect from 5 July 1948, the Unemployment Funds of Britain and Northern Ireland were virtually amalgamated, thus relieving the latter of much of the burden of a rapidly expanding insurance scheme which entitled insured persons (and in some cases their dependents) to cash payments during unemployment, sickness, maternity, widowhood, orphanhood, after retirement and at death. The Social Services Agreement, concluded in 1949 but also taking effect from 5 July 1948, relieved Northern Ireland of most of the cost of National Assistance, family allowances, non-contributory pensions and the health service. The unemployment and social services agreements were theoretically reciprocal, but in practice payments were made only from London to Belfast, and the beauty of the arrangement was that these sums did not appear in the budget to offset the imperial contribution, thus maintaining the fiction of an imperial contribution.

Internally, the same general policy was pursued. As made possible by the agreements, the step-by-step policy was continued in relation to social services, while the resultant discontent was softened by concessions in other directions to local manufacturers and by the knowledge that Britain has no wish to intervene in Northern Ireland's affairs. Nationalists and their sympathisers, who continued to make the mistake of linking well-founded grievances with demands for Irish unity, received no encouragement from the Labour government from whom they sought assistance on such matters as electoral law and practices, discrimination and the Special Powers Act. In fact, the one-sided nature of the state became more pronounced as Northern Ireland failed to follow Britain in implementing one man one vote for Stormont and local elections. After the war Britain abolished the various property qualifications and university seats which deprived some of the vote and gave others more than one, but in Northern Ireland the old qualifications were retained and even strengthened. The system favoured Unionists, as it was meant to, by restricting the votes of the poorer and largely Catholic sections of society and increasing those of the better-off and largely Protestant sections. The justification for the refusal to follow Britain was the one Unionists always gave on questions affecting representation, namely, that democracy did not mean mere head counting but also a stake in the community. The real reason was to prevent nationalists from gaining control of the three border counties and Londonderry city in either parliamentary or local elections. The same determination not to be outvoted remained uppermost in Unionist minds.

It is doubtful whether a more conciliatory attitude on the part of the government would have brought about an immediate reconciliation with Nationalists. The latter's former leader and regular attender in parliament, Campbell, was made a county court judge in 1945, but the abuse heaped upon him for betraying the cause of nationalism underlined how far in the post-war atmosphere many Catholics were from accepting the legitimacy of Northern Ireland. Little attempt was, therefore, made to associate the minority more closely with the work of government, although, as before the war, concessions were made in respect of education.

The efforts of the government in maintaining Unionist ascendancy and cohesion were assisted by those of the UUC. It remained a Protestant party, but towards the end of the war it had been revamped on more democratic lines to prevent the formation of splinter groups, and the

Young Ulster Unionist Council had been formed to try to tap the talent of a new generation. Above all, the UUC from 1941 until 1963 had in its secretary, William Douglas, a first-rate organiser. A man of narrow views but unsurpassed in techniques of electioneering, his main preoccupation and special talent was to know exactly where Unionist support lay and how to get it to the polls. Indeed, it was claimed that at any moment he 'knew, with as much certainty as was possible, the Unionist vote, not just in a constituency, but in every street and village in Ulster'.[11]

In fact, the war changed little politically and the continued polarisation of the community was all too evident in the 1949 general election. Held in February in response to the South's passing in the previous December the Republic of Ireland Act, declaring Eire a Republic and reiterating, if only by implication, the claim to jurisdiction over the whole island, it was virtually a referendum on the border. Brooke declared that 'Our country is in danger . . . today we fight to defend our very existence and the heritage of our Ulster children', while for the APL the outstanding issue was 'whether 65 per cent of the people in the six north-eastern counties of the nation's thirty-two can defy the will of the nation'.[12] Never before had the minority been so well organised both in the number of candidates put forward and the aid, not wholly welcome, received from the South, as all parties there subscribed to an anti-partition fund collected at church gates. In this feverishly sectarian atmosphere there was no room for parties or candidates who tried to cut across the religious divide or focus attention on other issues – not even a reformed Labour Party. The anti-partition campaign tore the party in two and in 1949, under pressure from Protestant trade unionists, the party finally made up its mind and declared for partition, stating on 31 January that 'being a democratic party' it 'accepts the constitutional position of Northern Ireland and the close association with Britain and the Commonwealth. Furthermore we are not seeking any mandate to change it.'[13] Neither this decision nor the red, white and blue rosettes of candidates could save what now became the Northern Ireland Labour Party and it lost votes from all sides. Its eight candidates polled only 26,831 votes compared with 66,053 in 1945 and it failed to keep the three seats it had then won. Anti-partition candidates won eleven seats (nine to the APL and two to anti-partition Labour candidates in Belfast) and 106,459 votes, while the official Unionists won 37 seats and 234,202 votes or 62.7 per cent of the poll.

A guarantee from Britain was soon forthcoming. Clause 1(1)B of the Ireland Act, passed in the following June to regulate the United Kingdom's relations with the new Republic, confirmed in the most emphatic fashion that Northern Ireland's existing status would be maintained:

Parliament hereby declares that Northern Ireland remains part of His Majesty's Dominions and of the United Kingdom and affirms that in no event will Northern Ireland or any part thereof cease to be part of His

Majesty's Dominions and of the United Kingdom without the consent of the Parliament of Northern Ireland.[14]

The declaration was not as watertight as appeared at first sight. Legislative supremacy remained with Westminster and 'what one statute of that parliament could ordain another statute could repeal'.[15] Nevertheless, it settled the anti-partition agitation and showed just how far constitutional security was rooted in the soil of devolution.

These events between 1945 and 1949 were significant ones in the history of Northern Ireland, showing just how little had been changed by the war. They determined not merely Northern Ireland's status, confirming its position within the United Kingdom, but also the course of its development into the 1960s. In many spheres of economic and social life, standards became geared to those of Britain, although Britain was not slavishly followed and advantage was taken of regional powers to innovate and to adapt measures to suit local circumstances. Such changes bound Northern Ireland even closer to Britain and separated it still further from the South. Yet, although in some respects Northern Ireland was transformed and its position vindicated, in other respects much remained the same. The traditional economy continued to decay and sectarianism and parochialism continued to riddle society, politics and administration.

III

The post-war agreements with Britain wrought a revolution in Northern Ireland's finances and hence some aspects of its administration. Henceforth, it had 'an expenditure-based system. The principal criterion was whether a particular development was justified in itself, rather than the pressure exerted by the notional idea of a balanced Northern Ireland budget.'[16] The consequent expansion and improvement of services was not without difficulties. Most changes had sectarian implications, while the question of state intervention was always capable of dividing Unionists. Nevertheless, within a decade Northern Ireland passed from 'the status of an exceptionally backward area to full membership of the welfare state'.[17]

Apart from the retention of long residential requirements, the major cash social services developed in line with those in Britain. The poor law, more than a century old, disappeared and boards of guardians were abolished. National insurance and industrial injuries insurance virtually operated as a single system in Britain and Northern Ireland, and, although Northern Ireland did not bind itself to keep exactly in step in national assistance, family allowances and non-contributory pensions, only to keep in general parity, there was little scope for differentiation. In 1956 it was proposed to depart from British practice by altering the rates of family allowances so as to favour smaller rather than larger families, most of which happened to be Catholic. The plan was, however, soon abandoned in favour of absolute uniformity in order to avoid charges of religious discrimination and, just as Craig had warned critics of contributory pensions in 1925, undesirable repercussions on financial relations with Britain.

Education was also a notable beneficiary of the change, although denominationalism became still further entrenched. The 1947 Education Act generally followed changes already implemented in England under the 1944 Butler Education Act: primary education ending at the age of eleven plus, and all children thereafter receiving secondary education until the age of fifteen in grammar, secondary intermediate or technical intermediate schools. Secondary education, which had received little attention before 1939, particularly benefited from the changes, while the provision of grants for university students was such that 'it might be said without too much exaggeration that the door to higher education was open to any child of sufficient ability to qualify for admission, regardless of what his social or economic background might be'.[18] Administratively, the biggest change was the much-needed abolition of the small regional education committees in Counties Antrim, Londonderry and Tyrone, so that the county councils and county boroughs became the local education authorities throughout the province. Within seventeen years the number of pupils in grant-aided schools rose from 213,211 to 295,855, an increase paralleled by the building and extension of many new schools, especially at the secondary level.

The 1947 act was remarkable not only for its educational achievements but also for the fact that it was the first time that the government defied its more volatile Protestant supporters on the question of religious education. It did not re-enact the provisions of earlier measures allowing management committees of transferred schools to require candidates for posts to express a willingness to give Bible instruction. A fierce and insulting agitation ensued and there were calls for the resignation of the Minister of Education, for the clause opened the possibility of Catholics being appointed to teach Protestant children. Yet, although the Minister of Education was eventually replaced, the government stood by this conscience clause on the grounds that previous requirements had contravened the written law of the Government of Ireland Act and the unwritten law of decency.

Nevertheless, the religious separation of schoolchildren – and teachers – was encouraged still further by the 1947 act. Although an increasing number of Protestant primary schools were transferred to public control, the voluntary schools, the great majority Catholic, remained obstinately under their own mainly clerical managements and even extracted further government help. Since the 1930s the Ministry of Education had been aware of the impoverished state of all voluntary schools, especially Catholic ones, and took advantage of the post-war atmosphere to increase from 50 to 65 per cent the state grants towards running costs, new buildings and reconstruction. The fact that they did not receive 100 per cent grants and had to continue to contribute towards the costs of their own schools was, justifiably or not, a major source of grievance to Catholics. In 1968 their bishops estimated that in the twenty-one years since the 1947 act, Northern Ireland Catholics had paid 'something in the region of £20m in present-day money towards the erection and maintenance of schools',[19] a considerable burden for what was the poorer section of society. What little evidence there is suggests that some able Catholic children were deprived of a grammar school education, but that Catholic schools were as academically successful as the state schools.

In respect of other services to the community, Northern Ireland on balance reaped the benefit of havings its own regional government. Some departures from British practice may not have been desirable, particularly the refusal to follow Britain in abolishing capital punishment, liberalising morality laws and giving grants to voluntary hospitals. Nevertheless, beneficial adaptations were made in the administration of some important services. Civil servants and nominated individuals were largely responsible for their administration but this lack of democratic accountability did not affect the high standard of services increasingly provided.

Housing became a high priority, after the first ever housing survey in 1943 had underlined the inadequacy of Northern Ireland's housing stock. Most houses would have been condemned if modern criteria had been strictly applied, but 100,000 new houses were immediately required, and a further 100,000 were needed to eliminate overcrowding and slums. The response was the payment of increased subsidies and a change of emphasis to the provision of public housing. Local authorities, albeit at the cost of sectarian tension, became much more involved, and a special government agency, the Northern Ireland Housing Trust, was created and charged with providing and managing houses built at the government's expense. The initial target of 100,000 was achieved within twenty years, and although much remained to be done, the sedate rate of progress was twice as fast as in the inter-war years. Of the houses built by 1963, all but 5,000 had been erected with the aid of the government subsidy: one-third by local authorities, one-quarter by the Housing Trust, and the rest by private builders.

In health, the old survivals of the poor law disappeared. A new Ministry of Health and Local Government was created in 1944 and within four years Northern Ireland had a General Health Services Board and a Hospitals Authority, both set up under the 1948 Health Services Act, and its own peculiar creation, the Tuberculosis Authority, established two years earlier under the Public Health (Tuberculosis) Act. Once again sectarian controversy obtruded, this time over the status and financing of the Catholic Mater Hospital, which feared that its Catholic principles would be compromised if it became part of the National Health Service. The government refused to follow the 1946 British National Health Service Act in providing for voluntary hospitals and simply said: 'They are either coming in 100 per cent, or they are staying out 100 per cent. There is going to be no half-way stage about this matter.'[20] The Mater opted out and actually lost some assistance it had hitherto received for such items as nurses' salaries and the treatment of venereal disease. The controversy continued into the 1970s and was a blot on the otherwise fine record of progress achieved by dramatic state intervention, which combined with fuller employment and improved medical knowledge, housing and diet to effect a remarkable change in the condition of Northern Ireland's health. The Tuberculosis Authority worked so vigorously as to undermine its own existence by 1959; there were substantial advances in environmental and mental health; and a £66.5m programme of hospital building was inaugurated. The up-shot was that the death rate, particularly among mothers, changed from being the highest to the lowest in the United Kingdom: 10.6 in 1962, com-pared to 11.9 in England and Wales and 12.2 in Scotland.

Yet the economic and social history of Northern Ireland after the Second World War was not one of unalloyed progress and achievement. Comprehensive regional planning remained neglected, and in the economic sphere the only outstanding success was once again agriculture. Increased modernisation may have been achieved at the cost of employment and the elimination of small, marginal and uneconomic holdings, but the rising vol-ume and value of agricultural output testified to the strength of a flourish-ing export industry. In 1952, 90,000 cattle and 1.3m cwt of fresh and processed milk were sent out from Northern Ireland: by 1965 the figures had risen to 216,000 and 1.5m respectively.

Less happy were the experiences of other sectors of the economy. Flinging aside any remaining reserve about the evils of socialism and public ownership, the government formed in 1948 the Ulster Transport Author-ity and brought all forms of public transport, including the once much-feared railways, under public control. Bold though the policy was, the problem of public transport remained both unprofitable and intractable. Even more intractable were the problems facing industrial policy, which had to take into account not only Northern Ireland's legal, geographical and economic limitations, but also the political problems posed by the declining industries. The obvious attractions to the Ministry of Commerce of diversifying the economy with new industries were somewhat offset by the demands of existing industries for whatever government money was available.

Dissatisfied since the mid-1930s with the previous industrial policy but overruled by Craig and Andrews, the Ministry of Commerce sponsored in 1944 a more flexible policy to attract larger enterprises. The 1944 Indus-tries Development Act, later renewed and extended, offered grants, fac-tory premises, equipment and some supporting services, and allowed the Ministers of Commerce and Finance considerable discretion in the type of assistance awarded. Owing to the lack of priority given to regional develop-ment in Britain, where the building of advance factories was stopped between 1947 and 1959, the new policy gave Northern Ireland an advantage over distressed areas in Britain and the initial response was encouraging. As early as January 1946, ten new plants had been established, including Courtaulds and Metal Box, which were expected to create 4,710 jobs.

The full potential of this policy was not, however, exploited. It failed to take an overall view of the province's economic circumstances and develop a regional plan, which would both improve the infrastructure and take into account the special problems of the South and West. Seventy per cent of new firms established between 1945 and 1963 were located within twenty-five miles of Belfast, and less than 10 per cent moved west of the Bann. Although the government had to be grateful for what it got, it did little to offset the obvious attractions for industrialists of the more developed east over the remoter western counties. By 1964 only 16 of the 111 advance factories built by the Ministry of Commerce were situated in the three western counties, and even these were simply plonked down in areas of high unemployment often ill-served by transport, housing and other amenities. More vitally, the policy of attracting new industries was not pressed with sufficient vigour in face of well-placed, if not well-founded, criticism from the champions and owners of existing enterprises who complained that the new and probably transient concerns were simply drawing scarce skilled labour away from the older industries which had stood the test of time but were overburdened by heavy taxation. Thus money and relief were provided for the older industries in the form of reductions in estate duties, a transferred tax, and the Re-equipment of Industry Act, 1950, which was replaced four years later by the more generous and less stringent Capital Grants to Industry Act. Both measures offered grants towards the re-equipment or modernisation of industrial undertakings, but the second act abandoned the requirement of the first that modernisation schemes would have to be substantial to qualify for grants.

The futility of relying on old industries instead of concentrating resources on recreating the infrastructure and environment to stimulate economic growth in new directions was underlined in two official reports critical of the economy and government policy. The *Economic Survey of Northern Ireland,* commissioned by the government in 1947 from two Queen's University economists, K. S. Isles and N. Cuthbert, was presented in 1955 and reluctantly published two years later. The Hall report, the *Report of the Joint Working Party on the Economy of Northern Ireland,* published in 1962, contained the by no means unanimous conclusions of a committee of Northern Ireland and British civil servants under an outside chairman, Sir Robert Hall. Neither report was very complimentary about traditional industry or government policy, Isles and Cuthbert making it abundantly clear that the lack of investment in the linen industry was due not to confiscatory levels of taxation but to an archaic industrial structure and the conservatism and timidity of local capitalists.

The justice of these strictures was fully borne out by events. A post-war boom temporarily buoyed up industry, but with its passing there was a sharp drop in economic activity and in the late 1950s and early 1960s Northern Ireland experienced a dramatic alteration in its manufacturing mainstays unequalled by regional economies in the rest of the United Kingdom. Between 1960 and 1964 no fewer than 11,500 jobs, some 40 per cent, were lost in shipbuilding, repairing and marine engineering, while in the period 1958-64 almost one-third of linen plants closed down and 27,000 employees, over 45 per cent of the labour force, lost their jobs. Furthermore, employment in the third old staple, agriculture, continued to contract as the consequence of modernisation. To cap it all, the very success of social policy after the war accentuated the problem of unemployment by raising an already high rate of natural increase. The consequent increase in the rate of unemployment was not as bad as the 1930s but was less tolerable because it underlined Northern Ireland's position as the most unfortunate part of the United Kingdom. Whereas in the 1930s Northern Ireland had been only one of several parts of the United Kingdom with heavy unemployment, by the late 1950s there was reasonably full employment in Britain where regional blackspots were faring considerably better than Northern Ireland. The unemployment figures for the 'Development Areas' spoke for themselves:

	1956	1958	1960	1962
Scottish	2.2	3.7	3.4	3.5
Welsh	2.2	4.1	2.5	3.0
Northern	1.4	2.2	2.5	3.2
Merseyside	2.0	3.6	3.1	3.9
South-West	1.8	2.8	2.8	2.2
Northern Ireland	6.8 (1955)	9.3	6.7	7.5

IV

Northern Ireland remained the most divided as well as the poorest part of the kingdom. Society was not static. The processes of economic diversification and decay and social reform did produce changes, but they were changes within each community rather than across them.

The traditional drift of the population from the west continued and Northern Ireland became more urbanised. The number of farm holdings diminished and agricultural employment contracted so that by the 1960s farming employed only 13 per cent of the workforce and an increasing majority of people lived in urban (administrative) areas (46.9 per cent in 1911, 50.8 in 1926 and 54 in 1961). The largest towns, apart from the two county boroughs, were in Counties Antrim (Ballymena, Carrickfergus, Larne, Lisburn and Newtownabbey) and Down (Bangor, Newry and Newtownards) and the industrial parts of Co. Armagh (Lurgan and Portadown). There were also changes in the denominational balance. During the course of the twentieth century, the balance between Catholics and non-Catholics, one-third to two-thirds, remained remarkably stable, although there was an increase in the Catholic proportion from 33.5 per cent in 1926 to 34.9 per cent in 1961. Overall, this was only a marginal increase, but it was more marked in some areas than others, particularly in the cities of Belfast and Londonderry, as the Catholic birth-rate, though falling, remained above that of Protestants and as a new generation refused to maintain the high level of emigration which had previously offset the higher Catholic birth-rate. The census returns for 1961 well illustrate the changing distribution of the population and show significant changes from 1911, when Catholics formed 24.1 per cent of the population of Belfast and 56.2 per cent of that of Londonderry city:

	Population	Catholics	Protestants	Others & Not stated
Antrim	273,905	66,929 (24.4%)	185,688 (67.8%)	21,288 (7.8%)
Armagh	117,594	55,617 (47.3%)	55,972 (47.6%)	6,005 (5.1%)
Down	266,939	76,263 (28.6%)	168,659 (63.2%)	22,017 (8.2%)
Fermanagh	51,531	27,422 (53.2%)	22,627 (43.9%)	1,482 (2.9%)
Londonderry	111,536	47,509 (42.6%)	58,861 (52.8%)	5,166 (4.6%)
Tyrone	133,919	73,398 (54.8%)	56,547 (42.2%)	3,974 (3.0%)
Belfast C.B.	415,856	114,336 (27.5%)	265,407 (63.8%)	36,113 (8.7%)
Londonderry C.B.	53,762	36,073 (67.1%	16,017 (29.8%)	1,672 (3.1%)
Northern Ireland	1,425,042	497,547 (34.9%)	829,778 (58.2%)	97,717 (6.9%)

The constant expectation that economic change or distress would foster new attitudes and a greater spirit of co-operation among Catholic and Protestant workers continued to be disappointed. Northern Ireland's labour force did become one of the most unionised in Western Europe by the end of the 1960s, with some 55 per cent of its workers belonging to sixty-five British-based trade unions, nineteen Northern Ireland unions and five with headquarters in Dublin. Attempts were also made to foster co-operation within Northern Ireland through trades councils and across the border through a series of all-Ireland organisations, the first of which had been the Irish Trade Union Congress (ITUC) formed in 1894 and its Northern Committee founded in 1943. The ITUC survived partition until 1945, when the conflicting claims of British-based and Irish-based unions led most of the latter to form a rival Congress of Irish Trade Unions, but unity was restored in 1959 with the establishment of the Irish Congress of Trade Unions (ICTU). It retained the Northern Committee, which the Brookeborough government refused to recognise, largely on the grounds that it was part of a Dublin-based congress. Nevertheless, this high degree of organisation still had surprisingly few consequences for politics and society and failed to inject life into the NILP. In the late 1950s and early 1960s there were hopes or fears that the effects of unemployment would give rise to a new working-class consciousness, as an increasing number of skilled Protestants in Belfast temporarily turned to the NILP for worldly salvation, but these expectations were short-lived.

More permanent changes occurred within the Catholic community, as its social structure expanded at both the top and bottom. In town and country before the Second World War, Catholics had been under-represented in the middle and upper classes but over-represented in the lower socio-economic groups. Similarly, they had been less well educated than Protestants who for long constituted the bulk of the grammar school and university populations. Thus Catholic farmers occupied the poorer land and the Catholic middle classes were a cut below the Protestant upper and middle classes. They were a small-town middle class, sharing local leadership with the clergy and serving the Catholic community largely as shopkeepers, publicans or solicitors, usually doubling up as undertakers, insurance brokers and the like. At the bottom end of the social scale, Protestants provided a disproportionate share of skilled workingmen, the aristocracy of labour, and although there were many unskilled and casual Protestant workers, they were proportionately fewer than Catholics.

After the Second World War, the Catholic middle classes were both diversified and expanded by the extension of secondary and higher education and the demands of new industries for professionally trained administrators and middle managers. To the small-town men were added graduates and new professionals, as over the years the proportion of Catholics in professional and managerial occupations rose more sharply than that for the population as a whole. Catholics never quite reached the upper crust, but at least some of them were rising and their more confident and more outward-looking attitude was re-inforced by liberalisation of the Catholic Church as exemplified by the short but eventful reign of Pope John XXIII, 1958-63, and the deliberations of the Second Vatican Council. On the other hand, working-class Catholics fared less happily from changes which affected the position of working men in industry in Northern Ireland as elsewhere in the twentieth century: the decline in agricultural employment, the dilution of craft skills, and the expansion of lower-grade non-manual occupations. They lost what little ground they had in the upper and middle reaches of the working classes, forming a diminishing proportion of lower-grade non-manual and skilled manual workers. Instead, an increasing proportion of Catholics became unskilled workers. By contrast, Protestants benefited from the changes. For them skilled manual labour was replaced not by unskilled work but by semi-skilled and even more by lower-grade non-manual work. In the lower social reaches there were few points of economic contact between Catholics and Protestants.

Such changes left the basic sectarian divide untouched. Whatever influence may be attributed to outside forces, the root cause of the divisions lay within the two communities whose beliefs, attitudes and habits made for neither social nor political harmony. Theologically, the fundamental incompatability between Irish Catholicism and Ulster Protestantism remained a live and all-pervasive issue in a society which, whatever happened in the rest of the United Kingdom, remained God-fearing and church-going. Moreover, spiritual separation was matched by temporal separation. Sectarian divisions were both hardened and made self-perpetuating as Protestants and Catholics segregated themselves in three vital areas of life, marriage, residence and education.

Marriages between Protestants and Catholics were infrequent and certainly discouraged. The mixed marriages that did occur did little to bridge the sectarian divide, for they were subject to considerable isolation and stress. Indeed, it has been argued that endogamy, marriage within one's own group, was the most powerful mechanism dividing people, at least in rural areas. The only people with whom an individual became intimate were his or her kin; all non-kin, regardless of denomination, were kept at a certain distance. If all one's kin belonged to the same religious group as oneself, the only way of becoming intimate with members of the other community was blocked off. How far this also applied to urban areas has not been determined, and it may be that in urban working-class areas residential segregation rather than endogamy was the more potent divisive force.

Residential segregations in towns, with Catholics living in some parts and Protestants in others, was not as total throughout Northern Ireland as is sometimes believed. Nevertheless, the largest towns, which contained the majority of the urban population, were highly segregated. The pattern was established well before partition but became more pronounced afterwards as a result of intimidation in times of crisis and the pressure of local politics. In the former instance, families of the 'wrong sort' were driven out of their homes or considered it advisable to leave, while local politicians were concerned to maintain if not enlarge their majorities by the careful allocation of houses among electoral areas. Segregation was most marked in Belfast. The Falls became almost exclusively Catholic, as Catholics of all social groups moved into the area, which in the nineteenth century had been a working class preserve. As a necessary corollary, the main Protestant districts became even more homogeneous, although without the same admixture of classes. In fact, parts of Belfast exhibited two types of segregation – residential and activity. Protestants and Catholics neither lived in the same area nor interacted with each other.

The completeness of this segregation was amply demonstrated by a study in the late 1960s of a small area of less than 5,000 persons between the Shankill and the Falls. The area as a whole was 44 per cent Catholic, but it contained two distinct parts. That nearest the Shankill was 99 per cent Protestant; that nearest the Falls 98 per cent Catholic. The lines of demarcation were clearly branded with such slogans as 'Taighs [Catholics] Keep Out', 'Prods [Protestants] Keep Out', 'No Pope Here', and 'No Queen Here'.[21] Most Catholics and Protestants could not be tempted into each other's territory either for convenient bus stops or better shops, and the tastes and habits of the two parts were entirely different. They read different newspapers, supported different football teams and led totally different lives. Not surprisingly, the study was prefaced with a quotation: 'I am . . . a bundle of prejudices – made of likings and dislikings – the veriest thrall to sympathies, apathies, and antipathies.'[22]

Segregated education, the education of Protestant and Catholic children in separate schools, reflected and re-inforced the prevalence of endogamy and residential segregation. Critics of the segregated system maintained that it perpetuated and re-inforced the division between Protestants and Catholics by physically separating children and by propagating different and perhaps hostile cultural heritages. Despite the controversy surrounding it, surprisingly little is known precisely about the workings of the denominational schooling system. Its statistical extent is unknown, although an estimate in 1961 suggested, without citing evidence, that at least 98 per cent of all Catholic primary children attended Catholic schools. Nor has much work been done on the actual learning experiences of children in segregated schools. Nevertheless, what evidence there is suggests marked differences in emphasis in the curricula studied by Catholic and Protestant secondary schoolchildren and even more significant differences in the way individual subjects were taught in primary and secondary schools.

The teaching of history, for example, reflected the different traditions of the two communities. In Catholic schools the emphasis was on Irish history, particularly the Gaelic revival and the national struggle, and in one 'very militantly Republican' girls' grammar school in Co. Tyrone these themes were the obsession of the vice-principal who '*hated* the English'.[23] By contrast, in Protestant schools the emphasis was on British and imperial history. Irish history was taught only where it impinged in a significant way on these other aspects and 'the impression generally was that Ulster children could be educated as if they were living in Chelmsford or Bristol or Haverfordwest'.[24] These different traditions were reflected in history textbooks, which displayed extensive bias, particularly by the deliberate use of emotionalism in some 'nationalist' textbooks and 'a strange blindness towards the rest of Ireland' in 'unionist' ones.[25] At least in a subject like history, children dealt with similar material, albeit from different perspectives. In other subjects, however, the content could be quite different, while sporting activities also separated schoolchildren. Although there was an increasing tendency for Catholic and Protestant schools to play each other at soccer, tennis, netball and basketball, other games remained taboo. Catholic schools played Gaelic games and showed little enthusiasm for rugby, cricket and hockey, whereas Protestant schools ignored the former and enjoyed the latter.

It would be a mistake to lay the blame for sectarian divisions entirely upon the educational system, as is sometimes done. The system reflected these divisions and many hostile attitudes were learned outside schools. Nonetheless, segregated education did nothing to heal the rift. Its very existence in law helped to confirm the attitude of adults and children opposed to any institutional *rapprochement* between Catholics and Protestants at any level, while, as a Londonderry survey showed in the late 1960s, at best the prejudices of schoolchildren were not dissolved by separate education and at worst were strengthened. Catholic and Protestant schoolchildren shared similar perceptions about Londonderry's industrial geography but showed very different attitudes on questions with a political flavour. More than two-thirds of the Protestant children named Belfast as the capital of the country in which Londonderry was situated, but more than half the Catholics named Dublin.

In many respects, Protestants and Catholics existed in mutual isolation and mutual ignorance. Unflattering stereotypes took the place of social intercourse and understanding, although the Catholic view of Protestants seems to have been less harsh and entrenched than that of Protestants towards Catholics. Peaceful co-existence was usually ensured not only by relative isolation but also by a host of habits and social mechanisms. When Catholics and Protestants did meet, the greatest efforts were made to prevent the discussion of any controversial topics — understandably so in view of the crudity that could distinguish political and religious comment even in sophisticated circles!

Much energy and ingenuity has been spent on trying to categorise the rift between Catholics and Protestants, to put it into some universal frame of reference. The long-favoured 'two-nations' theory remains as unhelpful to explain events after partition as before. Catholics might have been part of the Irish nation, but Ulster Protestants were not transformed into a separate nation by the creation of the new regime. Despite occasional references to Ulster nationalism and Ulster independence, Ulster Protestants and Unionists continued to regard political obligations in contractual terms and to have only a very hazy sense of nationality. Similarly, racial and ethnic explanations are more misleading than helpful, seeking as they do to compare Northern Ireland with such deeply divided societies as the American Deep South or the Caribbean, and frequently seeing religion as a mere expression of the racial distinction between colonists and natives. Such comparisons distort both the role of religion and the nature of Catholic-Protestant differences in Northern Ireland, which never cut as deep as those between Blacks and Whites in America or Hindus and Blacks in Trinidad. Protestants and Catholics in Northern Ireland did not deny each other's humanity and did share a common culture, holding similar views on such questions as emigration, the role of trade unions and big business, social class and attitudes towards authority. They regarded each other as equally and fully human, only misguided and perverted by heretical doctrines and evil institutions.

In the last analysis, it is impossible to escape from the basic religious and political questions. For Catholics the problem was largely political; for Protestants largely religious. Catholics looked to a united Ireland and objected to Protestant attitudes towards politics, but their standpoint could be negotiable, especially as there does not appear to be 'any underlying labyrinth of psychological fears supporting'[26] their attitude towards Protestants. By contrast, Protestant attitudes towards Catholics were more permanent and psychologically deep-rooted. Their strong objections to a number of aspects of Catholicism 'are underpinned by a complicated psychological network of fears and misapprehensions about the political power and dexterity of the Roman Catholic Church'.[27] These two separate problems were made the more insoluble and irreconcilable by the divisions within both communities, particularly the class, sectarian and geographical cleavages among Protestants. 'It is because Protestant distrusts Protestant, not just because Protestant distrusts Catholic, that the Ulster conflict is so intense.'[28]

V

All these differences found further expression and confirmation in politics and official life, which in the 1950s remained the almost exclusive preserve of Unionists and Protestants. Although the electoral law was somewhat softened, carefully drawn electoral boundaries and the retention of the property and other qualifications served to bolster up the Unionist vote and majorities on elected bodies. The extent to which legislation influenced voting was evident in the discrepancy between the different electorates in Northern Ireland. Had Stormont and local elections been conducted on the same franchise as in the rest of the United Kingdom there would have been more local government and fewer parliamentary electors. In 1956 the Westminster electorate, based on one man one vote, was 877,051; the Stormont electorate was 896,041, the local government electorate 600,765. The discrepancies were particularly significant in closely contested local government wards and tipped the balance in favour of the Unionist Party.

Moreover, the reformed UUC helped to hold Unionism together and provide younger, if not always young, blood for the government. The upper reaches of the party remained closed to men of the people, but no significant independent Unionist movement gained ground until the late 1960s, while the government was provided with a supply of recruits from the better-off sections of Unionist society throughout the province, including four ministers who later set about destroying one another. Two, Brian Faulkner and William Craig, were products of the Young Unionist movement. Born in 1921, a Presbyterian and son of a shirt manufacturer, Faulkner was first returned for East Down in 1949 at the age of twenty-nine, then the youngest member ever returned to Stormont. An able and ambitious pragmatist and no mean businessman, he was soon given responsibility, becoming Chief Whip, 1956-9, and making considerable impact as Minister of Home Affairs, 1959-63. Craig, born three years later, was a solicitor and although he did not enter parliament, for Larne, until 1960, he became Chief Whip within two years. Also ambitious, he was less wily than Faulkner and in his determination to uphold the Unionist ascendancy showed scant regard for the consequences of his words and actions. The two other controversial figures introduced by Brookeborough represented the farming and landed traditions of Unionism. Henry William (Harry) West, born in 1917, was a large-scale farmer, a Fermanagh man through and through, represented Enniskillen from 1954 and became Minister of Agriculture in 1960, having had a brief spell as junior minister two years earlier. The most senior of the four, Captain Terence Marne O'Neill, represented landed Unionism. Born in 1914 of aristocratic lineage, a member of the Church of Ireland, educated at Eton and a former army officer, he was returned for Bannside in 1946 and, with a short break as Deputy Speaker, 1953-6, remained a member of government from 1948 until 1969, including a long spell at the Ministry of Finance between 1956 and 1963.

Parliament thus continued to be dominated by official Unionists, the police forces and civil service by Protestants, and local authorities by Protestants and Unionists. The last became an increasingly controversial topic, because the expansion of local authority services after 1945 gave greater scope for discrimination in employment and housing. One admittedly propagandist source calculated that in 1951 965 or 88.1 per cent of the 1,095 non-manual workers employed in local government were Protestants. Catholics formed 34 per cent of the population but constituted only 11.9 per cent of non-manual employees, and most of those were employed by the five councils in Co. Down not controlled by Unionists. It was the same with the allocation of the houses constructed by councils as part of their enhanced role in house-building after the war. They were allocated less on the basis of social need than with a view to maintaining political control. Houses were given to co-religionists and political supporters in such a way as to ensure that the electoral geography was not upset. Great care was taken in the siting of houses and the selection of occupiers to bolster up majorities and to undermine the position of opponents. Nationalist-controlled councils did the same, but the effects of the actions of Unionist-controlled local authorities were the more widely felt for there were so many more of them in sensitive areas. Some councils, notably in Fermanagh, for long tried to avoid the problem by not building houses at all, which, it was alleged, had the effect of driving Catholics out of the area, but those that did build behaved very much like Dungannon Urban District Council. The council had built, it was claimed in 1965, '194 houses in the East Ward . . . and it allocated every single one . . . to a Unionist, to a Protestant. Not one Catholic managed to slip through the net, which shows how thoroughly the religious affiliations of the applicants were gone into.'[29]

Moreover, in the 1940s and 1950s there was a cruder, more uncompromising tone about the Protestant ascendancy. One reason for the deterioration may have been Westminster's increasing indifference to events there. After 1945 the Home Office abandoned whatever watch-dog role it may have had and settled into a routine of acting as spokesman for Northern Ireland among British departments and generally 'sponsoring the Unionist interest in British ruling-class circles'.[30] Full rein was thus given to the assertion of Unionist and Protestant principles or prejudices, a change also connected with Brooke's long leadership. Before the war Craig had at least shown a benign disposition towards the minority out of genuine concern for Catholics as well as for the sake of his government's image in Britain. Brooke was untroubled by such scruples and remained a party boss, never attempting to become a 'national' leader. Schooled in the hard frontier of Fermanagh, he was always vehemently opposed to anything smacking of nationalism and Irish unity and was notorious for his anti-Catholic speeches. He often cynically took the easiest options open to him, to play the Orange card, rather than educate his followers to a wider conception of their responsibilities as the party of government. Thus he refused to support those of his colleagues who sought accommodation with Catholics by associating them more closely with the Unionist Party. They argued in December 1959 that 'Toleration is not a sign of weakness, but proof of strength', but their suggestion that Catholics should be selected as Unionist parliamentary candidates died the death in face of swift and fierce reaction led by the Orange Order and endorsed by the Prime Minister. Catholics remained beyond the pale not necessarily because they were Catholics but because of their political traditions. As Brooke told a meeting of Young Unionists:

> There is no use blinking the fact that political differences in Northern Ireland closely follow religious differences. It may not be impossible, but it is certainly not easy for any person to discard the political conceptions, the influence and impressions acquired from religious and educational instruction by those whose aims are openly declared to be an all-Ireland republic. The Unionist Party is dedicated to the resistance of those aims and its constitution and composition reflect that basic fact. There is no change in the fundamental character of the Unionist Party or in the loyalties it observes and preserves. If that is called intolerance, I say at once it is not the fault of the Unionist Party. If it is called inflexible then it shows that our principles are not elastic.[31]

VI

Indeed, Unionists felt that they could afford to be unaccommodating. In the 1950s and early 1960s the position of Northern Ireland and the Unionist Party seemed more secure than ever. The six counties may have been the poorest part of the United Kingdom, but it had more to offer, at least materially, than the Republic. The advent of the welfare state considerably re-inforced partition by opening up a wide gap between the two parts of Ireland. Although its population was less than half that of the Republic, Northern Ireland had in 1964 95,000 children in secondary schools compared with 85,000 in the South; while expenditure on higher education was almost three times higher. There was also a discrepancy in welfare payments which were almost 50 per cent higher in the North, while the difference between the health services was so great that little comparison was possible. Admittedly, taxation was higher in the North, but the plain truth was that Northern Ireland enjoyed a high level of services and benefits because its position in the United Kingdom provided it with massive and ever rising financial contributions from Britain beyond the resources of the South.

Without British help life in Northern Ireland would have been very different indeed. In 1963 payments by the United Kingdom to Northern Ireland amounted to £46m, including £6.95m for social services, £8.36m for national insurance and as much as £28.55m in farming grants and subsidies. In addition, special measures to encourage industrial development cost the United Kingdom taxpayer some £15m, not by direct payment but by a reduction in the imperial contribution. Had Northern Ireland been independent and had to pay for its own defence and other 'imperial services', it would either have had to cut domestic spending by some £50m a year or raise that sum by taxation. Either course would have been catastrophic for a country whose expenditure was £119m and whose tax revenue was £116m. By the end of the decade the cost of independence would have been even higher, for in 1968-9, the last year of peace, British payments amounted to £72m. By the same token, Irish unity would have imposed an intolerable burden on the Republic. According to one estimate, had the Republic tried to bring its social services up to Northern standards in the year 1969-70, the then current expenditure of almost £143m would have had to be increased by about a further £150m, or by 105 per cent. If, in addition to raising its own standards, the Republic had to shoulder the cost of British payments to Northern Ireland, the effect would have been to raise the level of taxation by 60 per cent.

Within Northern Ireland, too, the opponents of partition and the Unionist Party were in a state of disarray and defeat. The NILP may have experienced a revival at the end of the decade, but it spent the 1950s licking its wounds and without representation in parliament and its later resurrection was short-lived. After the failure of the APL's campaign Catholics and Nationalists were in no position to offer effective opposition within Northern Ireland, let alone bring down the state. Admittedly, attitudes were changing, as a result of the benefits of the welfare state, the growth of a new generation, the changing social structure and the empty rhetoric of the South. Some Catholics began to consider that they could play a more positive role in public life without prejudicing the ultimate aspiration to Irish unity. The new middle class — the graduates, managers and teachers — sought a much wider role in the economy and in society than the old small-town middle class and were less ready to acquiesce in the acceptance of a position of assumed or established inferority and discrimination than had been the case in the past. The Catholic working classes, suffering more than Protestants from the dilution of skilled manual labour, also began to question traditional attitudes and to demand more from its leaders than nationalist and Catholic rhetoric. The change in working-class politics was evident in the late 1940s, but for the minority as a whole the new feeling first found coherent public expression in 1958 at a Social Studies Conference at Garron Tower, Co. Antrim. Then one of the most persuasive advocates of *rapprochement* with the state, Gerard Benedict Newe, dismissed as fallacious and a salve to the conscience the Republic's claim to be the *de jure* government of the North and claimed instead that Catholics had a duty to 'co-operate with the *de facto* authority that controls . . . life and welfare'.[32]

The trouble was that not until the 1960s did this new approach find more general acceptance and a measure of effective organisation. Until then Catholic politics remained confused and unorganised. The APL withered away and rural nationalism remained the preserve of the conservative local notables completely out of touch with events in Belfast. The graduates had their own ginger group, National Unity, formed in 1959 in an unsuccessful effort to reform the Nationalist Party, while Catholic working-class politics had a chaotic life of their own. In the Central, Dock and Falls divisions of Belfast, they were organised not on conventional party lines but on the basis of 'competition between hustling politicians with a labourist rhetoric and personal followings established by brokerage'[33] and patronage. The main field of activity was local politics, but the two most successful hustlers entered parliament and had their own parties. Harold (Harry) Diamond, an engineering fitter born in 1908 and a former Nationalist, founded the Irish Republican Socialist Party and sat for the Falls in Stormont from 1945 until 1969, but his later ally Gerard (Gerry) Fitt went one better. Born in 1926, self-educated, a former soap boy in a barber's shop and merchant seaman, Fitt was a likeable man with a keen sense of humour and a deep commitment to the problems of his native Dock Ward in Belfast, then a colourful but tough waterfront area. There in the 1950s he built up such a strong personal following that in 1962 he was returned to Stormont as the member for the Dock division and in 1966 to Westminster as member for West Belfast. Along with Diamond he formed in 1965 yet another Catholic-Labour party, the Republican Labour Party, which he led until 1970.

Above all, Northern Ireland successfully fought off an armed challenge launched by the IRA in 1956 in an attempt to overthrow British rule in 'occupied Ireland'. The campaign, which reached it speak in 1957-9, was confused and lacked both discipline and overall command. Nevertheless, it produced several ugly incidents along the border where policemen were killed in grisly circumstances, cost nineteen lives and led to heavy expenditure in both parts of Ireland on increased security precautions.

Apart from its own self-defeating division, the new campaign faced three obstacles which together proved insuperable. It had little support among the Northern minority, which was beginning to re-appraise its attitude towards the government of Northern Ireland and had no taste for Irish unity brought about by violence. No easy sanctuary was found in the Republic, where the government took vigorous action against the IRA, interning its members and exchanging information though not prisoners with the North. Finally, the reaction of the government of Northern Ireland was firm but calm. Wilder spirits were restrained from undertaking reprisals against Northern Catholics and indulging in counter-attacks across the border, while full advantage was taken of the powers and forces at the government's disposal. The repulsing of cross border raids, though theoretically the responsibility of the United Kingdom, was, as in the 1920s, carried out by the police, while 'the defeat of the indigenous IRA was brought about by good intelligence, RUC and USC vigilance and by internment'.[34] A total of 335 men were interned between 1956 and 1961, the maximum at one time being 187. It was a testimony to the strength and confidence of Northern Ireland that all were released well before the IRA called off the campaign in February 1962. Welcoming the announcement, the *New York Times* commented:

The original I.R.A. and Sinn Fein came in like lions . . . and now they go out like lambs . . . the Irish Republican Army belongs to history, and it belongs to better men in times that are gone. So does the Sinn Fein. Let us put a wreath of red roses on their grave and move on.[35]

Chapter 6

CHALLENGES TO ASCENDANCY

The relatively easy defeat of the IRA apparently left Northern Ireland more secure than ever. Yet appearances were deceptive, for the established pattern of government and politics – based upon Unionist partisanship, Catholic withdrawal, the cold war with the South and British indifference – was soon undermined by a series of challenges from within and without more potent than any armed action. In the 1960s the familiar props were removed. A new style of leadership confused and divided the Unionist Party; a new consciousness prompted the Catholic population to seek fairer government; the Republic began to see economic advantages in improved relations with the North; and the British government started to take more interest in the way Northern Ireland was governed. Such changes raised the question of how Northern Ireland should be governed and severely tested the capacity of the Ulster Unionists as a ruling party. The party failed the test with the result that by the end of the 1960s the regime they had so desperately wanted to maintain was once again fighting for survival.

I

On 25 March 1963, after a whisky and soda with the Governor, O'Neill, the Minister of Finance and senior minister, succeeded Brooke as Prime Minister of Northern Ireland and leader of the Unionist Party. Unionists had been growing increasingly dissatisfied with the ailing and ageing Brooke's indolent style and certainly wanted a change. Had a leadership election been held the party might have chosen a man of a very contrasting ilk, the businessman Faulkner, whose firm policy as Minister of Home Affairs during the IRA campaign had endeared him to local Unionist associations, particularly in the rural areas bearing the brunt of the campaign. As it was, the party still got a very different man in O'Neill. Anglican, English-educated and 'upper-crust' though he was, he differed from Brooke in his real Anglo-Irish ancestry, having both Gaelic and English forebears, and his quiet and professional approach to politics and government. A firm Unionist and upholder of partition, he nevertheless refused to rely on traditional methods of pandering to political and religious prejudices. Instead, he sought to maintain Unionist ascendancy by transforming the economy and changing the tone, if not the structure, of government, preferring the advice of professional administrators to that of the junta at party headquarters. Indicative of this new style was his insistence on adopting a code of practice regulating ministers' business

106

interests, a measure debated since the 1920s, and enforcing it in 1967 by sacking his Minister of Agriculture, West, on account of a land deal.

This new style, often dubbed 'O'Neillism', owed as much to changing circumstances as to O'Neill's urbanity and superficial liberalism. Changes within and without the Province meant that he had to be both more circumspect and more adventurous than his predecessors – more circumspect in his dealings with the minority and more adventurous in economic policy. The growth of the ecumenical movement created the possibility if not of church unity then at least of better contact and understanding between the different Christian churches. Ulster's Protestants and Catholics were, after all, part of the Church of Christ. Changes in personnel and policies in the Irish Republic opened the way for a *rapprochement* between the South and the United Kingdom, Northern Ireland included. In February 1957 Fianna Fail under de Valera was returned to power but reversed its traditional policy of trying to develop native industry by high tariff barriers. Two years later de Valera became President of the Republic and was succeeded as Taoiseach by his Minister for Industry and Commerce, Sean Lemass, a man not inclined to let Republican sentiments interfere with economic policies. In July 1959 he made an attempt to improve economic relations with the United Kingdom, Northern Ireland included. Brooke was not interested but others realised that the North could not afford to neglect opportunities to expand its markets and reduce its large annual trade deficit with the South. Moreover, cross-border co-operation on such items as tourist promotion and the generation of electricity could lead to considerable savings.

Renewed British interest in Northern Ireland in the 1960s also prompted change in the North and dictated its nature. One reason for the abandonment of long-established indifference to events in Northern Ireland was the increasing amount of money Northern Ireland was receiving from Britain. Ever growing since the Second World War, the sums soared in the 1960s with the result that aspects of government in Northern Ireland were subjected to even more critical scrutiny by the Treasury than ever before. Indeed, in the mid-1960s there was serious discussion on how to cope with the problems posed by Northern Ireland's lack of public accountability and one of the solutions canvassed was the transfer of some powers back to Westminster. No such re-transfer occurred but enhanced dependence on Britain meant that the North's autonomy was severely circumscribed and economic policy had to follow the general lines of regional development policy pursued in Britain. Thus a new emphasis on physical and economic planning in the 1960s followed British models and was adopted in response to the Treasury's refusal to countenance the continued subsidisation of the North's traditional industries, a refusal most categorically expressed in the Hall Report.

A second reason for heightened British interest in Northern Ireland was the return of Harold Wilson's Labour government in 1964. The Labour government as a whole was little interested in getting enmeshed in Irish affairs, but Wilson, long sympathetic to the idea of Irish unity, regarded Ireland as a suitable subject for fitful bouts of statesmanship and was wont to talk about a united Ireland, Catholic grievances and his abhorrence of discrimination and sectarianism. Furthermore, in June 1965 a vocal civil rights pressure group, the Campaign for Democracy in Ulster (CDU) was formed by Labour backbenchers to call for an inquiry into the North's affairs. Although not confined to parliamentarians, the CDU could occasionally count on the support of as many as 100 Labour MPs, including former and future government ministers, and it gained considerable bite and commitment when the hustling and bustling Fitt was returned to Westminster and became a regular speaker at CDU meetings.

Such developments at Westminster could not be ignored by any Prime Minister of Northern Ireland. The fears of some Ulster Unionists of a British takeover or sell-out were ill-founded, but what concerned O'Neill and his advisers was the supply of money from Britain, which often depended on appeals to British premiers to iron out the North's difficulties with the Treasury. This had been the case in Craig's day and continued to be the case in the 1960s, when O'Neill tried to keep on good terms with both the Conservative Sir Alec Douglas-Home and the Labour Wilson. He knew which side his bread was buttered on.

Even more compelling than these external reasons for change were two developments within Northern Ireland. The sharp drop in economic activity at the end of the 1950s underlined the inadequacies of existing economic policies, as humanitarian concerns were re-inforced by political ones with a Labour revival in Belfast. With increased lay-offs in the skilled trades dominated by Protestants, the NILP, which had returned no MPs since its re-organisation in 1949, won four seats from Unionists in Belfast in the 1958 general election. Two were former Labour seats with substantial Catholic populations but the other two – Woodvale and Victoria – were solidly Protestant and mainly working class. The party had little to say about such Catholic grievances as discrimination, was firmly unionist on partition, favoured strong measures against the IRA and was pervaded with a strong Protestant cultural ethos – the new members for Woodvale and Victoria both being ex-shipyard workers, Protestant lay preachers and ever proclaiming their 'loyalty'. The primacy given by them and others to Protestant principles later helped to ruin the party, but for a few years the gains in 1958 did seem to herald a triumph for what has been called the consensus-forming strategy pursued since 1949. The four MPs took up the position of official opposition and concentrated on the economic situation in an endeavour to build up a Protestant and Catholic working-class alliance within Northern Ireland. The position was maintained in the 1962 general election, when, although not gaining any more seats, the NILP won its highest ever total of votes and held the four seats won in 1958 with increased majorities. The revival, sustained through two elections, created considerable outrage and even panic among Unionists in Belfast who feared that the NILP had not reached the limit of the Protestant vote.

Movements within the Catholic community also provided a powerful incentive to try a new approach. The Protestant fear of being outbred and outvoted was re-activated by an increase in the Catholic population in such key areas as Belfast and Londonderry, but even more significant was a change in the mood of the Catholic community. The old fatalism and divisions which had long characterised Catholic politics in the North gave way to a greater degree of unity and self-confidence, demanding a place in whatever sun was available in Northern Ireland. This new-found and sometimes overweening and self-destructive confidence reached its peak at the end of the 1960s and the early 1970s, when leaders were wont to speak in outlandishly triumphalist terms, but it dated from the 1950s and the changes that had then begun to manifest themselves in the Catholic community. The Protestant monopoly of power and the economy was actively resented by professional Catholics excluded from public service, while other Catholics, conscious of their relative economic decline, had more material reason for complaint, especially about housing and employment. The changing attitude was re-inforced by the increasing British interest in the North's affairs, the changes in the Republic and O'Neill's new style. In addition, the political awareness of the Catholic working classes was further heightened by the violent clashes in inner urban areas that accompanied political demonstrations by the end of the decade.

The ideas of the Catholic graduate group formed in 1959, National Unity, began to find a more ready audience in the 1960s. Although almost as a reflex action supporting a united Ireland, it accepted the existence of the Northern Ireland constitution and sought reform from within. Centred around Belfast and with a high proportion of teachers, National Unity became a political party in 1965 capable of producing a variety of discussion papers, particularly on economic matters, but not of winning seats at elections. Its transformation into a political party reflected its failure to bring about a united front of all anti-partitionists. In April 1964 it had organised a conference in Maghery, Co. Armagh, at which was formed a 'National Political Front', but this front soon broke down in face of the Nationalist Party's refusal to give up its power in the countryside. Nevertheless, although not anxious to surrender its monopoly, the Nationalist Party did feel obliged to adopt a more disciplined approach to politics and published a 39-point policy statement, committing it to working within the constitution, demanding an end to discrimination and gerrymandering, and outlining an economic programme which included industrial training schemes, the attraction of new industries, agricultural co-operation and the public ownership of essential industries.

Similarly, the violent wing of Irish nationalism, the IRA, recognised the changes taking place in the Catholic community and adapted its policy accordingly. With the collapse of the 1956-62 campaign, many dropped out of the Republican movement but others, realising the need for mass involvement in the historic struggle, revived the radicalism of the early 1930s and turned to left-wing politics and social questions. They 'abandoned the formal legalism of the past, with its belief in the Army Council of the IRA as the legitimate government of Ireland',[1] and adopted instead the more flexible policy of working within the system to bring it down. As part of the new strategy two new organisations were established, the Wolfe Tone societies to act as a forum for discussion among Republicans, communists, socialists and radicals, and the Republican Clubs, banned in March 1967 by the Northern Ireland government, to organise open and legal political activity, including the contesting of elections.

Perhaps, however, the new consciousness and preoccupations of the Catholic community were best summed up in the formation in January 1964 of an energetic pressure group, the Campaign for Social Justice in Northern Ireland (CSJ). It had its origins the previous year in growing dissatisfaction with the distribution of council housing in part of Co. Tyrone and sought to collect and publicise information about discrimination in Northern Ireland, especially in employment, housing, electoral practices and boundaries and public appointments. Though non-political in origin and intention, the new body speedily established contacts with critics of the Unionist regime inside and outside Northern Ireland. It built up support within the British Labour Party and in 1965 affiliated with the National Council for Civil Liberties in London. Had the ordinary law provided a remedy, perhaps the CSJ's course might have been different, but early attempts to challenge Dungannon Urban District Council's housing allocation in the courts came to naught in face of the pusillanimity of lawyers.

These changes in the Catholic community presented both an opportunity and a challenge to Unionism, particularly in view of the contacts established by the likes of Fitt and Dr and Mrs McCluskey, the founders of the CSJ, with the Labour Party in Britain. Together with the economic changes in the North and changing attitudes in the South, they meant that Ulster Unionism could no longer continue in the old vein. O'Neillism was thus intended to put a new face on Ulster Unionism without jeopardising its control of the North.

II

The two outstanding aspects of O'Neillism were a more accommodating approach to the minority and a more systematic approach to economic planning. 'Our task,' he told the UUC, 'will be literally to transform Ulster. To achieve it will demand bold and imaginative measures.'[2] The basis of this 'new technocratic Unionism'[3] were two reports commissioned before O'Neill became premier — the Hall report and Professor Sir Robert Matthew's *Belfast Regional Survey and Plan* — and an economic plan drawn

110

up by Professor Thomas Wilson at O'Neill's request. This last provided the blueprint of the government's economic policy, energetically implemented by Faulkner who became Minister of Commerce and Deputy Prime Minister. Although the new economic policies have sometimes been dismissed as merely cosmetic, based upon faith in natural laws rather than rigorous economic calculation, the six-year plan nonetheless constituted a striking departure from previous piecemeal policies. For the first time regional planning became a reality and a serious attempt was made to counter the traditional concentration of industry and population in and around Belfast and to disperse industry and employment throughout the province. The aim was to attract new industries not simply by offering lavish grants but also by creating a modern economic infrastructure, a series of new growth centres and even a second university. It was thereby hoped to provide some 5,000 jobs in the construction industry, 30,000 in manufacturing and 30,000 in the service industries.

A limit was placed on the expansion of Belfast and growth was encouraged elsewhere. Growth centres were designated to the west and east of the Bann, but it was obvious that expansion would be more easily fostered in the east and the most ambitious projects were there, notably the building of a new city of 100,000 people out of the adjoining towns of Lurgan and Portadown in North Armagh. Attempts were, however, made to develop the West not merely, as had happened previously, by planting factories in areas of high unemployment, but by developing existing centres of population and providing them with industrial sites, a pleasant environment and adequate communications. This was a large part of the reason for the massive road-building and motorway programme undertaken in the 1960s – to facilitate speedy modern travel, as well as provide immediate employment. Of the towns west of the Bann, Londonderry received the most attention. A development plan produced in 1968 assumed a total population of 75,000 to 80,000 by 1981 with an additional 6,000 manufacturing jobs, but it was not chosen as the site for Northern Ireland's second university.

Whatever the limitations of O'Neill's first excursions into the field, he remained to the end an advocate of economic planning. In May 1968 his government commissioned three economic consultants, two of whom, Matthew and Wilson, had been involved in earlier exercises, to draft a five-year programme of economic development beginning in 1970. Published in June 1970 as the Northern Ireland Development Plan, it was a most comprehensive document prescribing a two-fold strategy of development for both the prosperous region of Greater Belfast and the rest of Northern Ireland.

Although under O'Neill the government's main priority was the attraction of new industries, the problem of the older industries could not be ignored. Here the response was to give financial aid, particularly to shipbuilding. Harland and Wolff received money from official sources in

111

Northern Ireland and Britain for re-organisation and re-equipment in the hope of restructuring the industry on a sound financial and economic basis to meet intense world competition. This aim was not achieved and the company's survival subsequently depended on continued government subsidies. Nevertheless, the yards were kept in operation and were at least physically transformed.

An even more striking departure from the practices of his predecessor was O'Neill's attitude towards Catholics. He was by no means convinced that Catholics were a down-trodden minority and thought that 'comments equating the lot of the Ulster Catholic with that of the American Negro are absurd hyperbole'.[4] Indeed, O'Neill shared many of the traditional Protestant and Unionist views of Catholics and had little genuine respect for their culture or aspirations, as was starkly revealed in a radio interview a few days after his resignation in 1969, during which he said,

> The basic fear of Protestants in Northern Ireland is that they will be outbred by Roman Catholics. It is as simple as that.
>
> It is frightfully hard to explain to a Protestant that if you give Roman Catholics a good job and a good house they will live like Protestants, because they will see neighbours with cars and TV sets.
>
> They will refuse to have eighteen children, but if the Roman Catholic is jobless and lives in a most ghastly hovel he will rear eighteen children on national assistance.
>
> It is impossible to explain this to a militant Protestant, because he is so keen to deny civil rights to his Roman Catholic neighbours. He cannot understand, in fact, that if you treat Roman Catholics with due consideration and kindness they will live like Protestants, in spite of the authoritarian nature of their church.[5]

Nevertheless, unlike his predecessor, O'Neill did not make crude bigotry the basis of his policy but did make some effort to win the minority over to Unionism, or, as he liked to put it, to build bridges with Catholics and nationalists. Within Northern Ireland he caused a sensation by visiting Catholic schools and homes, meeting Catholic priests and nuns and questioning the wisdom of segregated education. Even more sensational were the ministerial contacts O'Neill opened up with the South. Civil servants in both parts of Ireland had long been in touch on matters of mutual interest, but not ministers. An early sign of a new departure was the recognition in August 1964 of the Northern Committee of the ICTU, the Dublin-based co-ordinating body for trade unions in Ireland, thus opening the way for trade union co-operation in economic planning. This simple act was, O'Neill later recalled, 'one of the most difficult hurdles I surmounted during my premiership'.[6] In the following January he felt 'sufficiently secure' to take an even bolder initiative 'to try and break Northern Ireland out of the chains of fear which had bound her for forty-three years'.[7] He invited Lemass to lunch at Stormont Castle.

The historic encounter between the two Irish premiers took place on 14 January 1965 with both worried about the likely reactions of their followers. As O'Neill recalled,

> I helped Mr Lemass off with his coat and suggested that after his long drive he would probably like to wash his hands. Eventually, in the rather spacious loo at Stormont House he suddenly said, 'I shall get into terrible trouble for this.' 'No, Mr Lemass,' I replied, 'it is I who will get into trouble for this.'[8]

Nevertheless, the meeting, which avoided constitutional and political questions and concentrated on practical matters of common concern, was considered a great success – even when Lemass met other members of the government at tea. It inaugurated a series of ministerial meetings, including two visits by O'Neill to Dublin and a visit to Belfast by Lemass's successor, John 'Jack' Lynch, who was snowballed by O'Neill's critics.

O'Neill gave nothing away to the South and did little to improve the position of Catholics in the North, but he was inordinately proud of his policy of *detente* with Catholicism and nationalism and very conscious that he was 'blazing a trail'[9] in an effort to break down historic divisions, although not by reforming legislation. His constant refrain was that a new community spirit would be fostered not by state action but by voluntary action on the part of 'reasonable men' occupying a 'broad area of middle ground'. Even this was too much for some members of the Unionist Party, but O'Neill carried the party along with him by retorting that 'I came to the conclusion that if Mr Lemass was prepared to drive through the gates of Stormont and to meet me here as Prime Minister of Northern Ireland he was accepting the plain fact of our existence and our jurisdiction here.'[10]

The economic aspects of O'Neillism met with only limited success by the end of the decade. The targets for housebuilding and additional employment in the construction industry were met by 1968; some 29,000 manufacturing jobs were created; and the introduction of new forms of industry, such as light engineering, electronics and, above all, man-made fibres, reduced the traditional and dangerously narrow dependence on the old staples. Unfortunately, the failures were just as obvious. As expected, the east got the lion's share of new industries and jobs, while the jobs created by these new industries were not capable of taking up the slack created by the decline in the old staples. They did not require the skills possessed by those displaced from the contracting industries and, anyway, the employment created was insufficient to offset the volume of unemployment caused by continued contraction and closures. Thus by the end of 1969 the net improvement in manufacturing was only 5,000 jobs.

Many of these failures stemmed from long-standing disadvantages, but there was also some disquiet about the way the new policies were implemented. In 1970 it was calculated that the cost of each new job in Northern

Ireland was roughly twice the figure for Scotland and Wales, while the anxiety of the government to assist incoming industrialists held as many dangers as the close connections of ministers with the traditional industries. Recalling his years as Minister of Commerce, Faulkner recorded in his memoirs that 'Goodyear was another "blue chip" American firm which came to Ulster in 1966 after long negotiations . . . I was led to understand at the conclusion of these . . . that if ever I decided to get out of politics the Chairman of Goodyear would have a job waiting for me.'[11]

Whatever the reasons, Northern Ireland continued to have the highest rate of unemployment in the United Kingdom. In 1970 the overall level of unemployment in the kingdom was 2.7 per cent: in Northern Ireland it was 7 per cent, more than 2 per cent higher than the most depressed region in Britain, the North of England. The rate of unemployment was even higher in inner-city working-class areas such as West Belfast, and in the south and west in such places as Londonderry, Strabane and West Tyrone, Newry and South Armagh, it was over twice the provincial rate and almost seven times the United Kingdom figure. People thus continued to earn less in Northern Ireland than in Britain, though the gap had narrowed since the 1940s. Of all the regions in the United Kingdom, Northern Ireland still had the lowest level of earnings and the highest percentage of households in low income groups. In 1969-70 average male earnings in Northern Ireland were 81.4 per cent of the British average, £1,115 as against £1,369 – £113 less than the lowest region in Britain, East Anglia. The result was that household incomes in Northern Ireland were the lowest in the United Kingdom. In 1968-9 they were 89 per cent of the United Kingdom average, £27.18 per week as against £31.22. In the same year the percentage of households with a total weekly income of less than £20 was 36 in Northern Ireland but only 29 in the kingdom as a whole.

At one time it looked as though O'Neillism would pay political dividends and strengthen both the Unionist Party and the state. It certainly outflanked Labour in Belfast and stopped the leakage of the Unionist vote there. Admittedly, the NILP helped to cut its own throat. A dispute over the opening of swings on Sundays discredited and divided the party into Sabbatarians on the one hand and Catholics and liberal Protestants on the other, thus making it the less able to survive having its clothes stolen in the November 1965 general election by the economic policies of O'Neillism and the slogan 'Forward Ulster to Target 1970'. The poll showed an average swing to the Unionist Party of 7 per cent and reversed the Labour inroads of 1958 and 1962. Moreover, in the previous February, following the O'Neill-Lemass meeting and encouraged by Lemass, the Nationalist Party had for the first time in the history of the state taken up the position of official opposition and proceeded to act in a most conciliatory spirit. Ironically, it became so accommodating on becoming the official opposition that it virtually ceased to act as an opposition!

The thwarting of the Labour challenge and a temporary reconciliation with the Nationalist Party were the two demonstrable political achieve-ments of O'Neillism. They were not, however, sufficient to secure the continued peace and stability of Northern Ireland under Unionist rule. O'Neill went too far for many Protestants and Unionists but not far and fast enough for Catholics and others, and the normal constitutional pro-cesses became increasingly unable to cope with mounting discontent voiced not in parliament but on the streets.

Little was done positively to build bridges. As various opinion polls showed, the majority of all religious denominations, including some 69 per cent of Catholics, shared O'Neill's reservations about segregated education and favoured instead an integrated system to pull society together. It was hoped that the education of Catholics and Protestants in the same schools would help to alter basic social attitudes and to correct 'key contributory mechanisms in the development of outgroup hostility and prejudice',[12] such as the association of certain names and charac-teristics with opponents, which were learned at a very early age. No steps were taken, however, to integrate education. The obstacles, administrative, financial, religious and political, would have been massive, particularly since integration would have involved the disappearance of Catholic schools and encountered the determined opposition of the Catholic hierarchy who remained adamant that Catholic schools provided a reli-gious and moral ethos integral to Catholic education. This fundamental and constant religious objection continued to be re-inforced by distrust of public authorities in Northern Ireland. Criticism of Catholic schools was motivated, the Bishop of Down and Connor maintained in 1967, not by educational but by political considerations which 'belong to the darker areas of politics, in which religious prejudice is paramount'.[13] Some Catholics went so far as to argue that it was essential to preserve Catholic schools in a sectarian society, since

> One of the few opportunities there are for educated Catholics lies in being teachers within the Catholic school system . . . it would be mad-ness to lose control of the one large field of opportunity remaining in Catholic hands.[14]

The result was that the 1968 Education Act, forged after protracted negotiations between the government and the Catholic hierarchy, re-inforced segregation by increasing from 65 to 80 per cent the building grants to voluntary schools.

Concessions to the Catholic Church in respect of education had long been part of Unionist policy, but there was no sustained effort to associate the minority more closely with the state. Controversy continued over the financing of the Mater Hospital and there were no reforms of the police, housing or local government. Northern Ireland remained a Protestant state. Unionists had a majority of twenty in the Commons; all their MPs and all government ministers were Protestants and more were also Orangemen. Only three of the fifty-four Unionist MPs who became cabinet ministers between 1921 and 1969 were not members of the Orange Order. There continued to be a marked discrepancy between Catholics and Protestants in the civil service, particularly in the highest ranks. The Special Powers Act remained, as did the Protestant USC, which numbered 12,606 at the end of the IRA campaign in 1962. The percentage of Catholics in the RUC had fallen from 16.4 in 1936 to 12 in 1961, dropping still further to 9.4 by the following decade, while the courts continued to be manned by Protestants, many of whom were closely identified with the Unionist Party. In 1969 only six of the seventy-four posts from Clerks of Petty Sessions to High Court judges were held by Catholics, while two of the three judges in the Northern Ireland Court of Appeal had been Attorneys-General in Unionist governments.

Above all, local government remained an outstanding grievance, with Unionist majorities still bolstered up by discriminatory housing policies, carefully-drawn electoral areas and the persistent refusal to adopt the British practice of one man one vote. The business and university votes were abolished in Stormont elections by the Electoral Law Amendment Act of 1968, but changes in planning powers and the discussion of local government reform, such as the White Paper on *The Re-Shaping of Local Government: Statement of Aims,* published in 1967, were more concerned with structure than representation. Thus Unionists continued to control a disproportionate share of local authorities with disproportionately large majorities. In the predominantly Catholic county of Tyrone, urban and rural district councils remained under Unionist sway. For example, in the urban and rural districts of Omagh, Protestants were in clear minorities of 39 and 40 per cent respectively, but Unionists had majorities of 12 to 9 on the urban and 24 to 18 on the rural district councils. It was the same in the east: Protestant majorities were disproportionately large so that in Lurgan there were only Unionists on the council. Consequently, Protestants continued to receive preferential treatment in the allocation of local authority housing and a disproportionate share of local government jobs. Co. Fermanagh was some 53 per cent Catholic, but in 1969 it was claimed that of the 370 full-time employees of the Unionist-controlled county council, excluding those in schools, only 32 or 8.6 per cent were Catholics. In 1971 Catholics comprised about 26 per cent of the population of Belfast but only provided 61 or 4.3 per cent of the 1,407 people employed in the Corporation's Electricity Department.

The composition and behaviour of Londonderry Corporation were the most controversial of all. The city was two-thirds Catholic, but the Corporation was controlled by Unionists and Protestants got the plum jobs. In 1968 70 per cent of the Corporation's administrative, clerical and technical employees were non-Catholics, who also held nine of the ten best paid jobs. Unionist control of the Corporation was sustained by controversial ward boundaries, the restricted local government franchise and confining re-housed Catholics to the ward with an already large Nationalist majority. In 1966 the adult population was 30,376 – 20,102 Catholics and 10,274 Protestants – but the franchise qualification substantially reduced the Catholic majority in the electorate, which comprised 14,429 Catholics and 8,781 Protestants. The arrangement of wards did the rest. In the Waterside Ward 3,697 Unionists returned four councillors and in the North Ward eight councillors were elected by 3,946 Unionists, but it took 10,047 nationalist voters to return eight councillors in the South Ward. Londonderry was both the symbol of Unionist pride and the acme of minority grievances against the Stormont regime. It was the classic example of a process which continued to leave the minority in control of only two towns of any importance – Newry and Strabane.

Admittedly, in view of the importance the Unionist Party attached to the maintenance of the *status quo,* any major structural reform would have taken a good deal of courage and involved hard political graft. Other changes, however, such as the appointment of Catholics to public boards, required more will and imagination than effort, but O'Neill's government lacked that will and imagination. In 1969 it was calculated that the membership of twenty-one boards was 85 per cent non-Catholic: 283 non-Catholics to forty-nine Catholics. Moreover, the positive acts of O'Neill's government created resentment. Concentrating as it did on the development of the east, industrial policy and development served only to emphasise the economic imbalance between the predominantly Protestant east and the predominantly Catholic south and west. While it may be a matter of doubt as to how far government can control economic development and the precise location of industry, the naming of new towns and the siting of universities were nevertheless entirely within the power of the government. But here O'Neill's government made two provocative decisions. It named the new combined town of Lurgan and Portadown after the first Prime Minister, Craigavon; and, in accordance with the report of a committee on higher education, the Lockwood Committee, which contained no Catholics, the government sited the North's second university not in Catholic Londonderry, the second largest centre of population and already possessing a University College with an honourable academic tradition, but in the Protestant town of Coleraine, distinguished, if at all, as an agricultural market centre and totally innocent of academic traditions.

Catholic feelings of frustration were shared and re-inforced by Labour supporters in Northern Ireland. In the aftermath of its setback in the 1965 election, and under the influence of a strong Young Socialist movement, the NILP began to press hard for wide-ranging reforms but made little headway. When a delegation of the NILP and the ICTU met the cabinet in December 1966 and commented on the contrast between the restricted local government franchise in Northern Ireland and universal franchise in Britain, it was told that Britain was out of step with Northern Ireland!

Mounting frustration resulted in a crucial change of tactics on the part of those demanding reform. This was a switch from pressure group to protest politics, from a small body seeking to influence the holders of power by the collection and dissemination of evidence, to large numbers, supposedly non-violent but using the implicit threat of violence from fringe supporters or hostile counter-demonstrations. This transition was made in February 1967 when a new body, the Northern Ireland Civil Rights Association (NICRA), was formed by the Northern Wolfe Tone Society and the CSJ to spearhead a campaign for civil rights for Catholics. Modelled on the National Council for Civil Liberties, its membership covered a wide spectrum of political views, but it was predominantly Catholic. Eschewing violence and traditional nationalist aims, it sought to organise Catholic resentment towards clear social goals and its target was less the regional government than Unionist-controlled local authorities. Its basic aims were: one man one vote in council elections; the ending of gerrymandered electoral boundaries; machinery to prevent discrimination by public authorities and to deal with complaints; the fair allocation of public housing; the repeal of the Special Powers Act; and the disbandment of the 'B' Specials.

The slogan 'civil rights' deliberately invited comparison with the black liberation movement in the United States led by Martin Luther King. The analogy was, however, only partly appropriate and, unlike King's movement, NICRA was slow to take to the streets. Anxious to avoid charges of sectarianism and arousing active Protestant hostility, the leaders were reluctant to undertake marches which in the North were never regarded as neutral or secular events but as party occasions, as re-assertions of historic differences and territorial sectarian claims. Misrouted marches could easily unleash violent passions and re-create past battles. This was all the more likely in 1968 because, however much their organisers might protest to the contrary, civil rights marches could all too easily be seen as Catholic and republican demonstrations. During the first ever NICRA demonstration many marchers sang republican songs and Catholic hymns and the civil rights anthem 'We shall overcome' was drowned by the republican hymn 'A nation once again'.

Nevertheless, NICRA was forced onto the streets by mounting pressure for direct action from the Catholic areas in the west. At the beginning of 1968 the local Republican Club and left-wing Labour Party in Londonderry, led by Eamonn McCann, formed a Housing Action Committee and encouraged squatting and the disruption of traffic and Corporation meetings. In Caledon, Co. Tyrone, the local Republican Club also urged homeless families to squat in newly-built council houses which the Unionist-controlled Dungannon Rural District Council would not allocate to them. The result was that NICRA organised its first large-scale protest march from Caledon to Dungannon on 28 August 1968.

118

It was disastrous for the subsequent history of Northern Ireland that some Protestants and Unionists were fully prepared to challenge the civil rights movement on the streets. O'Neill may have been able to stay criticism within his party for a while, but he was unable to prevent the spread of a virulently Protestant and Unionist movement led by that large man with a very large voice, the Reverend Dr Ian Richard Kyle Paisley. Born in Armagh in 1926, the son of an Independent Baptist who had served in Carson's army and formed his own small church, Paisley lacked formal educational qualifications and almost desperately searched for letters to put after his name – his Doctorate of Divinity from the Bob Jones University of Greenville, South Carolina, was an honorary one. Nevertheless, he was an intelligent and able man and a talented orator capable of playing an audience with changes of tone, mood and devastating turns of phrase. These qualities enabled him to pursue a successful public career as a religious and political leader complete with his own church and party. 'By far the most complex character ever to cross the political scene in Ulster, Paisley has infuriated, perplexed, confused, amused, and fascinated his observers.'[15] He was, indeed, the embodiment of many of Ulster's complexities.

In religion he was an evangelical fundamentalist in the mould of a peculiarly Ulster line of Protestant political evangelists, such as Henry Cooke and Hugh Hanna. He was a bitter opponent of fashionable ecumenism and would have no truck with Rome or church unity. Determined to be no man's or church's creature, he formed in 1951, at the age of twenty-five, the Free Presbyterian Church of Ulster with himself as Moderator. As such, he quickly achieved notoriety at home and abroad by his assertion of Protestant principles and his resistance to Rome and ecumenism. His emergence as a political leader took longer, but he showed his determination to assert his political views from the very start of O'Neill's premiership. In the 1970s he was more flexible and thoughtful than some commentators have allowed, but before then he was an extreme Unionist and an uncompromising opponent of any suggestion or appearance of surrender to the evils of Catholicism and nationalism. Originally a supporter of official Unionism, which did not take him to its bosom, he soon became one of its fiercest critics and was particularly hostile to O'Neillism which he regarded as a betrayal of both Unionism and Protestantism.

He made his views and presence felt in 1963 when he narrowly escaped jail for defying the first ever Special Powers ban on a loyalist march and demonstrating against the lowering of the Union Jack on the death in June of Pope John XXIII. In the October of the following year, during the Westminster general election, his provocative protest against the illegal display of a tricolour flag in the Republican headquarters sparked off two days of serious rioting in Belfast and caused the police to use water cannon for the first time. He finally went to jail for three months in 1966 after a demonstration against the General Assembly of the Presbyterian Church, whose liberal and 'Romeward' trend he saw as the spiritual rationale of O'Neillism and appeasement. The protest caused insult to the Governor, Lord Erskine, and the assembly and precipitated rioting in Belfast. In fact, the year 1966 enabled Paisley to reach new heights or depths of political prominence, for it was the fiftieth anniversary of the Easter Rising. Lavish celebrations were planned in the South and, perhaps inappropriately in view of the new spirit obtaining among Northern Catholics, Northern Republicans also decided to mark the anniversary on a grand scale. Needless to say, there were ill-founded rumours of an IRA revival. At the same time, the Unionist past was also dredged up by a dispute over the naming of a new bridge over the River Lagan in Belfast, the Governor suggesting 'Queen Elizabeth', but traditional Unionists preferring to honour their dead leader, Carson, rather than their living sovereign.

To prove the steadfastness of the North, therefore, Paisley launched in February 1966 a weekly newspaper, the *Protestant Telegraph*, which poured forth a steady stream of hysterical anti-Catholic and anti-communist propaganda. In the following April he moved from propaganda to action by setting up a twelve-man Ulster Constitution Defence Committee (UCDC), a 'united society of protestant patriots',[16] to safeguard the Protestant constitution of Northern Ireland and to forward his 'O'Neill Must Go' campaign. Paisley did make some effort to engage in normal political activity and his supporters contested or threatened to contest local and parliamentary elections under the banner of the Protestant Unionist Party. Nevertheless, in the 1960s his was essentially a street movement relying on large and usually provocative demonstrations by supporters, and he was prepared to assert his position with little or no regard for the ultimate or wider consequences. Sometimes the consequences did alarm him, as when his oratory was said to have inspired Protestants to kill Catholics, and he was quick to disavow responsibility. Nevertheless, he was not deterred from keeping up a torrent of invective against opponents and seeking to confront them on the streets. His oratory may have been subtle but many of his hearers simply thought that victims were being pointed out to them.

Often, therefore, his activities were accompanied by a greater or lesser degree of violence or threat of violence. Some Protestants showed their determination to uphold the Protestant North by forming in 1966 a secret army, the Ulster Volunteer Force (UVF), thereby reviving the name of the force associated with resistance to the Third Home Rule Bill before the First World War. Opposed to appeasement, it declared war against the IRA and threatened that 'known IRA men will be executed mercilessly and without hesitation';[17] and in an effort to dispose of one Belfast IRA leader it mistakenly murdered one man on 28 May 1966 and another, a young

Catholic barman, on 26 June, as he left a pub in Malvern Street, Belfast. Denounced by O'Neill as 'this evil thing in our midst',[18] the UVF was declared illegal and went underground to organise on military lines and to play a prominent and destructive role in later events. Paisley vehemently denied O'Neill's accusation that he was associated with the UVF, although it shared his dislike of O'Neillism, its members included some of his closest associates, and one volunteer, when arrested for the Malvern Street murder, was reported as saying 'I am terribly sorry I ever heard of that man Paisley or decided to follow him.'[19] Most definitely associated with Paisley was another Protestant paramilitary force, the Ulster Protestant Volunteers (UPV), formed in May 1966 and controlled by the UCDC. Organised in local divisions on military lines, the UPV was open only to 'born Protestants' and was closed to members of the RUC but not, significantly, to those of the USC. Guided by the original UVF motto of 'For God and Ulster', it was supposed to eschew illegal violence. Nevertheless, there was some overlap of membership with the UVF and the men of the UPV were a formidable accompaniment to Paisley's many demonstrations and counter-demonstrations.

Paisley's new organisations were easily diverted from their original targets of republicanism and O'Neillism to the civil rights movement. To Paisley and his followers that movement was simply a cover for the traditional enemies of Northern Ireland and its reform programme amounted to a demand for the dismantling of the Protestant and Unionist ascendancy. Accordingly, the UCDC and UPV determined 'to confront the enemy at every opportunity', particularly by trying to thwart civil rights demonstrations. Counter-demonstrations were organised in the hope of getting the original marches banned by the government as prejudicial to public order and safety, and if this tactic failed Paisley's supporters sought to harass, hinder and break them up. Their capacity to do so was increased after 1966 with the conversion to Paisleyism of Ronald Bunting, a mathematics teacher at the Belfast College of Technology and a former British army officer who had retired with the honorary rank of major. An eccentric both personally and politically, Bunting nevertheless had a flair for organisation which he used in mobilising Paisley's forces, sometimes under such banners as the 'Loyal Citizens of Ulster' and the 'Knights of Freedom'.

The resort to the streets by two such mutually antagonistic groups as the civil righters and the followers of Paisley created a tense and volatile atmosphere, which the attitude of the authorities only made worse. The police force, or rather certain sections of the RUC re-inforced by the USC, could not be relied upon either to enforce the law impartially or to act with restraint. They were prepared to allow Unionists to dictate the course of many civil rights demonstrations, for when Paisley and his supporters occupied areas where the civil righters proposed to march, the police left the former in possession of the centre of towns and halted or diverted the civil rights demonstrators, often confining them to Catholic areas. And when they failed to keep the opposing sides apart, the police tended, on the grounds that loyalists did not attack them, to take up positions with their backs to the Protestants and facing the civil rights demonstrators. Thus, the latter took on the appearance of aggressors whom many policemen seemed only too willing to belabour with batons. Nor was the minister responsible for law and order, Craig, the Minister of Home Affairs since 1966, inclined to encourage more sympathetic or imaginative handling of civil rights demonstrations. A competent administrator, popular in the party and ambitious for the premiership, he was aggressively dismissive of critics of the regime. Like Paisley but more culpably as he was a minister, Craig showed little regard for the consequences of his words and actions, for he had an easy tongue and a penchant for the dramatic. To him protest was subversion which had to be suppressed at all costs, an attitude hardly likely to inculcate respect for the forces of law and order.

The combination of two determined but opposed sets of street politicians and inept if not blatantly partisan handling by the authorities produced an explosive situation. Although the police and Paisley's supporters together prevented it from completing its course, the first ever civil rights demonstration, from Caledon to Dungannon on 26 August 1968, passed off peacefully enough, with both Paisley and civil righters claiming victory. It was not so with the second demonstration, a march on 5 October through Londonderry, the citadel of discrimination, organised by local civil rights activists and intended to cross Protestant as well as Catholic areas on the grounds that the march was non-sectarian. The threatened rape of the Maiden City meant that Paisley's supporters were re-inforced by other Unionists and counter-demonstrations on a large scale were threatened. Ignoring a ban imposed by the Minister of Home Affairs, a section of the marchers collided with the large body of police which had been drafted into the city to ensure that there would be no repetition of events of the previous Easter, when Republicans had defied a ban in Armagh. The police broke ranks and used excessive and indiscriminate violence on the demonstrators who were batoned and hosed with water cannon. Some seventy-eight civilians and eighteen policemen were injured and television sent pictures of the scene round the world.

The march may have been ill-considered, but so also was the ban and the police action. Altogether the events in Londonderry on 5 October 1968 served to emphasise the frustration and mutual suspicion that continued to divide Northern Ireland. In protest on 15 October the Nationalist Party gave up its recently assumed role of official opposition. Six days earlier moderate civil rights leaders in Londonderry, led by a Protestant factory manager, Ivan Cooper, and John Hume, a Catholic teacher, organised the Derry Citizens' Action Committee to protest against the behaviour of the police and the partisan structure of the city's Corporation. Above all, the events of 5 October led to the formation of a new student group at Queen's University, Belfast, the People's Democracy (PD), which had a destructively uncompromising approach to politics.

Although in some respects part of the world-wide movement of student protest that occurred in the late 1960s, the PD was fundamentally a peculiarly Irish organisation in origins, concerns and eventual ideology. Its formation at the beginning of October 1968 was an emotional response by some 3,000 students to the events of 5 October and the subsequent frustration by the police and Paisley of peaceful protest. At first governed by mass meetings and part of the mainstream of the civil rights movement, the PD demanded the repeal of repressive legislation, one man one vote in local elections, and the end of gerrymandering and discrimination in jobs and housing. Most students probably supported the PD in the hope of extracting from the government some commitment to reform, but the new movement quickly fell under the control of former members of the university with pronounced left-wing views, such as McCann and Michael Farrell, a teacher. They generally followed Connollyite Republicanism, very different from the ideology developed by the continental student movement with its New Left emphasis on the writings of Sartre, Fanon and Marcuse.

The aims of these able but doctrinaire and frequently arrogant PD leaders went far beyond the redress of immediate grievances. Instead, they envisaged the eventual creation of a workers' and small farmers' republic for the whole of Ireland, which would dissolve the religious differences that had long divided the working class in the interests of the bourgeoisie. Although it professed non-violence, the PD was not averse to confrontation with the police and in the course of time developed the technique of 'defensive' violence with considerable expertise, achieving 'the defensive solidarity of a self-styled persecuted minority'[20] – a trait of other student movements. The PD's aims were scarcely realistic and its methods further divided rather than united Protestant and Catholic workers, but criticism that they were out of touch with reality was disregarded by PD leaders who gave short shrift to those who did not share their millenarian dreams. 'We're not concerned in the least,' Farrell once remarked, 'justifying ourselves to people who have proved by their theory and action that they are not socialists'.[21]

V

O'Neill now made an effort to retrieve the situation by taking the steam out of the civil rights movement. His response was not entirely voluntary. The governments at Westminster and Dublin reacted sharply to events in Londonderry, and on 3 November Wilson met O'Neill, Craig and Faulkner to demand the urgent introduction of reforms. Nevertheless, a large number of cabinet meetings were required before the government of

Northern Ireland could finally agree upon the reform package that was announced on 22 November 1968. Conceding some of the civil rights demands, the package included promises to ensure that housing authorities placed need in the forefront in the allocation of houses and made future allocation on the basis of published and readily-understood schemes; to appoint a Parliamentary Commissioner, an Ombudsman, to investigate citizens' grievances; to press on with the appointment of a Development Commission for the city of Londonderry and the abolition of the existing Corporation; to reform local government comprehensively within three years; and, finally, to withdraw the Special Powers Act as soon as this could be done without hazard. In addition, O'Neill made a Churchill-like television appeal for support, telling the civil rights demonstrators that 'Your voice has been heard, and clearly heard. Your duty now is to play your part in taking the heat out of the situation before blood is shed.'[22]

For a brief moment it looked as though the reform package and the appeal might restore order and decorum to the North. There was an overwhelming response to a newspaper campaign in support of O'Neill. The Unionist Parliamentary Party, with four abstentions, gave O'Neill a personal vote of confidence, and NICRA responded to his appeal with a month's moratorium on demonstrations. The package may not have conceded all that was being demanded, but it contained more concessions to Catholics than had been won in the first forty-seven years of the state. However, the mood of optimism quickly evaporated in face of mounting dissension within the Unionist Party and the growing influence of the PD in the civil rights movement. It may have enjoyed only a brief period of ascendancy but the PD left a lasting mark on the history of Northern Ireland.

The most determined members of the PD were not at all impressed by O'Neill's appeal for an end to agitation. They regarded the reform package as inadequate, especially since it did not immediately concede one man one vote; and they were incensed at the continued police toleration of counter-demonstrations, often illegal, organised by Paisley's supporters against civil rights marches. Moreover, obsessed with their own success to date and with 'the transitory attractions of illusory mass influence',[23] they preferred confrontation with the government to working through the reforms already granted. The militants thus sought to bring matters to a head by ignoring the NICRA moratorium and proceeding with a four-day march from Belfast to Londonderry at the beginning of 1969. In the words of the enthusiastic organiser, Farrell, the march was to be

The acid test of the government's intentions. Either the government would face up to the extreme right of its own Unionist Party and protect the march from the 'harrassing and hindering' immediately threatened by Major Bunting, or it would be exposed as impotent in the face of sectarian thuggery, and Westminster would be forced to

124

intervene, re-opening the whole Irish question for the first time in 50 years. The march was modelled on the Selma-Montgomery march in Alabama in 1966, which had exposed the racist thuggery of America's deep South and forced the US government into major reforms.[24]

About eighty marchers set off from the City Hall, Belfast, at 9 a.m. on 1 January 1969 and were harrassed at various points by loyalists, including off-duty members of the USC, the most serious incident occurring near Burntollet Bridge, Co. Londonderry. When the marchers eventually reached Londonderry on 4 January, they were ambushed as they entered the city, while after a meeting to mark the close of the march rioting broke out and culminated in an unprecedented police assault on Catholic houses in the Bogside. 'A number of policemen,' the Cameron Commission found, 'were guilty of misconduct which involved assault and battery, malicious damage to property . . . and the use of provocative, sectarian and political slogans.'[25] One result was a tacit agreement between leaders of the Catholic community and the Londonderry Commission that the RUC would stay out of the Bogside until calmer times. That night 'Free Derry' was born.

These latest and most dramatic clashes of the civil rights movement with Unionist die-hards and the police temporarily swung almost the whole Catholic population behind the most uncompromising of the civil rights leaders and completely disrupted the traditional pattern of political leadership in the Catholic community. Leading members of the PD were elected to the executive of the NICRA shortly after the general election of February 1969 had swept aside the 'Green Tories' of the Nationalist Party in several key areas, as the party paid the price for lapsing into a too easy acceptance of the Northern *status quo* and failing to respond to the growing militancy in its constituencies. McAteer, the party leader, was ousted from the Foyle division of Londonderry by one of the local civil rights leaders, Hume, with a majority of 3,653. A second Nationalist was defeated in Mid-Derry by Hume's civil rights colleague, Cooper, and a third succumbed in South Armagh. Even the PD took part in the election and its hastily improvised campaign achieved some notable successes, if not the return of any MPs; it only narrowly failed by 220 votes to defeat the sitting Nationalist member for South Down. The trend within the Catholic community to support different types of candidates was confirmed two months later in a by-election for the Westminster constituency of Mid-Ulster. Bernadette Devlin, then a twenty-one year old psychology student and member of the PD, won the nomination as a united anti-Unionist candidate and then became the youngest woman ever elected to Westminster by winning the seat with the biggest anti-Unionist majority since the seat had been created in 1950. She lost the seat in 1974 and any influence much before then, but for some months she enjoyed considerable popularity and prominence in Northern Ireland and at Westminster.

Some of the more moderate civil rights leaders, an older generation perhaps, were concerned about the growing influence of the socialist militants who spoke increasingly of the need to transform society and accused non-socialists of sectarianism. For their part, the moderates charged the militants with perverting the civil rights movement in pursuit of the will o' the wisp of socialism and working-class unity. According to Hume, the civil rights movement was not and never had been

A movement which seeks to promote either a socialist or a conservative society. It seeks only a just society, and the achievement of justice and democracy is surely a necessary first step in Northern Ireland to end for ever the equation of religion and politics before normal politics can take place.[26]

Yet, however distasteful and dangerous they found the views of the PD militants, the moderates were too divided among themselves by personal and local rivalries and past political commitments, and were too concerned lest they lose support, to present a united front and battle with the militants for leadership of the Catholic community. In the following year they did so, but until then the rifts remained unresolved. The Nationalist Party may have been pushed to one side, but in 1969 no leader or organisation was capable of delivering the support of the Catholic community for any political initiative.

On the Unionist side, too, there was dissension and disunity, as powerful and determined elements worked desperately against compromise and concessions to Catholics. O'Neill had learned to live with Paisley's denunciations, but the reform package and its failure to end agitation led to increasing dissatisfaction within the Unionist Party which became steadily more divided, with no one section in real control.

The challenge to O'Neill from within was led by Craig, critical of both the reform package and Westminster's role in forcing it on Northern Ireland. He denounced in public 'this nonsense centred around civil rights'[27] and demanded that Westminster's threat of interference should be resisted with a threat of independence. O'Neill dismissed him on 11 December wih the words 'Your idea of an Ulster which could "go it alone" is a delusion and I believe all sensible people will see it to be so.'[28] Just over a month later O'Neill lost two more ministers, Faulkner and William Morgan, the Minister of Health and Social Services and an MP since 1949. The issue was O'Neill's decision to appoint a commission of enquiry, headed by a Scottish judge, Lord Cameron, into the course and causes of the violence since the previous 5 October. Faulkner said that the commission was an abdication of responsibility and a political manoeuvre to ease the way to the concession of universal franchise. Having always opposed, although not necessarily on principle, one man one vote, Faulkner now argued that the government should make the decision itself and then sell it to the party. Backbenchers were proving equally truculent.

On 3 February 1969 twelve of them met in an hotel in Portadown, the 'Portadown Parliament', and called for O'Neill's resignation.

In retaliation, O'Neill called a general election, the 'crossroads election', on the question of reform. He did so less in the hope of winning substantial Catholic support than with the intention of rallying moderate Protestants and Unionists by taking up the gauntlet so boldly and provocatively thrown down by the 'Portadown Parliament'. He went to extraordinary lengths in doing so, even supporting opposition to official Unionist candidates. He certainly caught his critics unawares and must have enjoyed seeing his three late ministers, Morgan unsuccessfully, desperately fighting for their political lives. Nevertheless, the election was not an overwhelming victory for O'Neillism and served only to underline the rifts within Unionism. In the twenty-three constituencies where pro-O'Neill candidates were opposed by anti-O'Neillites and Protestant Unionists, O'Neill's supporters won 141,914 votes and eleven seats, while their opponents got 130,619 votes and twelve seats. O'Neill himself suffered a severe rebuff when he scraped home without an overall majority in Bannside, having been hard pressed by Paisley, standing as a Protestant Unionist, and Farrell standing for PD. Of the thirty-nine Unionists returned only twenty-six, including three Unofficials, could be considered as supporters of O'Neill and at least eight of these were unreliable.

Unionists preferring violent to constitutional opposition also took the field, largely unmolested. At the end of March onwards the UVF launched a bombing campaign, responsibility for which was generally and mistakenly attributed to the IRA. On 30 March 1969 a massive explosion rocked an electricity station at Castlereagh outside Belfast, causing damage estimated at £2m, and in the following month there were further explosions at the Silent Valley reservoir in Co. Down and an electricity link-up in Portadown. The IRA did, it is true, blow up a few post offices in Belfast in April, following rioting there, but the other explosions were the work of the UVF aiming to discredit reform and bring down O'Neill.

There is no one generally accepted explanation of this developing and bitter rift within the Unionist Party, of why some Unionists supported and others resisted the liberalisation of the regime. The neatest and most mechanical interpretation is a Marxist one, but its stress on the conflict between industrial capital and monopoly capital, between the old and the new industries, does not accord with the facts. More convincing are class explanations of the split. In and around Belfast O'Neill's critics were strongest in the working-class areas, his supporters strongest in the middle-class suburbs. In addition, there was resentment among the commercial Unionist middle class at the 'half a century of semi-oligarchical rule by the landed gentry',[29] a resentment embodied and made more specific in the personal ambitions of men such as Faulkner and Craig. However, such explanations do not explain the depth of feeling against O'Neill in the border areas of the west or the kind of protest that developed in the

127

Protestant working-class parts of Belfast. These two main centres of opposition to O'Neillism shared two vital characteristics. In both, Protestant communities were in close proximity to high concentrations of Catholics and Protestant dominance had been maintained partly by economic discrimination and partly by the manipulation of local government boundaries. Concessions to Catholics threatened to destroy a whole way of life in such areas. Protestants and Unionists not only feared the consequences of the dismantling of their traditional ascendancy, but they also felt that they were being discriminated against in the government's economic and social policies. Unionists in the west, long suspicious of Belfast Unionists, believed that too many jobs were being created in the east and not enough was being done to develop their area, while Protestant workingmen in Belfast disliked both the decision to limit the economic expansion of the city and the implications of certain housing and redevelopment plans.

In the border areas resistance to change was channeled through a new pressure group, the West Ulster Unionist Council, active between 1969 and 1971 in defending traditional Unionism. Opposing the reform of local government and demanding tough security measures, the council was spearheaded by the Fermanagh Unionist Association and the bulk of its membership was made up of Unionist Associations in West Ulster. It was led by the one and only victim of O'Neill's insistence on high standards of probity from ministers, West, the former Minister of Agriculture, whose opposition to reform and western perspective had been summed up in his constant refrain as minister: 'Fermanagh will never stand for it.'[30] In Belfast the spirit of resistance was summed up in the formation and subsequent growth of the Shankill Defence Association (SDA). Formed at the end of April 1969 by one of Paisley's supporters and a member of the UPV, John McKeague, the SDA's ostensible original object was to resist certain Belfast Corporation redevelopment plans which threatened to destroy the strong communal bonds of the Shankill area. Its real object was to preserve the Protestant purity of the Shankill by insisting that redevelopment took place 'within the existing, time-hallowed borders of the "loyalist" ghetto'[31] and that families displaced by slum-clearance be rehoused in the same area. It readily turned into a paramilitary group, patrolling the upper Shankill and the borders with the Catholic Falls, but its social aims were never neglected and Shankill's economic and social grievances were fully exploited by opponents of reform and concessions to Catholics.

The fundamental nature of the objections to reform and O'Neillism also explains the growing and lasting influence of Paisley. He was a man of the people willing to say out loud and in public what others only thought in private. O'Neill's rhetoric of reconciliation, his superficial *rapprochement* with the traditional enemies of Northern Ireland, and the consequent discouragement of the usual anti-Catholic and anti-Republican outpourings had stifled, confused and even demoralised many Unionists. They therefore welcomed Paisley's anti-ecumencial, anti-Republican speeches, which re-affirmed the traditional values and superiority of Protestantism and Unionism in ringing phrases. In fact, people knew where they stood with Paisley. It was otherwise with O'Neill. He remained a committed Unionist and partitionist, but his style and his rhetoric as much as his actual policies brought out again into the open all the deeply-held fears and antagonisms of old-style Unionism.

VI

By April 1969, therefore, matters were moving out of control. Both communities were divided among themselves. Advocates of compromise and conciliation on either side could not command a majority in their respective communities, and among others opinion was becoming more and more polarised, with mutual recrimination, demonstrations and counter-demonstrations, scuffles and even rioting in Belfast and Londonderry. Even those Catholics hitherto most sympathetic to O'Neillism abandoned all hope of reform in the North.

In these circumstances political initiatives were almost irrelevant. O'Neill's acceptance on 22 April of the principle of one man one vote provoked further Unionist opposition, including the resignation of his cousin, Minister of Agriculture since 1967 and soon to be his successor, Major James Chichester-Clark, a former army officer of solid landed Unionist stock but easily swayed by outside pressures. O'Neill resigned on 28 April in order, he later said, to ensure that he was succeeded as Prime Minister and leader of the Unionist Party by the more moderate Chichester-Clark, whom the Parliamentary Party did in fact elect by just one vote over Faulkner. Chichester-Clark tried in vain as Prime Minister to defuse tension by re-affirming the government's new-found commitment to one man one vote and by ordering an amnesty for those convicted or charged with political offences since the previous October.

Had these changes and gestures come at any other time of the year they might have had some effect, but they came just before the start of the Protestant marching season which brought to a head all the unresolved tensions of the previous months. There were serious riots in various parts of the province on 11 and 12 July, but they paled into insignificance beside the naked and unbridled sectarian warfare that broke out in Londonderry in the middle of August and spread soon afterwards to Belfast.

The 12 August was traditionally the date when the Apprentice Boys of Derry, one of the Protestant Loyal Orders, paraded in celebration of the action of thirteen apprentice boys in slamming the gates of the city on the army of King James II at the start of the famous siege of 1689. Usually such parades, often of 10 – 12,000 Orangemen from all over the North, passed off peacefully, but in the tense atmosphere of 1969 trouble was likely, particularly since the Orangemen were accustomed to march through the city and around the walls overlooking the Bogside, the Catholic quarter outside the walls where the besieging army had once camped. Unionist governments were always loathe to interfere with the Orange Order and Chichester-Clark was the more reluctant to do so at a time when the traditional marches assumed in Protestant eyes an even greater significance than usual, since they represented a re-affirmation of the Unionist ascendancy which had been threatened or 'betrayed' by O'Neill's policies over the previous twelve months. For their part, the Catholics of Londonderry were in no mood to tolerate such a reminder of their inferior position in the North and accordingly organised for attack as well as defence through the Bogside Defence Association (BDA), chaired by a veteran Republican, Sean Keenan.

The expected battle ensued. When the procession of Orangemen, heavily guarded by the RUC, reached the fringes of the Bogside, it was stoned by onlooking Catholics. The RUC baton charged and another siege was laid. The BDA had built barriers around the Bogside, which were defended with petrol bombs made from milk bottles. The siege went on all day and all night and was ended only when the 700 policemen were re-inforced by the British army. At 5 p.m. on 14 August fully-armed British troops moved into the centre of Londonderry and undertook hurried negotiations with the BDA, as a result of which the British commander agreed to pull back the RUC and the USC behind his troops and not to enter the Bogside. 'Free Derry' had been re-affirmed.

The agreement was hailed as a victory in the Bogside, but it was victory at a price, the price being paid by Catholics in Belfast. Belfast's Catholics, hemmed in by Protestants, had long been held hostage for the good behaviour of their co-religionists elsewhere in Ireland, and on the night of 14 – 15 August 1969 Protestants wreaked their vengeance on Catholics living in the Lower Falls Road, close to the Shankill. During the day tension had been at fever pitch, as Protestants filled the streets connecting the Shankill with the Falls, where Catholics were erecting barricades and forming local defence associations whose activities were soon co-ordinated by the Central Citizens' Defence Committee. At night Protestants surged down the side streets, firing guns, burning Catholic houses and eventually planting the Union Jack in the heart of a Catholic area. There were similar scenes across the city in the Ardoyne, a mainly Catholic area in North Belfast. Five Catholics and one Protestant were killed and 150 Catholic homes were burned out. Throughout the following day, 15 August, parts of the city were in a state of suspended war, as stronger barricades were erected in the Falls and guns were rushed up from the South. Once again the British army moved in to defuse the situation. Late in the afternoon of the fifteenth troops began to take up positions in the Falls Road but, as in Londonderry, made no attempt to breach the barricades. Instead, they erected a peace line, sometimes called the Orange-Green line, between the Falls and Shankill.

Events in Londonderry and the Falls were the most important of a series

130

of bloody incidents which rocked the North. Indeed, within the space of a few days the destruction was the most extensive and the death toll the heaviest since the 1920s. These four days in August 1969 may not have shaken the world, but they certainly shook Northern Ireland to its very foundations and decisively altered the course of its political history. They finally and emphatically underlined the inability of the Unionist regime to cope with the challenges that had emerged in the 1960s but which were born of historic divisions. Indeed, according to one view, a slide into violence was almost inevitable as Ulster's disturbed past and Ulstermen's selective history caught up with the present. Stripped of the protection of the state, 'The civil population turned instinctively to the only source of wisdom applicable to such circumstances — the inherited folk-memory of what had been done in the past, both good and bad.'[32]

Chapter 7

VIOLENCE AND DISINTEGRATION

The events of August 1969 marked the beginning of the end for Stormont. Northern Ireland's affairs ceased to be the sole concern of Northern Irishmen, as the British government became increasingly involved, as did, to a lesser extent, the government of the Republic. A re-alignment of opinion gave some grounds for optimism as new political parties and groupings emerged within both communities and even crossed the traditional divide, all seeking reform and reconciliation. Yet, on the other hand, traditional animosities were re-inforced by the revival of the IRA and a renewed determination on the part of many Unionists to uphold their accustomed ascendancy by any and every means. In the end, violence grew at the expense of constitutionalism, as politicians and advocates of compromise lost control to men with guns or industrial might. Between August 1969 and May 1974, therefore, the nature of the Northern Ireland question changed dramatically from one of forms of government to a more fundamental matter of power. The urgent question was no longer how Northern Ireland should be governed but who actually had the power to govern such a divided and violent province.

I

The most obvious consequence of the events of August 1969 was that the affairs of Northern Ireland ceased to be the sole prerogative of Northern Irishmen. The longer the conflict continued the more it had international ramifications, particularly in view of the Irish-American obsession with British policy in Ireland, the existence of the European Court of Human Rights, and the fact that Colonel Ghaddafi's Libya became a place of pilgrimage and a source of arms for Unionists and Republicans alike. Nevertheless, the two outside agencies most involved were the British government and the government of the Irish Republic.

Since Northern Ireland remained an integral part of the United Kingdom, and since control of the army lay with Westminster, the British government had a legal obligation to provide, if so requested by the police or government of Northern Ireland, troops to maintain law and order. Nevertheless, the obligation was only reluctantly admitted and the British government preferred to let Northern Ireland try to put its own affairs in order before sending troops in to contain the August rioting. Despite the wish for a quick withdrawal and a strictly limited engagement, Westminster was increasingly drawn into taking more and more responsibility for the affairs of the province, at first by committing itself, along with the government of Northern Ireland, to a programme of reform. On 19 August the Prime Minister of Northern Ireland and two of his colleagues were summoned to talks in London and after the meeting a communiqué was issued re-affirming the constitutional position of Northern Ireland and declaring that

Every citizen of Northern Ireland is entitled to the same equality of treatment and freedom from discrimination as obtains in the rest of the United Kingdom, irrespective of political views or religion.[1]

Between August 1969 and May 1974 three governments (two Labour headed by Wilson, 1966-May 1970 and February 1974 onwards, and one Conservative led by Edward Heath, May 1970-February 1974) held office in Britain. Although the mass of British people were largely indifferent to Britain's renewed role in Northern Ireland, the main parties agreed upon the fundamentals of a bi-partisan policy. While recognising that there was an Irish dimension to the Northern Ireland question, they accepted partition and agreed that Northern Ireland should remain part of the United Kingdom as long as the majority of Northern Irishmen so wished. They were also determined that every effort should be made to secure the Catholic minority's active acceptance of the existence of Northern Ireland, committing themselves at first to the reform of Stormont and then, after its suspension, the re-establishment of a regional government in which all sections of the community would participate. Finally, there was agreement that Northern Ireland should be governed by Northern Irishmen and that Westminster's role in the North should be a very limited one.

There was a similar basic continuity of policy in the Republic, where between 1969 and May 1974 two administrations held office. Until February 1973 a Fianna Fail, de Valera's party, government was headed by the Corkman, Lynch, after which there was a coalition of Fine Gael and the Labour Party under the premiership of Liam Cosgrave, an acquaintance of Faulkner's, and including one of the Labour leaders of international renown, Conor Cruise O'Brien. The Southern attitude towards the North after 1969 continued to be determined not simply by traditional claims to the whole island and concern for the Northern minority but also by the dictates of the Republic's internal politics. Generally, however, the government of the Republic confined itself to words in the tense early months of conflict. On the night of 13 August 1969 Lynch made a strong speech on television. He said that the Northern government had lost control of the situation which was the 'inevitable outcome of policies pursued for decades by successive Stormont governments'; that 'the Irish government can no longer stand by and see innocent people injured and perhaps worse'; and that the Irish army would establish field hospitals along the border for people injured in the North. He also called for a United Nations peace-keeping force in the North and for negotiations with Britain about the future of Northern Ireland, 'recognising that the re-unification of the national territory can provide the only permanent solution for the problem'.[2]

This speech set the basic tone of Southern policy towards the North: a repudiation of violence; an insistence upon reforms in Northern Ireland, at first civil rights for Catholics and later power-sharing; and the claim that there should be an Irish dimension to any solution of the Northern question. This last condition did not entail immediate re-unification. The *de facto* position of Northern Ireland was acknowledged and it was recognised that unity should be achieved not by coercion but only by the voluntary participation of Unionists in a single state. Meanwhile, however, the South demanded a voice in the North's affairs, a demand which was eventually, by September 1971, accepted by the British government as the most effective way of combatting the renewed violence of the IRA.

The effects of this new British and Southern intrusion into Northern Ireland's affairs were not always beneficial. The centre of debate was removed from Northern Ireland without really settling anywhere else. Instead of talking to one another, Northern Irishmen conducted slanging matches with a view to influencing Westminster or Dublin, whose attitudes were not entirely determined by what was in the North's best interests. This was a problem Northern Ireland politicians never resolved. Unionists who paid too much attention to Westminster found their support slipping, while the extent to which Lynch should be allowed to speak for them sometimes divided Catholics. On balance, intervention accentuated ancient divisions and resentments. The presence of British soldiers on active duty in the streets of Northern Ireland was like a red rag to republican bulls, while British insistence on the dismantling of their ascendancy was regarded by many Unionists as yet another act of betrayal and thus reinforced the siege mentality that had long characterised Ulster Unionism.

The attitude of the Southern government had a similar effect on Ulster Unionists. They preferred a Southern government eschewing violence to one threatening armed intervention, but Southern insistence that unity was the ultimate solution was totally unacceptable to Ulster Unionists, who continued to find repugnant many aspects of life in the Republic. The removal in 1972 of the clause in the constitution recognising the special position of the Catholic Church may have been a friendly gesture towards Protestants throughout Ireland, but it was not followed up by further measures dealing with other questions Protestants found intolerable, such as the importance attached to the social teaching of the Catholic Church and the constitution's claim to sovereignty over the whole island. Many Ulster Protestants from all classes and denominations thought that, instead of criticising the North, Southern politicians should set about making the idea of unity attractive. In fact, the Dublin government was seen as hostile and hypocritical, conniving at, if not secretly approving, the blatant use of its territory as a training-ground and refuge by the IRA in its offensive against the North. Not until the middle of 1972 did Lynch take a tougher line with the IRA in the Republic and even then Ulster Unionists remained sceptical in view of the retention of the provision in the Republic's constitution which made it impossible to bring fugitive offenders to trial. Since there could be no extradition for political offenders, the South continued to be a refuge for perpetrators of outrages.

Yet, though ultimately unhelpful, Southern and particularly British intervention did for a short while seem capable of creating conditions for a settlement. British intervention strengthened the hands of reformers among Unionists and gave new heart to Catholics, encouraging them to seek to work within a modified Stormont regime, while the government of the Republic lent support to and conferred prestige on those Northern Catholics and nationalists who preferred constitutional to violent methods and were willing to come to terms with Ulster Unionists.

II

The task of bringing out whatever reforming tendencies there were in Ulster Unionism continued to be slow and painful. Unionists and their government, loathe to recognise the extent and justice of Catholic grievances, were quite willing to dismiss the August rioting as merely a 'conspiracy . . . to overthrow a government democratically elected by a large majority'.[3] The British government's refusal to accept this interpretation was reinforced by the findings of the Cameron Commission, the three-man enquiry set up at the beginning of the year to investigate the violence of the previous months. Describing Stormont as hidebound and complacent, the Commission found a failure of leadership on all sides and listed among the causes of the disorders the well-founded grievances of which the civil rights movement had been complaining – the behaviour of the police, the use of the Special Powers Act and discrimination in public employment, representation and housing. Indeed, the more British ministers discovered over the next few months, the more they were convinced of the need for reform, for, as one said, 'The Augean stables were nothing to the mess he found at Stormont.'[4] Westminster's determination to see reform implemented was further strengthened by the conviction that timely changes could save Stormont. There were indications that the minority would welcome a new initiative and that members of the majority would assist, particularly with the formation of two new political parties.

One tried to cross the sectarian divide and form a centre party. This was the Alliance Party, formed on 21 April 1970 under the leadership of a Belfast solicitor and former Liberal, Oliver John Napier, and distinguished for its good intentions rather than its achievements. The first Irish political organisation to profess cross-sectarianism as its *raison d'être,* the Alliance

135

Party grew out of the New Ulster Movement, which had been established in April 1969 as a non-party ginger group professing traditional liberal values but firm on partition and Northern Ireland's place in the United Kingdom. Its initial leadership was drawn largely from people previously unknown in politics but it soon gained support from a section of Unionists who had backed O'Neill, including in 1972 three sitting Unionist MPs. It also succeeded in attracting support from all religious denominations roughly in proportion to their strengths in the population at large (except in the case of Presbyterians, always strongly Unionist), and its leading members showed a remarkable degree of unanimity on major issues of policy, including such controversial questions as integrated education. Although it absorbed some former members of the NILP, the Alliance Party was largely a middle-class affair with a restricted appeal. The fact that 'Ulster politics remained stubbornly soft-centred'[5] caused the party to lower its sights. It stopped seeing itself as a party of government and became committed to sharing power with moderate Catholic and Protestant parties and occupying a middle ground between them, a bastion against extremism and intolerance.

That changes were also taking place within the Catholic community was underlined by the formation in April 1970 of the Social Democratic and Labour Party (SDLP) among the more moderate Catholic politicians and laymen who had been involved in the 1960s agitation. It may be that 'self-preservation proved stronger than party loyalty'[6] in causing civil rights workers and members of the Republican Labour, Nationalist and NIL parties to co-operate to ward off the challenge to leadership posed by the militants of the PD and Bernadette Devlin. But it is also true that the founders of the SDLP were anxious to offer Catholics an organised opposition operating on constitutional lines, hitherto so conspicuously lacking.

The distinctive feature of the SDLP was that it did organise for the first time the Catholic community for sustained political action in Northern Ireland and within the confines of the constitution, deciding that the minority's interests and aspirations could be best served, at least in the short term, by co-operation with the government and by trying to gain a substantial share of power. When frustrated and angry, it was quick to resort, as in July 1971, to the old tactic of abstention, but its watchword soon became power-sharing and to that end it adopted the elaborate institutional structure of a mass political party, with fifteen branches in 1971 but as many as eighty-eight by 1974 (and 109 two years later). Although its membership was smaller than that of the other new party — 5,000 to 6,000 to Alliance's 10,000, the SDLP was far more effective in mobilising votes, at least Catholic votes, and it quickly came to monopolise Catholics' political representation.

The fact that, despite claiming to be non-sectarian, the SDLP remained a Catholic party reflected a certain naïvety. Believing that, as one of the founder-members said, 'a sustained run in office . . . could syphon off the sectarian poison from the atmosphere', it was slow 'to promote the image of a legitimate governmental partner',[7] so necessary to demonstrate its good faith to Protestants in view of the past. Thus it remained committed to Irish unity, although it made unity conditional upon the consent of the majority in Northern Ireland rather than asserting it, as did Republicans and Nationalists, as an absolute right. Moreover, although an explicitly socialist party seeking the public ownership and democratic control of essential industries, its socio-economic policies were not worked out in detail and what policies it had reflected the continued, albeit more muted, influence of Catholic social teaching. Party members may have lacked strong 'doctrinal' views on social and economic matters, but the Catholic Church did not. Consequently, particularly on such questions as integrated education, the attitude and possible reactions of the hierarchy had always to be taken into account by a party whose members and supporters 'pray as well as vote together'.[8]

Some of these weaknesses reflected political, personal and other differences among the leadership. Fitt, who resigned from the Republican Labour Party, became leader of the new party, but in many respects his leadership was nominal. The other founder-members were strong personalities with clearly defined views and local power bases and perspectives of their own. This was particularly true of two Catholic graduates of a younger generation, Hume and Austin Currie, born in 1937 and 1939 respectively. Hume, the party's theorist, was a Londonderry man and had first come to prominence in the city's civil rights movement. Currie, on the other hand, started his political life as a reforming Nationalist, being returned for East Tyrone in 1964 as the youngest MP ever elected to Stormont. East Tyrone, the area in and around Dungannon, was his hunting ground and it was from there that he had been catapulted into the headlines by engaging in the first direct action of the civil rights campaign. Among the older generation, closely involved in Catholic Labour politics in Belfast, Patrick Joseph (Paddy) Devlin, MP for Falls, 1969-72, was something of a political maverick who had several times switched parties – Republican, 1936-50 (interned 1942-5); Irish Labour Party, 1950-58, NILP, 1958-70 and its chairman in 1967-8. The existence of such independent men, mutual jealousies and varying local and political perspectives gave rise to the joke that the party's line on any issue depended on who answered the telephone. Even the clumsy and obscure title was a compromise, reflecting the difficulties of even founding the party at all: the title had to take account of Fitt's attachment to the Labour movement while preserving the preference of other MPs for social democracy.

Nevertheless, despite these weaknesses which did make for future difficulties, the rise of the SDLP introduced a new and hopeful element into political life. It transformed the nature of Catholic politics and converted the majority of Catholics into at least qualified supporters of Northern Ireland and the link with Britain.

Such changing currents of opinion gave grounds for hoping that a far-reaching reform programme could halt the slide into disorder by reconciling Catholics to a modified Stormont regime. British pressure thus turned Stormont into a reforming administration almost overnight. Most of the reforms were carried during Chichester-Clark's premiership, which lasted until March 1971, but the momentum was sustained by his successor, the erstwhile hardliner, Faulkner, whose rise and fall illustrated how a significant section but not a majority of the Unionist Party came to appreciate that traditional Unionism no longer sufficed in a changing world.

The reform programme at first favoured by the British government amounted to the virtual dismantling of the Unionist ascendancy by conceding most of the demands made during the civil rights campaign. The question of law enforcement received highest priority. During the Downing Street meeting on 19 August Northern Ireland ministers agreed that the army should control security operations, including the USC, and an enquiry into Northern Ireland's police forces, headed by Lord Hunt, the explorer, led to far-reaching changes. Published on 3 October 1969, the report recommended the civilianisation of the RUC; the establishment of a police authority representative of the whole community; the disarming of the RUC and the modification of its prosecuting role, since the impartiality of the police was liable to be questioned if they were responsible for both deciding who should be prosecuted and thereafter acting as prosecutor; the setting up of a Police Reserve; and, most controversially, the replacement of the USC by a new part-time security force. The recommendations were soon implemented. In the following March the Northern Ireland parliament instituted the new police organisation, headed no longer by an Inspector-General but by an English-style Chief Constable, an Englishman, Sir Arthur Young, the City of London Police Commissioner. The British government also acted quickly and set up the new part-time security force, the Ulster Defence Regiment (UDR), which became operational on 1 April 1970. The overhauling of the system of public prosecutions took longer, but early in 1972 the first Director of Public Prosecutions was appointed with full responsibility for the selection and prosecution of all serious criminal charges and for advising the courts on applications for bail throughout Northern Ireland.

Attempts were made to improve community relations by the establishment of both a Ministry of Community Relations and an independent Community Relations Commission, the latter supposedly to seek radical approaches to the problem; by the appointment in November 1969 of a Commissioner to deal with complaints against local authorities and public bodies – the local counterpart of the parliamentary Ombudsman appointed the previous June; and by the July 1970 Prevention of Incitement to Hatred Act which made incitement to religious hatred a statutory offence. Local government underwent dramatic changes in an attempt to root out sectarianism and inefficiency. The congeries of local bodies were abolished and their functions distributed between government departments, nominated Area Boards and twenty-six district councils elected by PR and on the basis of adult suffrage. The old property qualifications were abolished to concede the much desired one man one vote, while the electoral boundaries were drawn up by an independent commissioner. Accepted by Stormont in December 1970, these changes did not come into operation until October 1973. The new local authorities were not given any say in the allocation of public housing, which was placed entirely under the control of an appointed central body, the Northern Ireland Housing Executive, responsible to the Ministry of Development.

Finally, efforts were eventually made to associate the minority with the work of the regional government. On 22 June 1971 Faulkner announced to SDLP acclaim a scheme for three parliamentary committees to review policy and advise on legislation in respect of social, environmental and industrial services. Membership would be in proportion to party strength at Stormont but the opposition would provide two of the three chairmen who would be paid a salary. These proposals were repeated later in the year and included in a consultative document entitled *The Future Development of the Parliament and Government of Northern Ireland*. Moreover, in October 1971, the month the consultative document was published, Faulkner brought the first Catholic into the Northern Ireland cabinet, G. B. Newe, the secretary of the Northern Ireland Council of Social Services and well-known for his dedication to the cause of peace, welfare and reconciliation. He became Minister of State in the Prime Minister's Office to advise on minority matters, in face of denunciations from Nationalists and Catholics.

Unionists bitterly lambasted such changes as betrayal, but others criticised the reforms as giving too little too late. Certainly, the reform programme failed to create confidence in Stormont among those whom it was intended to benefit. The delay in altering local government lent substance to charges that no Unionist administration could be entrusted to reform itself and abandon its weapon of discrimination. Such comments under-rated both the commitment of some leading Unionists to reform and the difficulties they faced. Nevertheless, many of the changes were superficial and ill-conceived. There were significant omissions, such as the failure to examine the question of segregated education, and generally the reform programme injected Northern Ireland with a dose of the 'institutionitis'[9] then fashionable in Britain in the belief that problems did not need fundamental reform but could be administered out of existence by tinkering with a few institutions.

Thus community relations measures were not carefully devised to suit Northern Ireland's circumstances. Rather, they closely followed British legislation concerning its coloured minorities, regardless of whether or not the racial and ethnic conflict theories on which such legislation was based were adequate to explain the nature of conflict in the North. The establishment of a separate ministry encouraged the view that the problem of community relations could be compartmentalised into one department, instead of 'recognising that it was a central problem of government, which ought to be a consideration in almost every decision taken by every department'.[10] Admittedly, the Community Relations Commission was given wide terms of reference, enabling it to examine basic community conflict, but its independence was illusory and it was virtually ignored by the government. Similar comments can be made about the police reforms and Faulkner's proposals for involving the opposition in the work of government. Faulkner's committees might have provided good jobs for opposition MPs, but since they would have dealt only with uncontroversial topics and would have had in-built Unionist majorities, they would not have given the opposition any effective share in power. Above all, the police reforms did not gain for the forces of law and order general public confidence. At one time it looked as though a considerable number of Catholics would join the UDR, but the percentage of Catholic recruits dropped quickly from 18 to 3 to the accompaniment of complaints about the enrolment of too many ex-Specials. Catholic suspicions of the loyalist orientation of the new force were scarcely allayed by well-founded stories that some members of the UDR had close links with the Protestant paramilitary groups which abounded in the early 1970s.

III

The truth is, however, that the reform programme became almost irrelevant in face of growing violence. The record of violence spoke for itself:

	1969	1970	1971
Shootings	Not Available	213	1,756
Explosions	8	153	1,022
Armed robberies	NA	NA	437
Deaths (army and police)	1	2	59
Deaths (civilians)	12	23	114
Injuries (army and police)	733	811	707
Injuries (civilians)	NA	NA	1,838

Such violence challenged the very basis of the state and ruined any chance the reforms had of creating confidence in the justice of the Stormont regime and giving it legitimacy in the eyes of the minority. This was particularly true of the reforms relating to law and order, as the process of civilianising the police was interrupted and responsibility for law and order continued to be placed largely in the hands of the British army.

At first, only a few hundred troops were used in Northern Ireland to restore order in Belfast and Londonderry, but within a few months the number rose to seven units of 7,000 men and increased to as many as nineteen at one time in 1972. These included technical corps, such as the much-used and valiant bomb disposal squad as well as the controversial

Parachute Regiment and the Special Air Service, both feared for their ruthlessness. The soldiers were very different in appearance and equipment from those who had served in Northern Ireland during previous armed conflicts. They were more mobile with their ugly re-inforced Land Rovers, Ferret scout cars, Saracen armoured personnel carriers and Saladin armoured cars fitted with a 75mm gun and two Browning sub-machine guns. The troops were equipped to deal with both guerrilla warfare and community violence – dressed in flak jackets, plastic visors, shields and leg guards, and using two-foot riot batons, CS gas capable of causing serious temporary discomfort and five-ounce rubber bullets designed to bounce off the ground and strike at knee level. They usually operated in uniform, but in certain areas, where uniformed patrols were ineffective and liable to attack, plain clothes patrols from a special Military Reconnaissance Force operated in unmarked cars.

The army shared security duties with the reformed and enlarged RUC and the newly-formed UDR. The size of the RUC was increased from 3,500 in 1969 to 4,949 in 1970 and 6,500 in 1974, and was supported by a Reserve, usually of 1,500. The civilianisation of the RUC did not last long and the police were soon re-equipped with arms and found themselves travelling around in armoured cars. The locally-raised and part-time UDR slowly reached its target of eleven battalions by 1973 and assisted the army and police in guarding key installations, carrying out patrols and operating checkpoints. The hope was always that the role of the army and UDR would be gradually diminished and that the 'primacy of the police'[11] would be established, but this was a vain hope and for many years to come it was the army and not the police who dominated the peace-keeping effort in the province.

The main powers available to the security forces derived from the controversial Special Powers Act. There was some doubt as to the legality of the British army, an excepted service, operating under legislation passed by the Northern Ireland parliament, but the 1972 Northern Ireland Act authorised the Northern parliament to legislate in respect of the armed forces of the Crown and conferred retrospective validity on prior actions. Another useful piece of legislation was the 1969 Firearms Act, which laid down three broad categories of firearms charges, the most serious being possession with intent to endanger life, resist arrest or commit a crime, for which the maximum sentences ranged from ten to fourteen years imprisonment. The Criminal Justice (Temporary Provisons) Act, which was hurriedly passed in July 1970, introduced among other things a mandatory minimum prison sentence of six months for riotous or disorderly behaviour, although the latter was soon excluded since it transpired that people involved in domestic quarrels (which usually carried the charge of disorderly behaviour) were falling foul of the new act. Yet, although given wide powers, the security forces were not above the law. They were subject, as were all members of the public, to common law and were supposed to exercise their special powers with discretion and without unlawful force. These constraints were summed up in the famous Yellow Card of rules relating to the use of weapons by soldiers. The card set out the circumstances in which soldiers might lawfully open fire, as, for instance, 'against a person carrying a firearm, but only if you have reason to think that he is about to use it for offensive purposes and he refuses to halt when called upon to do so', or 'if there is no other way to protect yourself or those whom it is your duty to protect from the danger of being killed or seriously injured'.[12]

There is no doubt that the original decision to call on the army in August 1969 was fully justified. The army was needed to deal with a serious and immediate problem beyond the capacity of the RUC and indeed should have been called in earlier. The immediate problem was resolved by the army's intervention, but its presence created new problems which had not existed before. The revival of republicanism was greatly encouraged by the physical presence of the traditional enemy on the streets, particularly since the army was by its very nature little suited to the sensitive tasks of peace-keeping and restoring respect for the law in a divided community.

A basic trouble was that the use of the army both reflected and dictated a particular response to the problem of law and order – a 'military security'[13] approach which relied not on the normal system of justice but on methods often careless of ordinary legal rights. Normal police procedure is based upon certain conceptions of the grounds for arresting and charging subjects. Only people directly suspected of having committed a specific criminal offence could be legitimately arrested and brought to a police station for questioning, and only those against whom a specific charge could properly be preferred should be detained for custody. The military approach was much more cavalier, and the consequences were the more harmful in view of the unfamiliar circumstances in which the army was forced to operate in Northern Ireland, where the soldier did not have an identifiable enemy and was confronted daily by people of the same class as himself who spoke the same language but who at one time in the day would be quite friendly and at another would hurl stones and bottles at him.

Ironically, though, it was not Catholics and Republicans but Protestants and Unionists who initially constituted the greatest obstacle to the restoration of law and order and who first came into conflict with the army. Considerable resentment built up among Unionists at both the announcement of plans to dismantle the old Unionist ascendancy and the fact that the British army was protecting Catholics, even to the extent of respecting the existence of no-go areas in Belfast and Londonderry. The SDA went onto the attack; its chairman, John McKeague, was arrested and sentenced to three months imprisonment for unlawful assembly; and on the day the Hunt report was published the association declared that 'a day is fast approaching when responsible leaders and associations like ourselves will

142

no longer be able to restrain the backlash of outraged Loyalist opinion'.[14] That day came quickly, for on the following night, 11 October, rioting and loyalist sniping resulted in the first death of a member of the Crown forces, an RUC constable, in this particular phase of Northern Ireland's history. Protestant violence was not confined to Northern Ireland and seven days later a member of the UVF and Paisley's Free Presbyterian Church was blown up and killed planting a bomb at an electricity plant at Ballyshannon, Co. Donegal, in the Republic.

In the following year, however, the traditional battle lines were reformed, as the Catholic ghettos veered towards militant republicanism. The PD had never ceased trying to radicalise the proletariat, but it was swept aside and reduced to the role of IRA mouthpiece as a result of a dramatic split in the republican movement. Out of this split there emerged in Belfast and elsewhere in the North a new hardline organisation committed to the achievement of a united Ireland by military means – the Provisional IRA (PIRA).

The events of August 1969 had caught the IRA totally unprepared. The leftward and political trend pursued since the failure of the armed campaign of 1956-62 had left Republicans with neither the organisation nor the arms to defend the Catholics of Londonderry and Belfast when they came under loyalist attack in the summer of 1969. 'I.R.A. – I Ran Away' was chalked up on the walls of the beleagured ghettos. A sense of impotence and humiliation led some members of the Belfast IRA to take independent action. In September 1969 the staff of the Belfast brigade reorganised itself and broke away from the official Army Council, and three months later, in December, the split was formalised when the Army Council in Dublin voted by three to one to give at least token recognition to the three parliaments at Westminster, Dublin and Stormont. The minority seceded and set up a Provisional Army Council. A corresponding split occurred in January 1970 at the convention of the IRA's political front, Sinn Fein. The Provisionals (the 'Provos' or 'green' republicans) were those who followed the example of the Belfast brigade and adhered to the Provisional Army Council, while the Officials (the 'Stickies' or 'red' republicans) continued to recognise the Official Army Council.

The rift between the Provisionals and the Official IRA (OIRA) is often explained as a split between the political right and the political left, between fascists and marxists, between conservatives and social radicals. Such a simple characterisation ignores the fact that both wings of the IRA had several aims in common: the withdrawal of British troops from Ireland; the legalisation of all forms of republican activity in Northern Ireland; and the establishment, or what they saw as the re-establishment, of a thirty-two county Irish republic. Moreover, the simple explanation ignores the diversity of opinion within the Provisionals, particularly on economic and social issues. Nevertheless, the conventional labels do accurately reflect different emphases.

The Officials were more steeped in socialist ideology and more inclined to dabble in politics. They sought an all-Ireland workers' republic and, while not averse to guerrilla warfare, thought that their aims could be achieved through the ballot box. Thus they were willing to contest elections in Northern Ireland under the cover of the Republican Clubs and were willing for prolonged periods to suspend military action against the British government, as they did in May 1972. By contrast, despite some social democratic rhetoric, the Provisionals were cast in the dogmatic mould of the physical force nationalism established by the Fenians in the second half of the nineteenth century. For them the one vital issue was the overthrow of British authority in the North and the re-unification of Ireland. Once this was achieved, they assumed that all other problems, such as relations between different communities, would be resolved in a new democratic and socialist Ireland. 'Our aim,' the Provisional Army Council declared in Easter 1970, 'is to make the Irish people masters of their own destinies, controlling all the wealth of the nation, material and spiritual, in an independent republic of 32 counties, in which protestants, catholics and dissenters will have equal rights.'[15]

Moreover, the Provisionals would have no truck with parliamentary politics. Their methods remained military. At first they insisted that they were acting only defensively, to protect the Catholic community from outside aggression by loyalists or the Crown forces, but in February 1971 they went unequivocally on the attack, undertaking, as they put it, 'an offensive campaign of resistance in all parts of the occupied area'.[16] They did not necessarily believe that they could achieve a military victory, but they did intend to make government impossible in the North and break the will of the Northern Ireland and British governments. Like the Fenians they had 'no doubt of their moral right to wage war against Great Britain', for they saw themselves as the 'infallible interpreters of the will of the Irish people to achieve independence and unification, no matter what the cost'.[17]

Relations between the two wings of the IRA were bitter and often violent. The Provisionals accused the Officials of betraying republicanism, while the Officials charged the Provisionals with fomenting sectarian war instead of promoting solidarity among the workers. Often, however, at a local level, the differences between the two wings were expressed not dogmatically but more in terms of a domestic squabble about status, family and community allegiance and, later, as a feud or vendetta. This may help to explain the high level of violence between the wings, which sometimes erupted in open fighting, as in Belfast on 10 March 1971, when, with the British army standing carefully aside, a fierce battle in the Lower Falls resulted in one man shot dead and several wounded.

It was fatal to the peace of Northern Ireland that the Provisionals were more successful than the Officials in establishing themselves there. With their own six-counties organisation, based in Belfast, the Provisionals quickly assumed the leadership of Northern republicanism, becoming well entrenched in Belfast and in the Bogside and Creggan districts of London-derry. By the middle of 1971 the overall strength of the PIRA was believed to be around 1,500, including 800 in Northern Ireland, of whom 600 were in Belfast, 100 in Derry and 100 in other areas. The OIRA, numbering a couple of hundred in the North, claimed by 1971 to be in control of the Lower Falls area of Belfast. These IRA strongholds were the areas which from time to time were converted into barricaded no-go areas, from which the RUC was excluded and where the government's writ ceased to run.

The Provisionals saw themselves and acted as an army of liberation. The backbone were the full-time volunteers subject to a military code of discipline, obliged to obey orders from officers and liable to severe penal-ties for any infringements, including execution for 'bringing the movement into disgrace' by committing criminal offences like theft. In one area of Belfast volunteers were paid a minimal wage which had to be supple-mented by friends and relatives and even shopkeepers and club managers. Military operations were usually carried out by active service units com-posed of men from different companies who met to execute a pre-arranged plan. The full-time volunteers were backed up by auxiliaries, part-time volunteers not on twenty-four-hour call nor subject to the full discipline of the IRA. Furthermore, women and youths were mobilised through Cumann na mBan, the women's IRA, and two youth movements, Cumann na gCailini for the girls and Na Fianna Eireann, said in 1971-2 to have several hundred members, for the boys. These groups were assigned an important role in the campaign, from rioting to moving weapons and planting bombs.

At first both wings of the IRA were short of arms and expertise, often blowing themselves up with unstable bombs. Yet gradually sophisticated arms were acquired by the Provisionals, as was a deadly efficiency in the handling of explosives. In addition to the old stand-by, the Thompson sub-machine gun or 'Chicago piano', the IRA had some US-made M1 carbines and Garand rifles as well as a variety of .303 rifles and German and American pistols. Later Russian-made weapons came to hand through Libya. The most favoured explosives were the car bomb, the nail bomb, which usually consisted of a beer can full of nails and wrapped in ex-plosives, and the hold-all bag bomb often left outside business premises. There were also a number of ingenious and small devices which could be easily hidden in shops, such as the cigarette packet incendiary and the contraceptive fuse bomb. The work was costly and necessary funds came largely from America through such organisations as the Irish Northern Aid Committee, especially after the introduction of internment in the summer of 1971, as Irish-Americans with their basic hatred of all things British were easily persuaded that the PIRA was a liberation army.

With the growing ascendancy of the PIRA in the Catholic ghettos the period of fraternisation between Catholics and the army came to an end. The beginning of the end occurred on 2 April 1970, when rioting in the Catholic area of Ballymurphy was put down by troops, who were met with petrol bombs. The British General Officer Commanding in Northern Ireland, Lieutenant-General Sir Ian Henry Freeland, went on television and threatened to shoot petrol bombers dead. Henceforth, the PIRA increasingly appeared in action against the troops, and events at the beginning of July confirmed the dramatic change in Catholic-army relations since the previous summer. On the weekend of 3-5 July the army placed, illegally it transpired, some 20,000 Catholics in the Lower Falls under an around the clock curfew when an arms raid encountered armed resistance from the IRA, as a result of which five civilians were killed and sixty civilians and fifteen soldiers were injured.

In 1970 it was possible to argue that republican activity was largely defensive, but in February 1971 the PIRA went unambiguously on the offensive. The change followed the breakdown of secret talks between the army and the Provisionals about the control of rioting. On 6 February the latter shot dead a British soldier in the New Lodge Road, the first British soldier killed in action in the North for almost fifty years. The same night a Provisional officer was shot dead in a three-way battle between the PIRA, Protestants and the army in the Bone, a border area between Protestants and Catholics in Belfast. The Prime Minister, Chichester-Clark, announced on television that 'Northern Ireland is at war with the IRA Provisionals'.[18] The PIRA did indeed enter upon an extensive campaign of guerrilla warfare consisting of robbery, shooting, bombing and assassination. The object was to break the morale of the security forces and the will of the British and Northern Ireland governments by disrupting social and economic life and by murdering and maiming civilians as well as members of the Crown forces, primarily in Northern Ireland but occasionally in Britain as well.

Because of their violent tactics members of the IRA are often regarded as terrorists and/or psychopaths. Such labels the IRA vehemently refuted; it endeavoured instead to create the impression, especially among its own volunteers, that they were soldier-politicians, not merely gun-toting terrorists. Indeed, criticisms were frequently rendered ironic by the volunteers, such as the Belfast Provisional who once commented on the gall of a stray cat which had soiled his shirt, 'Fancy a cat pissing on a terrorist's shirt!'[19] It is also unhelpful to dismiss members of the IRA as psychopaths. Undoubtedly psychopaths are attracted to such organisations, but what evidence there is of the mentality of IRA volunteers hardly resembles either the popular image or the more clinical descriptions of psychopathy.

Sean MacStiofain has been described as the only real terrorist the IRA ever succeeded in producing. A Londoner with an Irish background, he was Chief of Staff of the PIRA from 1970 until 1972, when he fell from

146

grace in the republican movement for giving up a hunger strike during his imprisonment in the South for belonging to the IRA. His predominant personality traits were authoritarianism and fanatical devotion to the cause of nationalism, evident both in his hard work and his view that there would be no place for William 'Craig and his type in a United Ireland. There would be no place for those who say they want their British heritage. They've got to accept their Irish heritage, and the Irish way of life, no matter who they are, otherwise there would be no place for them.'[20] These were hard words, unlikely to reassure Ulster Unionists, but, as one Irish psychologist, Dr Heskin, has remarked, 'Authoritarianism is not psychopathy and fanatical dedication to a cause is quite inconsistent with psychopathic personality.'[21]

Similarly, it is difficult to describe as psychopathic the behaviour of members of the IRA described by an English sociologist, Dr Burton, who lived in a Provisional area of Belfast in 1972-3. Behaviour condemned by outsiders as evil or psychopathic was often viewed quite differently within this small community, while it proved impossible to typify members of the IRA as a group, apart from sharing a common and pervasive authoritarianism. Even the 'yahoo' or 'hood' elements, apparently matching the public image, were not of a uniform type. Some apparently remained 'wild men' but others had become 'politicised by the IRA and straightened out of their non-political behaviour'.[22] Bouts of depression, self-doubt and guilt were common among active IRA personnel and there was little evidence of the criminal racketeering of which the Provisionals were accused. On the contrary, dedication and material sacrifices seemed the norm.

Another source of controversy has been the nature of the support accorded to the PIRA in the Catholic ghettos of Belfast and Londonderry. The ghettos with their high proportion of unskilled workers and larger families constituted some of the most socially deprived parts of Northern Ireland with the highest rates of unemployment. In 1971 the rate of male unemployment in the Catholic Falls was almost two and a half times that in comparable Protestant working-class areas such the Shankill and Woodvale: 24 per cent as against 10 per cent. The relationship between violence and social deprivation was a complex one, as was that between the Catholic ghettos and the PIRA.

It is impossible to decide how far the strength of support derived from the loyalty the PIRA inspired or the intimidation it exerted. Certainly, strict discipline was maintained in PIRA areas by the meting out of summary punishments, but it is also true that the Catholic community looked to the IRA for protection against Protestants and the security forces and that the PIRA was able to capitalise on Catholic attempts at self-protection in 1969, when a network of local defence groups based on the parish had been established. Concerned Catholics used republican contacts to supply arms, while Republicans exploited Catholic concern to secure support and an operational base within the Catholic community. Indeed, the relationship between the IRA and the ghetto communities was kaleidoscopic and the degree of support for the IRA varied with the degree to which Catholics felt themselves to be victimised or protected by the forces and allies of the state. This put the IRA in a difficult position, for its role was not simply to act as an armed guard but also to fight an urban guerrilla war to end the British occupation. The contradictions of this dual role were clearly illustrated by the anger expressed by Catholics when the IRA shot two soldiers in their area. Some thought the killings morally wrong, while others blamed the IRA for the revenge the soldiers' colleagues exacted on the residents, because the IRA seemed to be using the community as a shield instead of protecting it. Still others added more cynically that the PIRA could not lose, as army retaliation, afflicting as it did the innocent, served to swell republican recruitment.

The ascendancy of the PIRA and its capacity for violence rendered difficult if not impossible any peaceful settlement of the Northern Ireland question and did much to change the nature of the question. Its uncompromising stance largely offset the more conciliatory position taken up by the SDLP, as members of the PIRA became prisoners of the role they had developed for themselves. Emphasising the soldier rather than the politician and preferring action, especially deeds of violence and destruction, to political discussion, they failed to appreciate the importance of taking advantage of political opportunities created by their military activity. Instead, they persisted in regarding political compromise as treachery, an insult to their dead comrades and a mockery to the toll of suffering. The result was that while they were able to destroy public order and bring down the Stormont regime, the Provisionals found it impossible to engage in constructive political action to achieve even part of their longer-term aims.

IV

The republican campaign destroyed what little chance Stormont had of saving itself. It did so by reducing the province to political chaos and by forcing the government to insist upon an ultimately self-defeating security policy, which compromised the advocates of settlement and caused a fatal rift between Westminster and Belfast.

The self-defeating security policy was adopted as a result of ever-growing pressure from Unionists in all parts of the province for the abandonment of reform and the implementation of drastic security measures considered so successful in the past. The reforms undertaken from October 1969 onwards had been enough to strengthen the position of some defenders of the status quo and to make others organise more effectively. Unionism, already divided by civil rights, now fell asunder. The Hunt reforms led directly to the formation of the Ulster Special Constabulary Association, an organisation of former B Specials which co-operated with loyalist paramilitaries and operated as a pressure group demanding more local control of security. And growing dissatisfaction with reform enabled Paisley to win O'Neill's old seat in Stormont, Bannside, in April 1970 and the Westminster constituency of North Antrim in the following June. Yet, it is doubtful whether the reforms alone would have led to the eclipse of the moderate Unionists. Rather, it was the question of security, the response to IRA violence, that provided the grounds for the effective mobilisation of intransigent Unionist opinion. It was in support of demands for the restoration of the USC and the introduction of internment that the most impressive demonstrations were organised, after the killing of three young off-duty Scottish soldiers on 10 March 1971 gave the Unionist hardliners the issue they wanted.

The arguments in favour of internment were emotive and political rather than practical. It had apparently proved effective in containing the disturbances of the early 1920s and the IRA campaign of 1956-62; it had the merit of simplicity; and it had an element of vengeance. The government as a whole shared these views and tried to curb the growing Unionist unrest by bringing critics into the administration and pressing Westminster for a more aggressive security policy. The former was easily accomplished but not the latter, for, moral and legal considerations apart, Westminster and the army reckoned that intensified repression, especially internment, would simply drive waverers in the Catholic community into the arms of the PIRA and complicate relations with the South. This view was adhered to, despite Chichester-Clark's resignation on 20 March 1971, but continued Unionist pressure and the insistence of the new Prime Minister, Faulkner, long an advocate of internment, eventually caused the British government to agree to more punitive measures. Troops were authorised to shoot 'with effect'[23] at anyone acting suspiciously and internment was introduced. The reason for the change of policy seems to have been fear of a Protestant backlash, fear that Protestants would take matters into their own hands, plus Westminster's reluctance to face the resignation of yet another Prime Minister of Northern Ireland. Faulkner inspired confidence and respect among British ministers and was the last of the acceptable alternatives.

The aim was to smash the IRA and at 4 a.m. on 9 August 1971 the British army swooped on the republican areas and arrested some 350 people, all but two of them Catholics, suspected of threatening the security of Northern Ireland. The swoop was quickly followed by serious rioting and shooting in Belfast and many other places, with twenty-three people, including four soldiers, dying in two days, but the policy was persevered with. Admittedly, many of those initially arrested were quickly released – some 116 within forty-eight hours – but many more were arrested and the number detained crept up to 500 by mid-November and to 900 by the time of the imposition of direct rule in March 1972. Altogether, it was an ill-considered and ill-executed policy. Owing to poor intelligence work those detained included many who were known by the communities in which they lived and worked to have no direct involvement in subversive activities, so that many wholly innocent people were roughly arrested and questioned as though they were terrorists. The sense of outrage was increased by the circulation of well-founded rumours of ill-treatment, particularly of those taken to a special interrogation centre at Holywood Barracks. There a number of suspects were subjected to what was euphemistically called interrogation in depth, a process designed to disorientate them and so break down their resistance. According to the European Court of Human Rights, the treatment was inhuman and degrading but did not constitute torture.

To the Catholic community internment was the final outrage in a system of law and order that had been pressing heavily upon it for years, particularly over the preceding eighteen months. It was not simply that the Catholic areas bore the brunt of emergency measures but also a feeling that the whole of the ordinary process of law continued to be weighted against Catholics. This was not an unfounded feeling. The authorities continued to regard Catholic violence more seriously than Protestant violence, as more dangerous to the state, and acted accordingly in the matter of arrests and charges, while there was also a tendency on the part of courts and jurors to accept the evidence, however nebulous, of the security forces in disputed cases. Most notably, the police tended to charge Catholic rioters with riotous behaviour, which carried a mandatory minimum six months prison sentence, but preferred to charge Protestants with only disorderly behaviour, for which the penalty might be a fine or even a suspended sentence. As one Catholic priest said, 'Our people are afraid of the courts; they believe the judicial system as it operates in the blatantly sectarian condition of life here is loaded against them.'[24]

The tough security policy pursued by the government with Westminster's backing proved a massive miscalculation, not least because it completed the alienation of the Catholic community from the Stormont regime. It weakened the will and support of those Catholics who favoured working within a modified Stormont system. There was an almost universal outcry from Catholics against internment. A campaign of civil disobedience, including the withholding of council rents and rates, was launched with the backing of opposition MPs and NICRA. The strike, at its highest involving only 23,190 or one-quarter of all Catholic council households, was never as extensive as its organisers claimed, nor did it inflict, as had been hoped, serious financial damage on the state. Nevertheless, it provided 'a non-violent alternative to the IRA' and embarrassed Stormont as 'a tangible expression of the virtual secession of many Catholics from the state'.[25] In addition, on 19 August prominent Catholics in Londonderry announced their resignations from public bodies, and three days later all anti-Unionist councillors decided to withdraw from local councils. Above all, the SDLP was severely discomfited, for the tougher security measures undermined its policy of *rapprochement* and almost destroyed the party itself.

The party had jumped eagerly and even optimistically at the mild offer of partnership made by Faulkner and on 7 July 1971 had taken part in the first of what was to have been a series of all-party discussions. Optimism quickly evaporated, for that same night and on the following day the army in Londonderry claimed the first two victims of the new policy of shooting with effect. Carried along with a tide of outrage, particularly in Londonderry, and fearing that it might lose the leadership of the Catholic community to the IRA, the SDLP, some members more reluctantly than others, withdrew from parliament on 15 July in protest against the refusal of Stormont and Westminster to hold a public enquiry into the two deaths. (The rest of the opposition, except an NILP member, quickly followed suit.) The SDLP's disenchantment with Stormont was completed by the introduction of internment. Its members pledged themselves not to return to Stormont or to co-operate in any way with the Belfast or Westminster governments until internment was ended. The minority's rejection of Stormont was symbolised by the holding on 26 October 1971 of an 'Alternative Assembly' in Dungannon, attended by some 100 people — local councillors and opposition MPs and Senators — with Hume as president. Although short-lived, the 'Dungannon Parliament' served to underline the lack of any political consensus in Northern Ireland. In a very short space of time the SDLP had gone from almost fulsome praise of the government to abstention, thus refusing, as its statement justifying its withdrawal from Stormont put it, 'to continue to give credibility to the system which in itself is basically unstable and from which derives the unrest that is destroying our community'.[26]

By contrast, the uncompromising opponents of Stormont increased in confidence and popularity. Far from being weakened the PIRA gained from what was seen as an assault upon the Catholic community. Its role as a defender of the Northern Catholics was enhanced, as the Bogside and Creggan, sealed off with barricades openly manned by the IRA, effectively seceded from the Northern Ireland state. And it was not only in the ghetto areas that attitudes towards the IRA became more sympathetic. Moreover, contrary to expectations, internment strengthened rather than undermined the PIRA and its capacity for violence. The replacement of older and more experienced officers by younger men resulted in a slackening of the tight military discipline which had long characterised the IRA and gave greater scope to local units to carry out retaliation and assassination. In addition, the gathering together of men in internment camps encouraged a greater sense of solidarity and facilitated further training 'without worrying that the Brits were likely to break in and carry you off to Long Kesh or somewhere ... and you knew some of us had to be let out.'[27] By the late summer of 1971 the Provisionals' confidence was such that they felt able to consider political initiatives and on 5 September announced five conditions for a truce: a cease-fire by the British army; the abolition of Stormont; free elections to a nine-counties Ulster parliament, to be called Dail Uladh; the release of detainees; and compensation for those who had suffered through the action of the security forces. Oddly enough, the conditions did not include a withdrawal of British troops or a united Ireland.

V

Internment failed to curb violence and destroy the IRA but alienated the advocates of accommodation among the Catholic community. It also failed to halt the disintegration of the Unionist Party. Although West did resign the leadership of the West Ulster Unionist Council on joining Faulkner's government, the adoption of an increasingly uncompromising security policy failed to satisfy the swelling ranks of Unionist critics who demanded even harsher measures, including the formation of a loyalist militia. What is more, the opponents of reforming Unionism became increasingly well organised as political parties formed around the two leading critics of O'Neillism — Craig and Paisley.

Paisley's Democratic Unionist Party (DUP), formed in September 1971, was not an entirely new creation. It arose out of the Protestant Unionist Party, formerly Ulster Protestant Action, a militantly Protestant group set up in 1959 to safeguard Protestant jobs at a time of rising unemployment. Nor was the DUP always the one-man show it later became. Paisley's closest mentor and co-founder of the party was Desmond Boal, a barrister of considerable influence and ability with a long record as a Unionist MP in working-class Belfast. The party, Boal said, would be 'right wing in the sense of being strong on the constitution and restoring security, but to the left on social policies'.[28] Nevertheless, its appeal lay largely in its strident anti-republicanism, which many of its followers regarded as synonymous with anti-Catholicism. Paisley clung to the traditional definition of loyalty, holding that 'If the Crown in Parliament decreed to put Ulster into a United Ireland, we would be disloyal to Her Majesty if we did not resist such a surrender to our enemies.'[29] Indeed, the distinctive feature of the DUP was its reversion to nineteenth-century Unionism and its advocacy, when Stormont's existence was threatened, of closer integration with Britain, including increased representation at Westminster to put Northern Ireland on a par with Scotland and Wales.

As leader of the DUP and a member of the Westminster parliament Paisley was capable of taking a distinctive view on such sensitive questions as the close relationship between the Orange Order and the Unionist Party, which he deplored, internment, which he opposed, and even attitudes to the South, which at one time he seemed willing to re-appraise. However, his own easy eloquence and fear of losing what support he had in the North prevented him from commanding general confidence even among

152

Protestants and Unionists. Thus in September 1971 he found it impossible to stand by remarks made to Southern press and radio to the effect that alterations to the Republic's constitution could bring significant changes in relations with the North. Acclaimed by nationalists throughout Ireland, these sentiments so dismayed and puzzled his supporters that Paisley back-pedalled, claimed he had been misreported, misquoted and misunderstood and reverted to the more familiar sounds of 'no surrender' and resistance to popish encroachments. Despite appearances to the contrary in the late 1970s, the DUP remained a minority party and Paisley a minority leader.

Craig's Vanguard Unionist Progressive Party (VUPP) was not formed until March 1973 but its roots lay in the events of the preceding three years. Its membership consisted largely of former members of the Official Unionist Party disgusted with the policies of recent leaders, O'Neill, Chichester-Clark and Faulkner, and it arose out of Ulster Vanguard, a pressure group within Unionism launched by Craig at the beginning of 1972 as a protest against government policy and rumours of the suspension or abolition of Stormont. Although it shared with the other Unionist parties a firm determination to keep the North out of a united Ireland, Vanguard's policy was distinctive in two respects. It flirted with the idea of a unilateral declaration of independence, arguing that an independent Ulster was the surest way of maintaining its British heritage. The party's symbol – the Red Hand of Ulster – emphasised its commitment to a mythical Ulster nationalism. In the second place, the Vanguard movement maintained open and close links with the various Protestant paramilitary groups which began to proliferate after August 1969.

At one time there was said to be some forty-six Protestant paramilitary groups, most formed in the years 1971-2 in response to increasing IRA violence. They did not constitute anything like an organised and co-ordinated army, but were rather a motley collection of local defence associations. In urban areas they patrolled neighbourhoods at night and erected barricades at checkpoints for motorists, while in the countryside they patrolled roads and guarded such buildings as Orange halls, which were likely objects of arson or bomb attacks. Such groups were strongest in the Protestant working-class areas of Belfast and in the adjoining areas of Newtownabbey, Dundonald and Lisburn, and achieved greater significance by affiliating to some wider body, such as the 10,000-strong Ulster Special Constabulary Association or the better-known Ulster Defence Association (UDA), which started life in September 1971 as a co-ordinating body for local associations. The formation of the UDA with the motto 'Law before Violence' reflected the growing anger and frustration of many Protestant working men and women at seeing 'the enemies of Faith and Freedom' destroying Northern Ireland to 'enslave the people of God'.[30] At its peak in 1972 it had some 40,000 members and took on a distinctively working-class image, excluding MPs and clergymen from membership.

Its massive military-style demonstrations were impressive reminders that Protestant volunteers were ready to defend their ideal Ulster should the Crown forces prove unwilling or unable to do so. Despite its initial strength, the UDA almost destroyed itself and its credibility by becoming associated with extortion, racketeering and gratuitous violence, but the appointment of a new commander in 1973, Andy Tyrie, born in 1940, a machine operator and former member of the UVF, resulted in a 'clean up' and the restraint of the most violent fringes.

Some Protestants had always believed that attack was the best form of defence but it was not until February 1972 that the long-feared Protestant backlash did get under way. Thenceforth, small Protestant groups assassinated or tried to assassinate Catholics suspected of IRA activities, placed bombs in public houses frequented by Catholics, shot Catholics associating 'improperly' with Protestants, and attacked Catholics more or less at random on the grounds that they were all rebels at heart. During the 1970s various murder squads emerged, but one of the most consistent was the old UVF, which picked up where it had left off in 1966. Said to have some 1,500 members by 1972 and to be well armed with a variety of weapons, its main centres of strength were the Shankill area of Belfast, East Antrim and Co. Armagh. It achieved considerable notoriety and in March 1977, after the costliest trial in Northern Ireland's criminal history, twenty-six UVF men were given a total of 700 years imprisonment, including eight life sentences.

The line between the paramilitaries and other Unionist groups was sometimes a very thin one. The UPV had accompanied Paisley's parades during the early civil rights period, but it was the Vanguard movement that most bridged the gap between political and other forms of action. In the first place, Vanguard collaborated closely with the Loyalist Association of Workers (LAW), formed at the end of 1971 to organise strikes protesting against the government's failure to stop the IRA bombing campaign. Based on several of the largest industrial plants in Belfast, LAW was associated with the UDA and led by William (Billy) Hull, the unofficial mayor of the Shankill, a former member of the NILP and a shop steward at the Belfast shipyard engine works. Vanguard also had close links with various paramilitary groups and even its own paramilitary organisation, the Vanguard Service Corps, which in 1973 became the Ulster Volunteer Service Corps. Indeed, the circumstances surrounding the formation of the original Vanguard movement in February and March 1972 were reminiscent of pre-war Germany and Italy. Rallies were organised, to which Craig frequently travelled in an open car with an escort provided by the Vanguard Service Corps, and on 18 March as many as 60,000 attended a demonstration in Ormeau Park, Belfast, the UDA and LAW turning out in strength with thousands marching in formation and wearing military-style uniforms. Unmoved by angry charges that the movement was neo-Nazi, Craig merely retorted that any paramilitary appearance was simply due to the symbolic gesture of men of different political affiliations standing together shoulder to shoulder to preserve their British traditions and way of life.

The closeness of the relationship between political parties and para-militaries throws some light on the nature of the Unionist violence. According to Dr Heskin, it was from the ranks of the Protestant paramilitaries that 'the preponderance of truly psychopathic terrorist activity has emanated, with the random and frequently grisly random assassinations of Catholics'. This phenomenon is explained by the fact that the Protestant paramilitary organisations 'lack the cultural traditions and historical respectability of the IRA and hence do not tend so readily to attract the stabilising element nurtured on those traditions and conscious to some extent, at least, of the ideals behind the conflict'.[31] Certainly, the question of what constituted an acceptable level of violence was often a matter of urgent debate within the Protestant community and para-militaries, with the result that one breakaway group from the UDA and UVF, the Ulster Citizen Army, issued handbills in October 1974 alleging that 'power-crazed animals have taken over control of the loyalist para-military organisations and have embarked on a programme of wanton slaughter, intimidation, robbery and extortion'.[32]

Nevertheless, just as it would be a mistake to dismiss IRA violence as psychopathic, so it would be misleading to regard all loyalist violence as gratuitous and perpetrated by people with disordered minds and no respect for conventional morality. Whereas the IRA had its higher justifica-tion in the concept of Irish freedom, so the Protestant paramilitaries resented the way they were described in the British and international press as narrow-minded and murdering fascists. On the contrary, they insisted that they were 'patriots ... fighting for Ulster's freedom' against 'the gangsters who have ravaged and raped our country' so that all Ulstermen might live and worship freely and in peace. Their fight was not against Catholics as such but against the 'animals you shelter' and their methods, they maintained, 'although extreme, are necessary. When the cancer within the human body lies deep, the surgeon must cut accordingly. If we must forfeit our lives, we will do so gladly, knowing that our cause is just.'[33] Moreover, the Protestant paramilitaries did not operate in a social and political vacuum but took encouragement from and sought justification in the attitudes of their own communities and the violent rhetoric of leaders such as Craig, who was forever threatening that force and even killing might have to be used to achieve normality. 'We must build up the dossier,' he told the Vanguard demonstration in Belfast in March 1972, 'on those men and women in this country who are a menace to this country, because one of these days, if and when the politicians fail us, it may be our job to liquidate the enemy.'[34]

There is insufficient evidence to support the view that the continued fragmentation of Unionism was a result of class differences, with the Van-guard movement speaking primarily for small local capitalists, and the

155

DUP and the paramilitaries for the Protestant working class. Still, whatever the explanation for the new alignments in Unionism, the proliferation of parties and organisations hardly made for peace and stability in Northern Ireland. Nobody could speak with confidence on behalf of the Protestant community or deliver its unanimous support for any political initiative. Furthermore, the failure of reforming Unionism meant that opinion in the province was more polarised than ever before. Most Unionists were as determined as ever to uphold their traditional ascendancy in some form or another, and many were prepared to resort to extra-constitutional methods to do so.

VI

With the break-up of the traditional Unionist Party, the alienation of the SDLP, and the growth of the PIRA and the Protestant parmilitaries, Northern Ireland was in danger of disintegrating into anarchy by the end of 1971. Whatever the wishes of community groups and the cries of moderate men, the outstanding feature of life in Northern Ireland was the escalation of violence, as communal rioting gave way to more organised violence. Internment had raised not lowered the incidence of death and destruction. From 1 January to 8 August 1971, thirty-four people had been killed — eleven British soldiers, four RUC men and nineteen civilians; but from the introduction of internment until the end of the year 139 people died as a result of political violence — thirty-two soldiers, seven policemen and ninety-five civilians. The situation was reminiscent of that in 1921-2, when the existence of the new state had been threatened, but in 1971-2, there was a crucial difference. In 1921-2 the government of Northern Ireland had been able to save itself by presenting a united Unionist front and by relying, with the connivance of a British government anxious to avoid direct embroilment in the North, on its own security force, the USC. In 1971-2, however, Unionists were in disarray and the government of Northern Ireland was entirely reliant upon the security forces of a British government which was becoming increasingly concerned at the extent to which its support of the Stormont regime was committing resources to the North, losing men and bringing British liberal democratic traditions into disrepute. The events of Bloody Sunday brought home both the extent of this involvement and the price being paid.

On Sunday, 30 January 1972, thirteen people were shot dead in Londonderry's Bogside by soldiers of the First Parachute Regiment. The shootings occurred during rioting following an illegal and provocative march organised by the Londonderry Civil Rights Association to protest against internment. The army claimed that someone had fired on the soldiers first and that the dead were terrorists and gunmen, but an official enquiry, conducted by Lord Widgery, the Lord Chief Justice of England, while not doubting that the army had been fired on first, did not find proved its allegation that the dead and wounded had been shot while handling firearms. Nationalist and Catholic Ireland exploded with anger at the events of what was quickly dubbed 'Bloody Sunday'. The British Embassy in Dublin was burned down on 5 February while there were strikes and demonstrations in Northern Ireland and bomb attacks in both Northern Ireland and Britain. The OIRA planted a bomb in the officers' mess of the 16th Parachute Brigade at Aldershot on 23 February 1972, which killed five cleaning women, a chaplain and a gardener. Both wings of the IRA, however, disclaimed responsibility for one of the cruellest of the many violent incidents that occurred in Northern Ireland – the bombing of the crowded Abercorn restaurant in the centre of Belfast on 4 March 1972. The casualties were mainly women and children having a break from Saturday afternoon shopping. Two women died and 130 people were injured, many being seriously mutilated. Two sisters each lost both legs and one of them, who was buying her wedding dress, also lost an arm and an eye.

Such incidents brought to a head the rift between Belfast and Westminster that had been increasingly evident since Chichester-Clark's resignation the previous March. The hostile reaction to internment had caused MPs of all parties in Britain to question the wisdom of continuing to prop up Stormont, and Heath's Conservative government began to consider ways of extricating itself from what was increasingly being represented as a colonial war, even Britain's Vietnam. After rejecting as an unwarrantable interference in the affairs of the United Kingdom Lynch's call for an end to internment, Heath had invited the Irish Prime Minister to London, first to bilateral talks on 6-7 September 1971 and then to tripartite talks, which included Faulkner, three weeks later. Not only was the Irish dimension being increasingly explored but so also was the idea of the suspension of Stormont. The obstacle to decisive action was said to be the Home Secretary, Reginald Maudling, forever counselling caution if not inaction. It was also said that the events of Bloody Sunday removed this obstacle by shattering Maudling's optimism and convincing him that time was on no-one's side.

Thereafter events moved swiftly. On 22 March 1972 Faulkner and his deputy were called to Downing Street and told bluntly that Stormont was to be deprived of all worthwhile power in respect of law and order and would be left with little to govern. A shocked Faulkner returned to Belfast to tell his colleagues who found it difficult to give up office but even more difficult to accept the erosion of their power, especially since Unionists at large wanted more not less repression and only a week before Unionist backbenchers had voted to oppose any reduction in Stormont's powers. On the morning of 24 March, therefore, Heath announced that the government of Northern Ireland was resigning; that the Stormont government and parliament was to be suspended; and that Westminster would undertake direct responsibility for Northern Ireland. The Northern Ireland parliament met for the last time on 28 March.

Unionists, even the most moderate, were horrified at the suspension of the government and parliament so long regarded as their security against a united Ireland. There were no riots, nor clashes with the British army, but at the end of March there did occur a significant demonstration of the strength and depth of traditional Unionism. Following the announcement of the suspension of Stormont, Vanguard called a two-day protest strike and a rally at Stormont on 28 March to coincide with the old parliament's last sitting. The strike was effective, shutting-off power supplies, stopping public transport and closing most of the major industries. The Stormont demonstration was massive. Admittedly, Craig was upstaged by Faulkner and did not advocate, as he had previously threatened to do, the formation of a provisional government to take over the province. Nevertheless, the strike and the demonstration suggested that, although Unionists could not save Stormont, they had the resources to thwart any future plans for the government of the province which they considered a betrayal of traditional Unionism.

The IRA may have brought down Stormont but Unionists were strong enough and organised enough to prevent their traditional enemies, be they Republicans, Nationalists or Catholics, from capitalising on the death of a fifty-year-old regime that had disintegrated in violence. The Northern Ireland question was no longer a matter of forms of government. It had become a question of power.

Chapter 8

DEADLOCK

The suspension of Stormont and the imposition of direct rule took power away from the Unionists but did little to restore order and failed to achieve widespread agreement upon the way Northern Ireland should be governed. There were moments of optimism, when both wings of the IRA declared a truce and when some Unionists co-operated with members of the SDLP and the Alliance Party in a power-sharing executive, but these moments were short lived. Peace initiatives petered out. Violence continued unabated. Direct rule, envisaged as only a temporary measure, became the form of government that divided Northern Irishmen least but which could not command complete acceptance. Indeed, it is difficult to disagree with Professor Rose's verdict that 'The power to govern did not pass to Westminster with Britain's assumption of responsibility for direct rule of the Province. Instead, it sank almost out of sight.'[1]

I

The imposition of direct rule in March 1972 meant that Northern Ireland was for the first time wholly ruled from Westminster with its own Secretary of State, similar to those for Scotland and Wales, who had a seat in the cabinet. The first holder of the new office was William Whitelaw, a senior Conservative politician, assisted by a small team of junior ministers, each of whom had responsibility for at least two of the old Stormont administrative departments. The province was governed bureaucratically rather than democratically under a Temporary Provisions Act and Northern Ireland legislation was brought forward by way of Orders-in-Council, which could not be amended on the floor of the Commons. There was an attempt to make direct rule more palatable locally by establishing an advisory commission but this was boycotted by Unionists who objected to the province being treated, as Faulkner put it, like a 'coconut colony'.[2]

The new regime's most pressing task was the restoration of order, and the intention was to be firm but conciliatory. Conciliation was certainly much in evidence in the first few months, especially on the vexed question of internment. Among Whitelaw's first acts were the release of forty-seven internees on 7 April, the abandonment of the prison ship, *Maidstone,* as a detention centre and the establishment of a new advisory committee to consider applications for release from internees. By mid-August the number of men held under the Special Powers Act had been cut to 243. In addition, Whitelaw made what he later admitted was a mistake by agreeing to special privileges for convicted terrorists belonging to paramilitary groups, the 'special category' system instituted following a hunger strike in Belfast Prison which brought one IRA leader, Billy McKee, close to death. The hope was that the phasing out of internment and other concessions would evoke a friendly response from the IRA and persuade it to reduce the level of violence and even to switch from military to political activity. Even if this did not happen, the government could argue that it had made every reasonable effort to secure peace and the IRA would be revealed as being concerned only with the perpetration of violence.

Initially, there was little prospect of the IRA responding to Whitelaw's overtures. Internment continued; the army of occupation remained; and both wings of the IRA declared that they would fight on. They even undertook joint action after an army patrol had shot dead a prominent member of the Officials. Yet the chance of a breakthrough occurred in the middle of May, when the OIRA overstepped the mark in Londonderry by killing a young Catholic soldier home on leave in the Creggan from his regiment in Germany. The fierce reaction of local women led the Officials to declare an unconditional ceasefire. The Provisionals were also under pressure from their own 'war-weary' areas and from the South. A premature explosion in Anderson Street in the Short Strand in Belfast killed four volunteers and two local civilians and wrecked part of the street, while the Southern government, taking heart from the suspension of Stormont, began to try to break up Republican organisations in the South. On 22 June the Provisionals announced that they would cease fire at midnight on 26 June if the British would reciprocate.

The British did reciprocate, however guardedly, and on 7 July a party of six Provisional leaders was given safe-conduct and flew to London for talks with Whitelaw. The journey was taken as a sign of the Provisional's willingness to move away from military action, but like most signs it was misread. The IRA did have a peace plan but it was unacceptable to the British government, requiring of Britain an acknowledgment of the right of the Irish people to self-determination, a commitment to withdraw its army by a specified date, and the declaration of a general amnesty. No agreement was reached at this meeting and before talks could be resumed the truce was called off by the Provisionals on 9 July, when the army became involved in conflict between Catholics and Protestants over the allocation of houses to displaced Catholics at Lenadoon, near Belfast. Faced with the need to respond, the IRA did so in the only way it knew how — by military action — and threw away an opportunity to establish itself as a constructive political force in Northern Ireland. Prisoners of their role as freedom fighters or soldier politicians, 'Instead of turning their chips into money when they could, they staked them on another throw; and they lost the lot.'[3] Their *pièce de résistance,* a bombing blitz on Belfast on 21 July with twenty-six explosions, went disastrously wrong. Eleven people, two soldiers and nine civilians, were killed and 130 injured, many badly mutilated. Known as 'Bloody Friday', it was the most devastating day of violence in Belfast up to that time and is often regarded as the point at which the PIRA put itself outside the pale of political negotiation. Certainly, it was the day when one of the leaders of the most effective Protestant murder gang 'started turning bitter. . . . I saw it all in colour on the BBC news. . . . Very few people here had colour TVs at the time. But they should have seen what I saw: people putting pieces of bodies into plastic bags. I will never forget it.'[4]

Westminster, under much pressure from disgruntled, frightened and angry loyalists, responded on 31 July with 'Operation Motorman', the code name given to the attempt to clear barricades in no-go areas in Belfast and Londonderry. Some 21,000 troops, 9,000 mobilised members of the UDR and 6,000 policemen were involved in the exercise which, despite forecasts of at least 100 deaths, passed off comparatively peacefully. Loyalists helped to dismantle their own barricades, which they claimed were simply a response to the existence of republican no-go areas. The determination to 'remove the capacity of the IRA to create violence and terror',[5] as Whitelaw put it, was further continued by heightened activity on the part of the security forces, increasing the number of houses searched from 17,262 in 1971 to 36,617 in 1972 and 74,556 in the following year; and by the retention of internment and the assumption of wider powers. After various changes in 1972, the Emergency Provisions Act of July 1973, which broadly followed the recommendations of the Diplock Committee on the means of dealing with terrorists, retained an arrangement for interim custody but also brought in new powers for the short-term holding of suspects. The army was given power to arrest and detain for up to four hours any person suspected of terrorist activity.

This more forward policy did break up the no-go areas, yielded good intelligence and put the IRA under considerable pressure in the North. In the South, too, the Provisional leader, MacStiofan, was jailed and a clampdown made it difficult for the PIRA to obtain arms and explosives. Yet the PIRA remained in business and by 1973 had become better armed and organised. It received Russian-made arms through Libya and seemed to enjoy using that most prestigious weapon, the RPG7 rocket launcher. Competence increased, too, for there were fewer premature bombs and fewer casualties among the volunteers.

The resilience of the PIRA was due in part to the attractions of the cause, but it was also due to the effects of a security policy which continued to bear most heavily on Catholics and Catholic areas. Although Westminster was fully prepared to intern Protestants, extraordinary powers were still more frequently used against Catholics so that between 1 February 1973 and 30 October 1974 interim custody orders were served on only ninety-nine Protestants but 626 Catholics. Under the ordinary processes of the law Catholics still tended to be charged with the more serious offences and to suffer harsher sentences than Protestants. This differential treatment was not necessarily the result of deliberate discrimination but rather of differences between police and military procedures. Security in Protestant areas was largely in the hands of the RUC and these areas were subjected to normal police procedure which concentrated on the investigation of specific incidents. By contrast, because of the unpopularity of the police, Catholic areas were largely policed by the army and were subject to an independent security policy, the policy of communal screening. Using its power of arrest and detention for four hours, the army hoped to establish as complete a record as was practicable of the population of all militant republican areas. To this end, a large-scale screening operation was undertaken in the Catholic areas to discover who was and was not involved in or sympathetic to IRA activities.

Occasionally the process paid dividends and resulted in the capture of maldoers, but more often than not it was counter-productive. Large numbers of people were arrested and questioned on no other grounds than their residence or presence in an area and the presumption that they would have some knowledge of terrorist organisation and activity. Apart from its doubtful legal validity, the procedure tended to antagonise the population in the Catholic enclaves where it was applied and is said to have ensured a steady flow of recruits for the IRA, especially from among those who had been abused or maltreated in the course of their, in some cases, frequent arrests. Soldiers did, of course, have a difficult task, but the evidence suggests that many were hardly models of tact and restraint when enforcing the law. As Dr Burton, the English sociologist, recorded on the basis of his experiences in a republican area of Belfast in 1972-3:

This 'enforcement' can be terrifying, as when the Paratroop Regiment entered Anro. Reports came in hourly about the latest beating, intimidation or act of destruction. A discotheque was interrupted by a foot-patrol who attacked the teenage dancers, putting one boy back into the hospital from which he had just been released. He had the stitches from a routine operation on his stomach reopened by the troops. A baker's hand was broken by the soldiers as he went about his delivery round. A store of furniture belonging to homeless, intimidated families was wrecked during the search. Local mill workers were kicked in the genitals as they were searched, twice daily, as they went to and from their workplace. I was hit in the ribs with a rifle as two Paratroopers asked me if I was in the IRA. I said that I was not and they replied, 'Well, fucking well join so we can shoot you.' The friend I was living with was beaten up in the back of a Saracen tank by a Paratroop sergeant. After being interrogated and cleared he was taken back to Anro by the same soldier who apologised, 'I'm sorry about that lad on the way down, we do it to everyone. People soon start talking after we soften them up.'[6]

Even when not applying undue force, soldiers managed to create a startling degree of resentment even among those who did not sympathise with the Provisionals but who disliked being ordered around by the army.

For these reasons the security forces were unable to break up the PIRA whose campaign of violence continued. Between 1 April 1972 and 31 January 1973, the Provisionals were said to have been responsible for some 300 deaths, including those of 120 members of the security forces. Such continued activity also meant a prolongation of the Protestant backlash begun in earnest in February 1972. Of the 104 factional or sectarian assassinations occurring between 1 April 1972 and 31 January 1973, the Provisionals were blamed for thirty-four and Protestants for seventy, including some very grisly and ritual ones involving the use of pitchforks and blowlamps. Catholics continued to be the main victims of the Protestant backlash, but a novel feature in 1973 was that for the first time loyalist groups began to admit responsibility for and to justify the killing of Catholics. One of the most active of these murder gangs was the Ulster Freedom Fighters, formed in June 1973 either as a breakaway group from the UDA or as an organisation of convenience to enable members of the UDA to carry out killings without besmirching the good name of the parent group. Whatever their origins, there was a ruthlessness about the Freedom Fighters who liked to identify their cause and methods with those of militant Zionism in Israel and threatened that 'each time an act of aggression is committed against our people, we shall retaliate in a way that only the animals of the IRA can understand'.[7] One of their earliest victims was the SDLP Senator, Gerard Paddy Wilson, whose body and that of a Protestant woman friend were found on 26 June 1973 with multiple stab wounds in a lonely quarry on the outskirts of Belfast.

Altogether, direct rule witnessed not a diminution of violence but an increase. In the fifteen months prior to direct rule there had been 253 deaths as a result of political violence. In the fifteen months following the suspension of Stormont there were as many as 471. Of course, the nature and effects of the violence changed over the years: the inter-communal rioting of 1969-71, the IRA bombing campaign, the activities of paramilitary groups and sectarian murders all affected different parts of the province in different ways. Nevertheless, the extent to which law and order had broken down was underlined by the rise in the number of unsolved murders from two in 1969 to 900 in 1976. Although large areas were little touched directly and parts of Belfast, Londonderry and later South Armagh bore the brunt, the prolonged and high level of violence could not fail to have repercussions throughout such a small society. By the mid-1970s more than one Ulsterman in every hundred had been killed or wounded by political violence. 'Given the size of extended family networks in the Province, this means that nearly one family in every six has had a father, a son, a nephew or an aunt killed or injured in the Troubles.'[8] Not surprisingly, there was and is considerable concern about the consequences for individuals, the community at large and the economy, as many people

163

lived in conditions of endemic fear, social and public services were frequently disrupted and amenities eroded.

The economic and social planning of the 1960s was almost brought to nought by the prolonged political crisis. It undermined confidence and investment and accentuated the damage that any international depression quickly inflicts on peripheral parts of economies. The new town of Craigavon languished, failing to attract or even retain sufficient industries and inhabitants. Bankruptcies reached a record level in 1971. There was hardly any private investment in the early 1970s, as some firms cancelled plans for expansion or the establishment of new businesses. Income from tourism was almost halved between 1968 and 1972. Northern Ireland thus remained the most deprived region in the United Kingdom with the highest rate of unemployment, the lowest level of personal income and lower standards of services and amentities. In 1974 20 per cent of all dwellings, and as many as 47 per cent in one large area of Belfast, were defined as unfit for human habitation compared with only 7 per cent in England and Wales. 'Urban blight' was in fact a major problem compounded by sectarianism as different areas competed for limited public funds for renovation and modernisation, and as Protestants became increasingly suspicious that preference was being afforded to republican areas.

Less susceptible to precise description was the effect of violence upon people. Many commentators have endorsed the view expressed in 1974 by one historian that 'One of the most tragic and horrifying features of the present troubles is that, in the ghettos of Derry, Belfast and elsewhere, young people, both boys and girls, have become habituated to violence.'[9] Some social psychologists believe that even a political settlement would not end Northern Ireland's troubles in view of certain evidence suggesting that problems of anti-social behaviour among the young may emerge as a major feature of life. Others, however, doubt whether such pessimism is warranted considering the North's low rate of criminality and delinquency in the past and the strength of the churches' influence and fundamentalist religious values, particularly respect for, or at least compliance with, the authority of elders. Those in search of the dramatic may have maintained that respect for authority had broken down completly, but 'Other observers with noses rather closer to the ground, have taken the opposing view that, in fact, mutual respect has increased as young and old have become involved in the problems of their community.'[10]

There is similar uncertainty about the effect of the Troubles on adults, particularly in areas most affected by communal violence and military intervention. Early newspaper reports after the initial outbreaks in Belfast in the summer of 1969 claimed that there was a dramatic rise in the incidence of mental illness in the troubled areas, while studies by two Belfast psychiatrists pointed to an increase in the number of psychiatric cases not in the worst trouble spots but in adjacent areas of intermediate disturbance. On the other hand, there were also widespread indications of people's ability

164

to cope with stress, such as the decrease in depression and suicide rates and, most strikingly, the rapid rate of recovery of bomb victims. Such resilience, such adaptation to stress, may, however, have stored up future problems, by eroding traditional values and qualities, or by masking and further creating inestimable strains, just as in the 'legendary grief-stricken performer' who insists that 'the show must go on'.[11] What will be the eventual effect on the people and community of Northern Ireland when the show is over can only be a matter of speculation. What is certain is that the violence and the deep divisions it reflected scarcely provided a propitious background to the attempts of the British government to bring about new political alignments in the North.

II

Never intending that direct rule should be other than temporary, the British government almost immediately began to look for ways of restoring regional government to Northern Ireland. As well as having talks with the IRA, Whitelaw initiated a flood of consultations and discussions, but the difficulty of reconciling entrenched viewpoints was underlined in August 1972 by the reaction of the seven Stormont parties to his invitation to a conference. Four declined – the Nationalist Party, the Republican Labour Party and the SDLP representing the Catholic community, and Paisley's DUP. Only three parties, the Official Unionists, Alliance and Northern Ireland Labour, attended the conference held on 25-27 September amidst tight security in a hotel outside Darlington, Co. Durham, and even these three could not agree among themselves.

The initiative thus remained with the British government which responded in the following month with a discussion paper, a green paper, on the fate of Northern Ireland. Applauded by some for 'its restraint, its insight, its informativeness, its flexible approach, its brevity and its readability',[12] the paper reviewed the various proposals that had recently been made; sought to identify the 'unalterable facts'[13] of the situation; and laid down the vital conditions which, in the British government's view, any settlement would have to satisfy. These conditions included both confirmation of Northern Ireland's position as an integral part of the United Kingdom and recognition that there was an 'Irish dimension' to the problem; the close association of all sections of the community with the work of government; fair play and civil rights for all; and, for the time being, control of security by Westminster. The proposals eventually hardened into a White Paper containing a detailed plan for ending direct rule and restoring a measure of regional autonomy, which was then incorporated into the Northern Ireland Constitution Act of August 1973. The act also finally abolished the Stormont parliament.

The proposals were controversial. A new Executive was to be responsible to a new single-chamber Assembly of seventy-eight members, about the same size as the old parliament but elected by PR and with fewer powers. The Executive and Assembly were to have no control over the security forces, special powers dealing with terrorism, the police, the appointment and removal of judges, or parliamentary and local elections, while there was provision for a standing advisory commission on human rights to prevent discrimination on the grounds of religious belief or political opinion. Even more controversial was the insistence on a compulsory coalition. Majority rule had been the guiding principle of Stormont, but the new proposals provided that power should be shared between the various parties. A committee system, 'designed to create a strong link between the assembly and the executive' and 'to involve majority and minority interests alike in constructive work',[14] was to be established. Each political head of a government department would act as chairman of a committee, whose membership would reflect the balance of parties in the Assembly, and the committee chairmen would collectively form the Executive of Northern Ireland. On top of all this there was a recognition of the Irish dimension. Not only were there to be periodic plebiscites to enable the people of Northern Ireland to declare their views on the border issue, there were also to be institutional arrangements for consultation and co-operation between Northern Ireland and the Irish Republic.

Like the 1920 act, however intellectually satisfying such proposals appeared on paper, they were little likely to lead to any radical changes in Northern Ireland politics. The motives behind the withholding of security powers were obvious and worthy enough, but it did make nonsense of the concept of power-sharing to withhold from the proposed new regime one of the fundamental functions of government. The story of the Northern Ireland Assembly might have been very different 'if an SDLP leader such as Paddy Devlin or John Hume had appeared regularly on television as, say, Attorney-General or Home Secretary, to announce how many terrorists had been arrested and how many rounds of ammunition captured during the preceding week'.[15] Shared real responsibility might have helped to create the consensus the British government was aiming at and enabled Protestants and Catholics to see each other in a new light as genuinely desiring to create a new political order within Northern Ireland.

Nevertheless, many Catholics welcomed the new proposals as a dramatic change from the bad old days of Stormont when Unionists ruled supreme without interference from either Dublin or Westminster. The Provisionals rejected it, but the SDLP gave it general approval, at the same time demanding an end to internment and the early establishment of a powerful Council of Ireland. Unionists were divided, more against than for, especially since Northern Ireland's position had on 8 March 1973 been once more assured by the overwhelming 'yes' given in a constitutional referendum, the border poll, on the question 'Do you want Northern Ireland to remain part of the United Kingdom?'[16] The verdict seemed to make the White Paper and talk of an Irish dimension irrelevant. Official Unionists may have equivocated, but the White Paper was roundly condemned by the Orange Order, Paisley and Craig, who also announced the further evolution of his Vanguard movement into the VUPP to fight the Assembly elections in opposition to the White Paper.

Westminster refused to be discouraged and took great heart from the successful holding on 30 May 1973 of elections to the new district councils, the first local elections for six years and the first elections under PR since 1925. A call by Provisionals and the PD for a boycott was heeded only in a few hard-core republican areas, and elsewhere the poll was fairly high. The anti-Unionists were worse off than under the old system, gaining an outright majority on only one council; the centre parties, Alliance and NILP, were weak; and the Unionists were strong but divided. Nevertheless, the fact that the SDLP virtually eliminated all other anti-Unionists groups and that the elections had run smoothly was taken as boding well for the future of power-sharing and the Assembly elections, which took place on 28 June. As far as the minority was concerned, the contest was straightforward. The Provisionals' and PD's call for a boycott was even less effective than in the local elections. The handful of candidates put forward by the Nationalist and Republican Labour parties were defeated, as were the ten candidates put up by the Official Republicans. In contrast, the SDLP nominated twenty-eight candidates and won nineteen seats. 'There was no doubt that they had become the official voice of the Northern minority, with the biggest anti-Unionist parliamentary group in the history of the state.'[17] The rest of the results were less encouraging. The centre virtually collapsed. The NILP's eighteen candidates won only a single seat, while the Alliance Party with thirty-five candidates got eight. Among Unionists there was still confusion. The forty-four Official Unionists were nominally committed to Faulkner and pledged to support the re-negotiation of the White Paper, but, as in 1969, many remained ambiguous. Craig's Vanguard and Paisley's DUP, with twenty-four and sixteen candidates respectively, stood allied in determined opposition to the White Paper, as did a handful of Independent Loyalists and twelve hard-line Unionists led by two members of Faulkner's defunct administration, West and John Taylor. Such opponents of power-sharing secured the majority of Unionist votes and seats, with 235,873 votes and twenty-seven seats to the Official Unionists' 211,362 votes and twenty-two seats.

These results rendered difficult the answer to the question, who should form the new Northern Ireland Executive. The various brands of Unionists with a total of forty-nine seats had an overall majority in the seventy-eight-man Assembly but could not alone, according to the White Paper, form an Executive. Most rejected power-sharing as capitulation to Republicanism and demanded instead the restoration of the former Stormont regime with unimpaired powers. Even the Official Unionists, the followers of Faulkner, had pledged themselves not to share power with anyone whose primary object was to break the Union with Great Britain, a condition that might or might not include the SDLP, without whose support no Executive could be formed. Neither the Alliance Party nor the NILP had any bargaining power, while the SDLP had said that it would participate in the Executive only if internment were ended. The White Paper's prospects were indeed grim, as was all too clear during the noisy scenes which characterised the first meeting of the Assembly on 31 July 1973. It needed some tough talking by the British and Southern governments and some readjustment on the part of Official Unionists and the SDLP to give the White Paper a reprieve, albeit a temporary one. After much haggling a coalition was slowly but surely cobbled together and equipped with an anodyne social and economic programme. On 22 November Whitelaw announced the formation of an Executive-designate of eleven members: six Unionists, four SDLP and one Alliance, with Faulkner as Chief Executive and Fitt as his deputy. There seemed to be jobs for all, for in addition to these voting members of the Executive there were five non-voting members: one Unionist, two Alliance and two SDLP.

Supported by some twenty Official Unionists, nineteen members of the SDLP and eight members of the Alliance Party, the coalition had a clear majority in the Assembly, even though the loyalty of some of Faulkner's nominal followers was doubtful. The whole arrangement was a tribute to Whitelaw's optimism and persistence — or to the strength of politicians' desire for office. Pledged not to participate in Northern institutions while internment lasted, the SDLP agreed to serve while it continued and under the very man who had introduced it. Faulkner had come to power in Stormont as a hard-liner and had fought the Assembly elections on a policy of not sharing power with supporters of a united Ireland, but now agreed to work with the SDLP.

Had matters been allowed to rest with the formation of the Executive, its fate might have been a happier one. But matters were not so allowed to rest, for the price of Southern and SDLP co-operation had to be paid — a consideration of the Irish dimension. Before 1973 the SDLP had scarcely endeared itself to Protestants and Unionists by pressing Britain for ringing declarations in favour of Irish unity and by advocating the establishment of joint British-Republic sovereignty, a condominium, over Northern Ireland. With an eye to power-sharing, although remaining committed to ultimate unity, it dropped the idea of condominium and demanded instead the immediate establishment of a Council of Ireland with wide powers to bring about Irish unity 'by planned and agreed steps'[18] within the context of the European Economic Community. On 6 December 1973 members of the Executive-designate met representatives of the British and Southern governments at Sunningdale, Berkshire, in order to hammer out arrangements for consultation and co-operation between the two parts of Ireland. After four days agreement was reached on the formation of a two-tier Council of Ireland, consisting of a fourteen-man Council of Ministers, seven from each side, and a sixty-member Consultative Assembly, half elected by the Dail and half by the Assembly.

The Council's powers were ill-defined, but its initial task was mainly to foster social and economic co-operation, and the whole agreement was couched in terms to reassure all parties in the North. The Northern minority was supposed to take comfort from the provision that the Council of Ministers should be consulted on appointments to the Irish police forces and the British government's promise to review internment. In return, the Southern delegates stated that 'The Irish government fully accepted and solemnly declared that there could be no change in the status of Northern Ireland until a majority of the people of Northern Ireland desired a change in that status.'[19] They undertook to step up the offensive against the IRA and to increase co-operation between the Gardai and the RUC. Finally, in view of Southern laws prohibiting extradition for political offences, an Anglo-Irish law commission was to be established to devise ways of dealing with 'fugitive offenders' from the North who took refuge in the South. The whole agreement was to be formally ratified and implemented in the New Year.

Sunningdale really was 'the high point of British strategy in Ireland . . . a masterpiece of balance and ambiguity'.[20] Unionists could justify the Council to their followers by arguing that the North's position had been strengthened by Southern recognition and co-operation against the IRA and that the Council had no real power anyway. On the other hand, the SDLP and the Southern government could maintain that they were getting a measure of control over the RUC and that the Council of Ireland was a major step towards the re-unification of the country. 'But they were contradictory arguments. The success of the agreement depended on neither side listening to what their allies were saying about it.'[21] And this was increasingly difficult to do, especially when within a few days the agreement regarding the status of Northern Ireland was challenged in the Republic's courts as inconsistent with the constitution and the government's legalistic defence, hardly in accordance with the spirit of Sunningdale, raised doubts about the status of the guarantees.

The insistence upon the Irish dimension ruined whatever chance Faulkner had of persuading a majority even of Official Unionists to accept the Executive as a genuine attempt to achieve a lasting settlement in the North and remove the Southern bogey. His own party had only narrowly voted in favour of power-sharing, when a motion of opposition had been defeated in the UUC by just ten votes. On 4 January 1974, however, the UUC rejected the Sunningdale agreement by 427 votes to 374, whereupon Faulkner resigned as leader and later founded his own party, the Unionist Party of Northern Ireland, committed to power-sharing and willing to heed Westminster's wishes as to the way Northern Ireland should be governed. West became leader of the UUC, which henceforth voiced the demand of traditional Unionism that the province should be governed by and in accordance with the wishes of the majority: 'While we proclaim loyalty to the British Crown, we do not necessarily follow the dictates of any British political party at Westminster.'[22] By January 1974, therefore, all Unionist organisations were in the hands of the opponents of the new initiative – the White Paper and the Sunningdale Agreement – and, while preserving their separate existences, the DUP, UUC and VUPP came together to form the United Ulster Unionist Council (UUUC) with the object of bringing down the Executive.

The Executive, which formally took office on 1 January 1974, found it impossible to establish credibility in face of mounting evidence of the extent and depth of Unionist opposition. On 7 February, after the Executive had been in office for less than six weeks, Heath announced a general election in the United Kingdom for 28 February. Talk of excluding Northern Ireland from the turmoil of an election came to naught. The issue at stake in the rest of the United Kingdom was the government's right to control the economy, but in Northern Ireland Sunningdale was made the dominant issue by the UUUC, which by careful planning took 51 per cent of the poll and eleven of the twelve seats, while the power-sharing parties fought one another. The announcement of the results co-incided with the publication of the final judgement of the Dublin courts upholding the legality of Sunningdale and reiterating the point that the government of the Republic had not been party to any agreement regarding the status of Northern Ireland.

The election results and events in Dublin emboldened the UUUC to adopt an all-out offensive against the Executive on the grounds that it constituted a violation of democracy and a subversion of the will of the majority of the people of Northern Ireland. In place of the Executive and the 1973 Northern Ireland Constitution Act, it demanded immediate elections, a Northern Ireland parliament with full security powers and large increases in the sizes of the RUC and UDR. Should Westminster not agree, selective sanctions, including industrial action, were threatened. The UUUC did not have sufficient Assemblymen to bring down the Executive by vote in the Assembly – and on 14 May its motion opposing Sunningdale was defeated by forty-four votes to twenty-eight. But this did not matter, for the UUUC had powerful allies outside among the Protestant paramilitaries and the industrial workforce in the shape of the Ulster Workers' Council (UWC) and the Ulster Army Council (UAC). The UWC had been formed towards the end of 1973 from among former members of the defunct LAW, but, unlike LAW, it made no attempt to build up an unwieldy mass movement and concentrated instead on recruiting shop stewards and key workers, especially in the power stations. The UAC was also formed towards the end of 1973 as a co-ordinating committee of Protestant paramilitaries and fully identified itself with the demands of the UUUC for an end to power-sharing and any discussion of a Council of Ireland. It warned that 'If Westminster is not prepared to restore democracy, i.e., the will of the people made clear in an election, then the only way it can be restored is by a *coup d'état.*'[23] The strength of these bodies made pointless the deliberations of the Assembly, for on the evening of its endorsement of Sunningdale a constitutional stoppage or general strike was called. In view of talk of Ulster nationalism and an independent Ulster, the strikers' main demand was surprisingly limited – an immediate general election, which, in the light of the recent United Kingdom election, would have meant the return of a large anti-Sunningdale, anti-power-sharing majority.

The strike lasted for fourteen days. In organising it, the UWC operated through a co-ordinating committee, headed by a Vanguard Assemblyman from Londonderry and member of both LAW and UDA, Glen Barr, and representative of all shades of Unionists opposed to Faulkner, including such leading politicians as Craig, Paisley and West, and paramilitaries such as Tyrie of the UDA. The behaviour of the paramilitaries and the UAC was one of the most controversial aspects of the strike, as they set up road blocks all over Belfast and tried to prevent workers from entering or leaving factories. Yet the UWC's control of power stations rather than intimidation made the strike effective. Electricity was the key weapon and one by one the output of power stations was reduced so that industry could not operate. Back-to-work marches organised on 21 May by the ICTU, one of them led by Leonard Murray, the general secretary of the British Trades Union Congress, attracted only a couple of hundred workers. The next day the UWC tightened its grip on the city by banning petrol supplies to all but essential users. As Craig boasted, 'We are in effective control of the country.'[24] Nor was the South immune. On 16 May Craig, the least restrained of the three party leaders, had demanded the scrapping of Sunningdale and went on to threaten action 'against the Irish Republic and those who attempt to implement the agreement'.[25] The next day three car bombs exploded in Dublin and one in Monaghan.

All this went on over the heads of the Executive. It had no security powers and thus decisions as to how to deal with the strike remained with Westminster. The Labour government, returned to power in the previous February, refused to negotiate with the strikers and responded on 19 May by declaring a state of emergency and promising to use the army to maintain essential services. Wilson, once again Prime Minister, appeared on television on 25 May condemning the strike and abusing the strikers for sponging off the British taxpayers:

> It is a deliberate and calculated attempt to use every undemocratic and unparliamentary means for the purpose of bringing down the whole constitution of Northern Ireland so as to set up there a sectarian and undemocratic state, from which one-third of the people of Northern Ireland will be excluded. . . .
>
> The people on this side of the water – British parents – have seen their sons vilified and spat upon and murdered. British taxpayers have seen the taxes they have poured out, almost without regard to cost – over £300 million a year this year with the cost of the Army operation on top of that – going into Northern Ireland. They see property destroyed

by evil violence and are asked to pick up the bill for rebuilding it. Yet people who benefit from all this now viciously defy Westminster, purporting to act as though they were an elected government; people who spend their lives sponging on Westminster and British democracy and then systematically assault democratic methods. Who do these people think they are?[26]

The words reflected widespread British frustration and even disgust, but no decisive action was taken against the strikers, much to the bitter chagrin of the power-sharing parties. They were deeply disappointed that the army could not provide the expertise to run the power stations and did not prevent the erection of road blocks by supporters of the strike. The army's inaction was a source of bitter controversy, but at bottom the failure to act decisively was part and parcel of British reluctance to be saddled with full responsibility for Northern Ireland. The whole aim of British policy since 1969 had been to create conditions that would enable it to disengage from the North's affairs. To have taken on the majority community might well have opened up a very unpleasant Pandora's box.

To have attempted to break the strike would indeed have involved taking on the Protestant community, because by the end of the first week the strikers did have the support of the Protestant middle classes. Whether or not the rallying behind the strikers represented irreconcilable hostility to power-sharing in any form, it certainly reflected resentment at an experiment which had been hailed as a victory for Catholics. Several weeks before the strike, Barr had warned the SDLP members of the Assembly against continuing to 'rub the noses of Loyalists in the dirt', and in a post-mortem on the Executive Faulkner noted that 'People were showing that we have had five years of being kicked around.'[27] The strike and the support it received were expressions of a long-growing sense of siege and betrayal on the part of the Protestant ascendancy whose power had been dismantled and who saw some of its traditional opponents elevated by outside intervention into positions of authority, while others persisted in a campaign of violence against all that Ulster Unionism had stood for. As some leaders of the UDA had said the previous June, 'For four hundred years we have known nothing but uprising, murder, destruction and repression. We ourselves have repeatedly come to the support of the British Crown, only to be betrayed within another twenty years or so by a fresh government of that Crown . . . Second-class Englishmen, half-caste Irishmen.'[28]

Unable to persuade the British government either to act decisively against or to negotiate with the strikers, the Unionist members of the Executive resigned on 28 May, so bringing down the Executive. As Faulkner admitted in his resignation statement, 'From the extent of support for the present stoppage . . . the degree of consent needed to sustain the Executive does not at present exist.'[29] The next day the UWC called off the strike and Westminster prorogued the Assembly. Its downfall summed up all the difficulties of achieving a workable political consensus in Northern Ireland: a too narrow basis of agreement, excluding all contentious issues and not underpinned by strong economic and social policies; reliance upon Westminster and Dublin, unable or unwilling to 'deliver the goods'; and the determination of Ulster Protestants and Unionists to have nothing to do with Irish unity. As the historian of the SDLP, Dr McAllister, has commented, 'The ultimate expression of this opposition, the UWC strike, was similar in aim but different in form to the Protestant veto originally used to prevent the application of the third Home Rule Bill to Ulster in 1912.'[30]

III

The second suspension of a government in two years produced deadlock in the search for a settlement of the Northern Ireland question. Sections of both the Catholic and Protestant communities had shown that they had the will and the power to frustrate any peace initiatives or reform programmes remotely capable of acceptance by members of both communities. The old Stormont regime had been finally destroyed by the violence of the IRA, while its radically different successor was brought down by the industrial action of Protestant workers. Extra-constitutional protest had destroyed two constitutions and was always likely to destroy others in the future. Once more there was a reversion to direct rule from Westminster as the form of government that least divided Northern Irishmen. The trouble was that it was the form of government that least appealed to people in the rest of the United Kingdom. Thus a state of deadlock remains, as Northern Ireland continues to search for a constitution in fruitless open convention or private negotiations, and seems condemned to suffer a level of political violence totally unacceptable in part of the oldest parliamentary democracy in the world. Indeed, the annual toll of murders, shootings and bombings is distressing but eloquent testimony of both the intractability of the Northern Ireland question and the failure of statesmanship throughout the British Isles.

173

NOTES

Preface
1. K. Heskin, *Northern Ireland: A Psychological Analysis*, Dublin 1980, 111.

Chapter 1: Unionism versus Nationalism
1. A. T. Q. Stewart, *The Narrow Ground: Aspects of Ulster 1609-1969*, London 1977, 180.
2. F. Wright, 'Protestant Ideology and Politics in Ulster', *European Journal of Sociology* XIV (1973), 224.
3. P. Buckland, 'The Unity of Ulster Unionism 1886-1939', *History* LX (1975), 213.
4. D. W. Miller, *Queen's Rebels: Ulster Loyalism in Historical Perspective*, Dublin/New York 1978, 117.
5. ibid., 110.
6. P. Buckland, *Irish Unionism 2: Ulster Unionism and the Origins of Northern Ireland 1886-1922*, Dublin/New York 1973, xxxiii.
7. J. C. Beckett to author, 11 September 1975.
8. S. E. Baker, 'Orange and Green. Belfast 1832-1912', *Victorian Cities: Images and Realities*, ed. H. J. Dyos & M. Wolff, London 1973, I, 803.
9. P. J. O'Farrell, *Ireland's English Question: Anglo-Irish Relations 1534-1970*, London 1971, 245.
10. Buckland, *Irish Unionism 2*, xxxiii.
11. ibid., 44.
12. P. Buckland, *James Craig*, Dublin 1980, 24-5.
13. ibid., 27.
14. P. Buckland, *Irish Unionism 1885-1923: A Documentary History*, Belfast 1973, 261.
15. Buckland (1980), 32.
16. Miller, 102.
17. A. T. Q. Stewart, *The Ulster Crisis*, London 1967, 135.
18. P. N. S. Mansergh, *The Irish Question 1840-1921: A Commentary on Anglo-Irish Relations and on Social and Political Forces in Ireland in the Age of Reform and Revolution*, rev. ed. London 1965, 192.
19. Buckland, *Irish Unionism 2*, 104.

Chapter 2: Partition and Devolution
1. J. Bowman, 'De Valera and the Ulster Question: 1917-1973', Ph.D. thesis University of Dublin (1980), 2.
2. ibid., 254.
3. T. Jones, *Whitehall Diary, Volume III, Ireland 1918-1925*, ed. K. Middlemas, London 1971, 129.
4. Buckland, *Irish Unionism 2*, 111.
5. ibid., 114.
6. ibid., 116-17.

7. ibid., 117-18.
8. R. H. S. Crossman, *The Diaries of a Cabinet Minister, Volume III, 1968-70,* London 1977, 187.
9. P. Buckland, *The Factory of Grievances: Devolved Government in Northern Ireland 1921-39,* Dublin/New York 1979, 169.
10. J. Darby, *Conflict in Northern Ireland: The Development of a Polarised Community,* Dublin 1976, 151.
11. Buckland (1979), 17.
12. ibid., 76.

Chapter 3: Struggle for Survival
1. Buckland (1980), 50-1.
2. ibid., 58-9.
3. ibid., 60.
4. D. G. Boyce, 'British Conservative Opinion, the Ulster Question, and the Partition of Ireland 1919-21', *Irish Historical Studies* XVII (1970-1), 104.
5. ibid.
6. Buckland (1979), 187.
7. Boyce (1970-1), 104.
8. *Daily Express,* 12 November 1921.
9. Buckland (1980), 69-70.
10. Buckland (1979), 199.
11. H. Calvert, *Constitutional Law in Northern Ireland: A Study in Regional Government,* London 1968, 381.
12. F. H. Newark, 'The Law and Constitution', *Ulster under Home Rule,* ed. T. Wilson, London 1955, 48.
13. Buckland, *Irish Unionism 2,* 166-7.
14. Buckland (1979), 184.
15. P. Bew, P. Gibbon & H. Patterson, *The State in Northern Ireland 1921-72. Political Forces and Social Classes,* Manchester 1979, 59.
16. Buckland (1979), 201.
17. Buckland (1980), 77.
18. ibid., 74.
19. A. C. Hepburn, *The Conflict of Nationality in Modern Ireland,* London 1980, 152.
20. Bew *et al.,* 67-8.
21. Buckland (1979), 195.
22. ibid., 212.
23. ibid., 210.
24. ibid., 199.
25. Buckland, *Irish Unionism 2,* 172.
26. T. Jones, 210.
27. C. Younger, *Ireland's Civil War,* Fontana ed., London 1968, 309.
28. Bew *et al.,* 65-6.
29. Buckland (1980), 78.
30. ibid., 73.
31. ibid., 88.
32. *Fermanagh Herald,* 27 November 1920.

33. Buckland (1975), 220.
34. Buckland, *Irish Unionism 2*, 177.
35. Buckland (1979), 193.
36. ibid., 61.
37. A. Hezlet, *The 'B' Specials: A History of the Ulster Special Constabulary*, Pan ed., London 1973, 92.
38. Bew *et al.*, 72 n.66.
39. Buckland (1979), 232.
40. ibid., 233.
41. ibid., 272-3.
42. ibid., 273.

Chapter 4: A Protestant State

 1. Buckland (1979), 72.
 2. Buckland, *Irish Unionism 2*, 174.
 3. Buckland (1979), 252.
 4. M. Farrell, *Northern Ireland: The Orange State*, London 1976, 110.
 5. F. S. L. Lyons, *Ireland since the Famine*, Fontana ed., London 1973, 635.
 6. ibid., 547.
 7. Farrell, 360.
 8. ibid., 153.
 9. J. F. Harbinson, *The Ulster Unionist Party 1882-1973. Its Development and Organisation*, Belfast 1973, 56.
10. Buckland (1979), 236.
11. Hepburn, 160.
12. Buckland (1979), 246.
13. ibid. 23.
14. ibid.
15. ibid., 220.
16. Hezlet, 135.
17. Calvert, 386.
18. Farrell, 117.
19. D. Kennedy, 'Catholics in Northern Ireland 1926-1939', *The Years of the Great Test 1926-39*, ed. F. MacManus, Cork 1967, 148.
20. Buckland (1979), 265.
21. Harbinson (1973), 221.
22. E. Rumpf & A. C. Hepburn, *Nationalism and Socialism in Twentieth-Century Ireland*, Liverpool 1977, 195-6.
23. Farrell, 116.
24. Kennedy, 145.
25. Buckland (1979), 26.
26. ibid.
27. Farrell, 145-6.
28. ibid., 119.
29. ibid., 122.
30. Buckland (1979), 152.
31. ibid., 174.

32. R. J. Lawrence, *The Government of Northern Ireland: Public Finance and Public Services 1921-1964,* Oxford 1965, 135.
33. Buckland (1979), 264.
34. Lawrence, 61.
35. Buckland (1979), 1.
36. ibid., 121.
37. ibid., 102.
38. ibid., 47-8.
39. Kennedy, 144.
40. Buckland (1980), 107.
41. ibid., 121.

Chapter 5: Change without Change
1. Lyons (1973), 728.
2. ibid.
3. J. W. Blake, *Northern Ireland in the Second World War,* Belfast 1956, 232-3.
4. T. O'Neill, *The Autobiography of Terence O'Neill,* London 1972, 40.
5. Lyons (1973), 730.
6. Bew *et al.,* 112.
7. ibid., 119.
8. Farrell, 178.
9. ibid., 179.
10. ibid., 180.
11. Harbinson (1973), 52.
12. Farrell, 184, 185.
13. ibid., 194.
14. ibid., 188.
15. Lyons (1973), 738.
16. A. J. Green, *Devolution and Public Finance: Stormont from 1921 to 1972,* Centre for the Study of Public Policy No. 48, University of Strathclyde, Glasgow 1979, 17.
17. Lyons (1973), 741.
18. ibid., 743.
19. Darby, 131.
20. M. Wallace, *Northern Ireland: 50 Years of Self-Government,* Newton Abbot 1971, 112-13.
21. F. W. Boal, 'Territoriality on the Shankill-Falls Divide in Belfast', *Irish Geography* VI (1969), 41.
22. ibid., 30.
23. B. Devlin, *The Price of My Soul,* London 1969, 58, 62.
24. J. Magee, *The Teaching of Irish History in Irish Schools,* Belfast 1971, 5.
25. Darby, 134.
26. Heskin, 44.
27. ibid., 51.
28. J. Whyte, 'Interpretations of the Northern Ireland Problem: An Appraisal', Paper prepared for a seminar at the Institute of Irish Studies, Queen's University, Belfast, 29 October 1977, 26.

29. Darby, 74-5.
30. Bew *et al.*, 177.
31. Harbinson (1973), 44.
32. I. McAllister, *The Northern Ireland Social Democratic and Labour Party: Political Opposition in a Divided Society*, London 1977, 10.
33. Bew *et al.*, 165.
34. Hezlet, 199.
35. T. P. Coogan, *The I.R.A.*, Fontana ed., London 1970, 418.

Chapter 6: Challenges to Ascendancy
 1. Farrell, 244.
 2. T. O'Neill, *Ulster at the Crossroads*, London 1969, 41.
 3. Farrell, 230.
 4. O'Neill (1969), 127.
 5. Hepburn, 182.
 6. O'Neill (1972), 63.
 7. ibid., 68.
 8. ibid., 72.
 9. ibid., 73.
10. O'Neill (1969), 130, 158.
11. B. Faulkner, *Memoirs of a Statesman*, London 1978, 32-3.
12. Heskin, 147.
13. Darby, 128.
14. ibid., 128-9.
15. Heskin, 111.
16. D. Boulton, *The UVF 1966-1973: An Anatomy of Loyalist Rebellion*, Dublin 1973, 34.
17. ibid., 40.
18. W. D. Flackes, *Northern Ireland: A Political Directory 1968-79*, Dublin 1980, 146.
19. Boulton, 51.
20. P. Arthur, *The People's Democracy 1968-73*, Belfast 1974, 102.
21. ibid., 109.
22. O'Neill (1969), 144.
23. Arthur, 105.
24. Farrell, 249.
25. Boulton, 85.
26. Arthur, 64.
27. Boulton, 76.
28. ibid., 80.
29. Lyons (1973), 766.
30. O'Neill (1972), 92.
31. Boulton, 109.
32. Stewart (1977), 185.

Chapter 7: Violence and Disintegration
 1. J. Callaghan, *A House Divided: The Dilemma of Northern Ireland*, London 1973, 58.
 2. Farrell, 261.

3. ibid.
4. C. H. King, *The Cecil King Diary 1970-1974,* London 1975, 194.
5. Darby, 103.
6. Farrell, 275.
7. McAllister (1977), 146.
8. ibid., 63.
9. Bew *et al.,* 181.
10. Darby, 193.
11. Flackes, 200.
12. K. Boyle, T. Hadden & P. Hillyard, *Law and State: The Case of Northern Ireland,* London 1975, 139.
13. ibid., 43.
14. Boulton, 127.
15. T. W. Moody, *The Ulster Question 1603-1973,* Dublin/Cork 1974, 69.
16. F. Burton, *The Politics of Legitimacy: Struggles in a Belfast Community,* London 1978, 82.
17. Moody, 71.
18. Farrell, 276.
19. Burton, 125.
20. Heskin, 80.
21. ibid., 81.
22. Burton, 117.
23. McAllister (1977), 91.
24. Boyle *et al.,* 50.
25. McAllister (1977), 101.
26. Farrell, 281.
27. Burton, 81.
28. Heskin, 122.
29. R. Rose, *Northern Ireland: A Time of Choice,* Washington/London, 1976, 40.
30. Boulton, 144.
31. Heskin, 85.
32. Flackes, 138.
33. M. Dillon & D. Lehane, *Political Murder in Northern Ireland,* Harmondsworth, 1973, 285-6.
34. Boulton, 156.

Chapter 8: Deadlock
1. Rose (1976), 28.
2. Flackes, 57.
3. J. Whale, 'Modern Guerrilla Movements', *Community Forum* III (2) (1973), 6.
4. Dillon & Lehane, 285.
5. Flackes, 103.
6. Burton, 107.
7. Dillon & Lehane, 286.
8. Rose (1976), 24-5.
9. Moody, 68.
10. Heskin, 140.

11. ibid., 73.
12. Moody, 51.
13. ibid.
14. ibid., 52.
15. Miller, 163-4.
16. Flackes, 29.
17. Farrell, 308.
18. McAllister (1977), 58.
19. Moody, 106.
20. Farrell, 311.
21. ibid.
22. Rose (1976), 39.
23. Flackes, 138.
24. Farrell, 318.
25. ibid.
26. Hepburn, 211.
27. Miller, 163.
28. Dillon & Lehane, 281.
29. McAllister (1977), 145.
30. Ibid., 146.

SELECT BIBLIOGRAPHY

This bibliography lists only those works quoted in the text plus a few other important works. Those marked with an asterisk contain useful bibliographies, particularly J. Darby's *Conflict in Northern Ireland* which draws together and evaluates much of the vast literature now available on Northern Ireland.

1. Reference Works and Collections of Documents

Buckland. P., *Irish Unionism 1885-1923. A Documentary History*, Belfast 1973.

Compton, P. A., *Northern Ireland: A Census Atlas*, Dublin 1978.

*Deutsch, R. R., *Northern Ireland 1921-1974: A Select Bibliography*, New York 1975.

Deutsch, R. & Magowan, V., *Northern Ireland: A Chronology of Events 1968-74*, 3 vols, Belfast 1973-5.

Elliott, S., *Northern Ireland Parliamentary Election Results 1921-72*, Chichester 1973.

Flackes, W. D., *Northern Ireland: A Political Directory 1968-79*, Dublin 1980.

Hepburn, A. C., *The Conflict of Nationality in Modern Ireland*, London 1980.

Maltby, A., *The Government of Northern Ireland 1921-1972: A Catalogue and Breviate of Parliamentary Papers*, Dublin 1974.

Magee, J., *Northern Ireland: Crisis and Conflict*, London 1974.

O'Neill, T., *Ulster at the Crossroads*, London 1969.

2. General Histories

*Coogan, T. P., *Ireland since the Rising*, reprint, Connecticut 1976.

*Farrell, M., *Northern Ireland: The Orange State*, London 1976.

Harkness, D., 'England's Irish Question', *The Politics of Reappraisal*, ed. G. Peele & C. Cook, London 1975, 39-63.

Kee, R., *The Green Flag: A History of Irish Nationalism*, London 1972.

*Lyons, F. S. L., *Ireland since the Famine*, Fontana ed., London 1973.

Macardle, D. *The Irish Republic*, Corgi ed., London 1968.

MacManus, F. (ed.) *The Years of the Great Test 1926-39*, Cork 1967.

Mansergh, P. N. S., *The Irish Question 1840-1921: A Commentary on Anglo-Irish Relations and on Social and Political Forces in Ireland in the Age of Reform and Revolution*, rev. ed., London 1965.

*Moody, T. W., *The Ulster Question 1603-1973*, Dublin/Cork 1974.

O'Farrell, P. J., *Ireland's English Question: Anglo-Irish Relations 1534-1970*, London 1971.

Phillips, W. A., *The Revolution in Ireland 1906-1923*, London 1923.

Rumpf, E. & Hepburn, A. C., *Nationalism and Socialism in Twentieth-Century Ireland*, Liverpool 1977.

Wallace, M., *Northern Ireland: 50 Years of Self-Government*, Newton Abbot 1971.

3. Autobiographies and Biographies

Buckland, P., *James Craig*, Dublin 1980.

Callaghan, J., *A House Divided: The Dilemma of Northern Ireland*, London 1973.

Crossman, R. H. S., *The Diaries of a Cabinet Minister, Volume III, 1968-70*, London 1977.

Devlin, B., *The Price of My Soul*, London 1969.

Dwyer, T. Ryle, *Eamon de Valera*, Dublin 1980.

Faulkner, B., *Memoirs of a Statesman*, London 1978.

Gwynn, D., *The Life of John Redmond*, London 1933.

King, C. H., *The Cecil King Diary 1970-1974*, London 1975.

Marrinan, P., *Paisley: Man of Wrath*, Tralee 1973.

O'Neill, T., *The Autobiography of Terence O'Neill*, London 1972.

Stewart, A. T. Q., *Edward Carson*, Dublin 1981.

4. Partition

*Bowman, J., 'De Valera and the Ulster Question: 1917-1973', Ph.D. thesis University of Dublin (1980).

Boyce, D. G., 'British Conservative Opinion, the Ulster Question and the Partition of Ireland 1919-21', *Irish Historical Studies* XVII (1970-1), 89-112.

Boyce, D. G., *Englishmen and Irish Troubles: British Public Opinion and the Making of Irish Policy*, London 1972.

Buckland, P., *Irish Unionism 2: Ulster Unionism and the Origins of Northern Ireland 1886-1922*, Dublin/New York 1973.

Gallagher, F., *The Indivisible Island: The History of the Partition of Ireland*, London 1957.

Gibbon, P., *The Origins of Ulster Unionism: The Formation of Popular Protestant Politics and Ideology in Nineteenth-Century Ireland*, Manchester 1975.

Heslinga, M. W., *The Irish Border as a Cultural Divide*, Assen 1962.

Jalland, P., *The Liberals and Ireland: The Ulster Question in British Politics to 1914*, Brighton 1980.

Jones, T., *Whitehall Diary, Volume III, Ireland 1918-1925*, ed. K. Middlemas, London 1971.

Lyons, F. S. L., 'The Irish Unionist Party and the Devolution Crisis of 1904-5', *Irish Historical Studies* VI (1948-9), 1-22.

McDowell, R. B., *The Irish Convention 1917-18*, London 1970.

Pakenham, F., *Peace by Ordeal: The Negotiation and Signature of the Anglo-Irish Treaty 1921*, N. E. L. ed., London 1967.

Report of the Irish Boundary Commission 1925, with an introduction by G. J. Hand, Shannon 1969.

Stewart, A. T. Q., *The Ulster Crisis*, London 1967.

5. Discussions of the Northern Ireland Question

Barritt, D. P. & Carter, C. F., *The Northern Ireland Problem: A Study in Group Relations*, 2nd ed., Oxford 1972.

Birrell, D., 'Relative deprivation as a factor in conflict in Northern Ireland', *Sociological Review* XX (1972), 317-43.

*Darby, J., *Conflict in Northern Ireland: The Development of a Polarised Community,* Dublin 1976.

*Heskin, K., *Northern Ireland: A Psychological Analysis,* Dublin 1980.

Miller, D. W., *Queen's Rebels: Ulster Loyalism in Historical Perspective,* Dublin/New York 1978.

Nelson, S., 'Protestant "Ideology" Considered: The Case of "Discrimination"', *British Sociology Yearbook, Volume II, The Politics of Race,* London 1975, 155-87.

Rose, R., *Governing without Consensus: An Irish Perspective,* London 1971.

Rose, R., McAllister, I. & Mair, P., *Is There a Concurring Majority in Northern Ireland?,* Centre for the Study of Public Policy No. 22, University of Strathclyde, Glasgow 1978.

Stewart, A. T. Q., *The Narrow Ground. Aspects of Ulster 1609-1969,* London 1977.

*Whyte, J., 'Interpretations of the Northern Ireland Problem: An Appraisal', Paper prepared for a seminar at the Institute of Irish Studies, Queen's University, Belfast, 29 October 1977, subsequently published in *Economic and Social Review* IX (1978), 257-82.

Wright, F., 'Protestant Ideology and Politics in Ulster', *European Journal of Sociology* XIV (1972), 213-80.

6. The Government of Northern Ireland

Bew, P., Gibbon, P., & Patterson, H., *The State in Northern Ireland 1921-72: Political Forces and Social Classes,* Manchester 1979.

*Birrell, D. & Murie, A., *Policy and Government in Northern Ireland: Lessons of Devolution,* Dublin/New York 1980.

Boyle, K., Hadden, T., & Hillyard, P., *Law and State: The Case of Northern Ireland,* London 1975.

*Buckland, P., *The Factory of Grievances: Devolved Government in Northern Ireland 1921-39,* Dublin/New York 1979.

Calvert, H., *Constitutional Law in Northern Ireland: A Study in Regional Government,* London 1968.

Clark, W., *Guns in Ulster: A History of the B Special Constabulary in Parts of Co. Derry,* Belfast 1967.

Darby, J. & Williamson, A., *Violence and the Social Services in Northern Ireland,* London 1978.

Elliott, S., 'The Electoral System in Northern Ireland since 1920', Ph. D. thesis Queen's University, Belfast (1971).

Green, A. J., *Devolution and Public Finance: Stormont from 1921 to 1972,* Centre for the Study of Public Policy No. 48, University of Strathclyde, Glasgow 1979.

Hezlet, A., *The 'B' Specials: A History of the Ulster Special Constabulary,* Pan ed., London 1973.

Lawrence, R. J., *The Government of Northern Ireland: Public Finance and Public Services 1921-1964,* Oxford 1965.

Mansergh, N., *The Government of Northern Ireland: A Study in Devolution,* London 1936.

Newark, F. H., 'The Law and Constitution', *Ulster under Home Rule,* ed.

T. Wilson, London 1955, 14-54.

Northern Ireland Office, *The Future of Northern Ireland: A Paper for discussion,* London 1972.

Northern Ireland Office, *Northern Ireland Constitutional Proposals,* London 1973, Cmd. 5259.

Wilson, T. (ed.), *Ulster Under Home Rule: A Study of the Political and Economic Problems of Northern Ireland,* London 1955.

7. Parties and Politics in Northern Ireland

Arthur, P., *The People's Democracy 1968-73,* Belfast 1974.

Blake, J. W., *Northern Ireland in the Second World War,* Belfast 1956.

Boulton, D., *The UVF 1966-1973: An Anatomy of Loyalist Rebellion,* Dublin 1973.

Buckland, P., 'The Unity of Ulster Unionism 1886-1939', *History* LX (1975), 211-23.

Budge, I. & O'Leary, C., *Belfast: Approach to Crisis: A Study of Belfast Politics 1603-1970,* London 1973.

Burton, F., *The Politics of Legitimacy: Struggles in a Belfast Community,* London 1978.

Dillon, M. & Lehane, D., *Political Murder in Northern Ireland,* Harmondsworth 1973.

Edwards, O. Dudley, *The Sins of Our Fathers: Roots of Conflict in Northern Ireland,* Dublin 1970.

Feeney, V. E., 'The Civil Rights Movement in Northern Ireland', *Eire-Ireland* IX(2) (1974), 30-40.

Fisk, R., *Point of No Return: The Strike that Broke the British in Ulster,* London 1975.

Graham, J., 'The Consensus Forming Strategy of the Northern Ireland Labour Party 1949-68', M.S.Sc. thesis Queen's University, Belfast (1972).

Harbinson, J. F., 'A History of the Northern Ireland Labour Party 1891-1948', M.Sc.(Econ.) thesis Queen's University, Belfast (1966).

Harbinson, J. F., *The Ulster Unionist Party 1882-1973. Its Development and Organisation,* Belfast 1973.

Kennedy, D., 'Catholics in Northern Ireland 1926-1939', *Years of the Great Test 1926-39,* ed. F. MacManus, Cork 1967.

McAllister, I., 'Political Opposition in Northern Ireland: The National Democratic Party 1965-70', *Economic and Social Review* VI (1975), 353-66.

McAllister, I., *The Northern Ireland Social Democratic and Labour Party: Political Opposition in a Divided Society,* London 1977.

McAllister, I. & Wilson, B., *Bi-Confessionalism in a Confessional Party System: The Northern Ireland Alliance Party,* Centre for the Study of Public Policy No. 8, University of Strathclyde, Glasgow 1977.

McCann, E., *War in an Irish Town,* Harmondsworth 1974.

Report of the Commission on Disturbances in Northern Ireland (Cameron Commission), Belfast 1969, Cmd. 532.

A Commentary by the Government of Northern Ireland to accompany the *Cameron Report,* Belfast 1969, Cmd. 534.

Report of the Tribunal of Inquiry into Violence and Civil Disturbances in 1969 (Scarman Tribunal), 2 vols, Belfast 1972, Cmd. 566.

Rose, R., *Northern Ireland: A Time of Choice,* Washington/London 1976.

Sunday Times Insight Team, *Ulster,* Harmondsworth 1972.

Thompson, J., 'The Northern Ireland Civil Rights Movement', M. A. thesis Queen's University, Belfast (1973).

Whale, J., 'Modern Guerrilla Movements', *Community Forum* III (2) (1973), 3-6.

8. Society and Economy in Northern Ireland

*Akenson, D. H., *Education and Enmity. The Control of Schooling in Northern Ireland 1920-1950,* Newton Abbot/New York 1973.

Baker, S. E., 'Orange and Green: Belfast 1832-1912', *Victorian Cities: Images and Realities,* ed. H. J. Dyos & M. Wolff, I, London 1973, 789-814.

Beckett, J. C., 'Belfast. A General Survey', *Belfast: The Origin and Growth of an Industrial City,* London 1967, 213-80.

Beckett, J. C. & Glasscock, R. E. (eds.), *Belfast: The Origin and Growth of an Industrial City,* London 1967.

Boal, F. W., 'Territoriality on the Shankill-Falls Divide in Belfast', *Irish Geography* VI (1969), 30-50.

Busteed, M. A., *Northern Ireland,* Oxford 1974.

Fraser, R. M., *Children in Conflict,* Harmondsworth 1974.

Freeman, T. W., *Ireland: A General and Regional Geography,* 4th rev. ed. London 1972.

Harris, R., *Prejudice and Tolerance in Ulster: A Study of Neighbours and 'Strangers' in a Border Community,* Manchester/New Jersey 1972.

Isles, K. S. & Cuthbert, N., 'Ulster's Economic Structure' and 'Economic Policy', *Ulster under Home Rule,* ed. T. Wilson, London 1955, 91-114, 137-82.

Isles, K. S. & Cuthbert, N., *An Economic Survey of Northern Ireland,* Belfast 1957.

Jones, E., *Social Geography of Belfast,* Oxford 1960.

Magee, J., *The Teaching of Irish History in Irish Schools,* Belfast 1971.

Mogey, J., *Rural Life in Northern Ireland,* London 1947.

Robinson, A., 'Londonderry, Northern Ireland: A Border Study', *Scottish Geographical Magazine* LXXXVI (1970), 208-21.

Belfast Regional Survey and Plan: Recommendations and Conclusions (Matthew Report), Belfast 1961-3.

Report of the Joint Working Party on the Economy of Northern Ireland (Hall Report), Belfast 1962, Cmd. 446.

Economic Development of Northern Ireland (Wilson Plan), Belfast 1965, Cmd. 479.

Northern Ireland Development Programme 1970-1975, Belfast 1970.

9. The South

Bell, J. B., *The Secret Army,* London 1970.

Carroll, J. T., *Ireland in the War Years 1939-45,* Newton Abbot/New York 1975.

Coogan, T. P., *The I.R.A.*, Fontana ed., London 1971.
Fanning, R., *The Irish Department of Finance 1922-58*, Dublin 1978.
Harkness, D., *The Restless Dominion*, London 1969.
Meenan, J., *The Irish Economy since 1922*, Liverpool 1970.
Murphy, J. A., *Ireland in the Twentieth Century*, Dublin 1975.
Nowlan, K. B. & Williams, T. D. (eds), *Ireland in the War Years and After 1939-51*, London 1969.
Whyte, J., *Church and State in Modern Ireland 1923-70*, Dublin 1973.

189

Hull, W., 154
Hume, J., 122, 125, 126, 137, 151, 166
Hunt, Lord, 138, 148
Hunt report, 138, 142, 148

imperial contribution, 22, 39, 49, 79–80, 87, 103
Independent Unionists, 51, 57, 67–8, 100, 167
industry, 5–6, 15, 25, 27, 28, 32, 73–4, 82, 83, 96, 113; location, 28, 74, 93, 113, 117, 122; industrial policy, 27–8, 58, 74, 80, 92–3, 107, 110–11, 114, 117, 120, 164
internment (1920s), 46–7, 51, 56, 72; (1940s), 84, 85, 137; (1956–62), 105; (1970s), 149–51, 152, 156, 159–60, 161–2, 168
Ireland, 1–9, 14, 15, 17–24, 38, 50
Irish Americans, 18, 132, 145
Irish Congress of Trade Unions, 95, 112, 117, 171
Irish convention (1917–18), 18
Irish Free State, 29–30, 38, 39, 43, 45, 46, 47, 48, 49, 50, 52, 53, 55–6, 58–9, 61, 64–5, 69, 70, 73, 74
Irish Labour Party, 133, 137
Irish National Land League, 7
Irish National League, 7
Irish nationalism, nationalists (pre-1921), 1, 6–8, 9–10, 12, 14–18, 19, 20, 35
Irish nationalism, nationalists (Northern Ireland), 23, 43, 52, 63, 71, 72, 98, 99–100, 102, 137, 142; divisions, 45, 66, 104, 109; in Belfast, 104; organisation, 58, 66, 85–6, 88, 103–4, 109; leadership, 80–1, 114, 125; local government representation, 52, 62, 101, 116–17; parliamentary representation, 33, 62, 67–8, 88; and Irish unity and legitimacy of Northern Ireland, 29–30, 31,

33, 35, 43, 45, 50, 57–8, 70, 84, 85, 87, 88, 103–4, 109, 114–15; 150; and role of official opposition, 66, 114, 122; responsive to events in South, 29–30, 70, 86, 88, 134; identified with Catholicism, 35, 57, 66, 85; social and economic policies, 58, 85, 109; internment, 47, 56, 149–50; eclipse of old constitutional Nationalist Party, 125, 126, 136–7, 165, 167; see also Irish Republican Army
Irish News, 85
Irish Northern Aid Committee, 145
Irish Parliamentary Party, 7, 8, 9, 14, 15, 17, 18, 33, 45, 57
Irish Republic, 17, 29–30, 88, 89, 103, 106, 107, 109, 123, 132, 133–5, 153, 157, 160, 161, 166, 168, 169, 170, 171, 173
Irish Republican Army (1919–22), 18, 31, 35, 37, 39, 44, 45–6, 48, 51, 149; (1930s and 1940s), 59, 65, 71, 84; (1956–62), 104–5, 106, 108, 116, 149; (1960s and 1970s), 109–10, 120, 127, 132, 134, 135, 143, 149, 151, 152–5, 158, 160, 161, 165, 169, 173; see also Official Irish Republican Army and Provisional Irish Republican Army
Irish Republican Socialist Party, 104
Irish Trade Union Congress, 95
Irish Union Association, 66
Irish Unionists, 7, 8; see also Southern Unionists and Ulster Unionists
Isles, K. S., 93
Israel, 163

James I, 2
James II, 3, 129
John XXIII, 96, 119
Joint Exchequer Board 22
Judicial Committee of the Privy Council, 78, 79
judiciary, see courts

Kafka, F., 9
Keenan, S., 130
Kerry, Co., 50
King, M. L., 118
Kipling, R., 14

Labour Party (British), 57, 69, 71, 72, 84, 85, 86, 107–8, 110, 133, 171
Labour Party (Northern Ireland), see Northern Ireland Labour Party
Lagan, River, 3, 69, 120
Larne, 12, 95, 101
law and order: disorder and violence, 11, 31, 35–6, 37, 44, 45–6, 59, 71, 84, 104–5, 120–1, 122, 125, 127, 129–31, 143, 144, 146, 154, 156–7, 161; casualty figures, 46, 104, 105, 140, 156, 163; steps to maintain, 12–13, 40–3, 46–8, 51, 65–6, 71, 84, 105, 121, 130, 132–43, 149–50, 157–62; consequences of violence, 49–50; 163–5; see also army, courts, internment and police
Law, A. Bonar, 11, 49
Leech, Judge, J., 62
Legion of Mary, 67
Leinster, 8
Lemass, S., 107, 112–13, 114
Lenadoon, 160
Liberal Party, Liberals, 7, 12, 14, 17
Libya, 132, 145, 161
linen, 5, 6, 27, 28, 32, 34, 73, 94
Lisburn, 95, 153
Liverpool, 83
Lloyd George, D., 17, 18, 19, 20, 23, 30, 36, 38, 40, 44, 47, 49, 50
local government, 56–7, 100; structure, 21–2, 79, 80, 116–17, 138–9; electoral areas and franchise, 52–4, 57, 61–2, 63, 72, 116–17, 118, 123, 124, 135, 139; Unionist domination, 60, 116–17; conservative and partisan, 22, 35, 79; employment, 22, 63, 101, 110, 123, 135; housing, 101, 110, 118, 123, 124; reform, 79, 116, 124, 138-9; rates and rent strike, 150

194